DEBUSSY REMEMBERED

Debussy Remembered

ROGER NICHOLS

Amadeus Press
Reinhard G. Pauly, General Editor
Portland, Oregon

First published in 1992
by Faber and Faber Limited
3 Queen Square London WC1N 3AU

First published in North America in 1992
by Amadeus Press (an imprint of Timber Press, Inc.)
9999 S.W. Wilshire, Suite 124,
Portland, Oregon 97225, U.S.A.

Phototypeset by Intype, London
Printed in England by Clays Ltd, St Ives plc

ISBN 0–931340–41–1 (cased)
0–931340–42–X (paper)

Contents

Illustrations

Acknowledgements

I should like to express my gratitude to various friends who have assisted in the preparation of this volume: firstly, and principally, to Robert Orledge for his help in finding many of the items and for his constant interest and encouragement; to Marie Rolf for allowing me to quote from the letter sent her by François Gillet; to Henry Thompson for translating from the Russian the souvenirs of Ninon Vallin; and to Margaret Cobb, Roy Howat, Jean-Michel Nectoux, Joan Redding, Nico Steffen and John C. G. Waterhouse.

I am also grateful for permission to quote from the following copyright material (detailed source references are given at the end of each extract):

Jane Bathori, 'Les musiciens que j'ai connus', tr. Felix Aprahamian; Dolly Bardac (Mme Gaston de Tinan), 'Memories of Debussy and his circle', *Recorded Sound* (British Library National Sound Archive); Sir Arnold Bax, *Farewell, My Youth* (Longmans, 1943); articles by Raymond Bonheur, Maurice Emmanuel, Robert Godet, Charles Koechlin, Edward Lockspeiser, André Messager, Gabriel Pierné, Marguerite Vasnier, Paul Vidal, *La Revue Musicale*; M. D. Calvocoressi, *Musicians Gallery* (Faber and Faber, 1933); Erik Satie, *Ecrits* (Champ Libre, 1977); Igor Stravinsky, *Expositions and Developments* (Faber and Faber, 1962); Dame Maggie Teyte, 'Memories of Debussy', *Music and Musicians*; *Star on the Door* (Rita O'Connor); Ricardo Viñes, diary entries, *Revue internationale de musique française* (Champion-Slatkine); Sir Henry Wood, *My Life of Music* (Gollancz, 1938).

Introduction

There is a story about Bartók arriving in Paris for the first time and telling a friend that he was keen to meet Debussy. 'But he's a very prickly sort of person. Do you really want to run the risk of being insulted?' 'Yes, please!'

It is probably fair to say that Debussy had never been a great lover of the human race, and as the years went by his patience with it seems to have decreased rather markedly. In the 1890s he proposed a Society for Musical Esotericism, to make music less available to the masses, who, in his view, were not only incapable of understanding true art but offered unwelcome encouragement to products like Charpentier's *Louise*, a work about which Debussy never missed the chance to say an unkind word. He himself claimed he was 'as simple as a blade of grass', which was pure nonsense. The memoirs that follow show friend after friend grappling with his elusive, complex, contradictory character, not to mention his well-developed gift for upsetting people. Debussy did not believe in God, the Establishment or bourgeois convention, and those who enjoy symbols will relish references to his strange forehead, jutting forward like the prow of a ship and cleaving its single-minded way through hitherto calm waters. And yet for most of those friends it was worth the struggle. Paul Dukas reckoned that, in order to appreciate Debussy's character fully, you had to have known him when he was young, before *Pelléas* brought fame and, more damaging still, responsibility. But as these memoirs amply testify, even in later life he remained a man of huge personality and extraordinary charm.

Like Ravel, he did not much like talking about music, preferring 'life' in all its aspects. He was no superman: good at rolling cigarettes, bad at tennis, a superb cook, an infuriatingly slow and incompetent bridge player. One of the biggest question marks of all hovers over the real nature of his second marriage. One hears rumours that he indulged in table-tapping and that Emma disapproved, and certainly she did her best to make his life difficult whenever he escaped from her immediate control, as on his tour of Russia in 1913. On the other hand, he cannot have been the easiest of husbands (his charm was not turned exclusively upon the male sex) and she did provide for him the privacy that he needed in order to do his work – the incomparable quality of which was yet another reason for his friends and fellow musicians, like Bartók, to forgive him his sins against the social order.

As in *Ravel Remembered*, I have omitted irrelevant or uninteresting passages without notice, but sources at the end of each extract are quoted as exactly as possible. Where no translation of a source is acknowledged, the translation is mine. Some two-thirds of the material appears here in English for the first time.

ROGER NICHOLS
Docklow, Herefordshire
January 1992

Chronology

Debussy's Life and Works
Contemporary Figures and Events

1862   22 *August* Achille-Claude Debussy born at Saint-Germain-en-
        Laye, near Paris

1862   Delius, Klimt born
                Halévy (63), Thoreau (45) die
                First performances of *Béatrice et Bénédict* (Berlioz), *La forza
                del destino* (Verdi)
                The Companies Act introduced

1863   Cavafy, Mascagni, Edvard Munch, Pierné born
                Delacroix (65), Alfred de Vigny (66), Thackeray (52) die
                Renan's *La vie de Jésus* published
                First Salon des Refusés in Paris
                Gounod's *Faust* produced in London, Dublin and New York
                First performances of *Les troyens à Carthage* (Berlioz), *Les
                pêcheurs de perles* (Bizet)
                French troops occupy Mexico
                First underground railway completed in London
                Poles rebel against Russia

1864   Richard Strauss born
                Nathaniel Hawthorne (58), Meyerbeer (73) die
                First performance of *Mireille* (Gounod)
                Civil war in Japan
                Papal Syllabus of Errors

1865   Dukas, Glazunov, Sibelius, W. B. Yeats born
                Pierre Proudhon (56) dies
                First performance of *L'africaine* (Meyerbeer), *Tristan und
                Isolde* (Wagner)
                End of American Civil War
                Lincoln assassinated
                Massachusetts Institute of Technology founded

1866   Busoni, Kandinsky, Satie born
                Rückert (78) dies
                Le Parnasse contemporain first published
                First performances of *The Bartered Bride* (Smetana), *Mignon*
                (Thomas), Symphony No. 1 (Bruckner)
                Prussia defeats Austria
                Submarine telegraphic cable completed between Ireland and
                Newfoundland
                Alfred Nobel invents dynamite

1867   Family settles in Paris

1867   Bonnard, Granados, Emil Nolde, Pirandello born
                Charles Baudelaire (46) dies
                Exposition Universelle in Paris
                First performances of *Roméo et Juliette* (Gounod), *La grande
                duchesse de Gérolstein* (Offenbach), *Cox and Box* (Sullivan),
                Don Carlos (Verdi), Symphony No. 1 (Borodin), Symphony
                No. 1 (Tchaikovsky)
                Dominion of Canada established
                Sholes invents the typewriter

1868   Stefan George, Scott Joplin, Vuillard born
                Rossini (76) dies
                First performances of *Mefistofele* (Boito), *Dalibor* (Smetana),
                Die Meistersinger von Nürnberg (Wagner), Piano Concerto
                (Grieg), Piano Concerto No. 2 (Saint-Saëns)
                Trade Union Congress founded

1869   Gide, Matisse, Pfitzner, Roussel, Frank Lloyd Wright born
                Berlioz (66), Dargomizhsky (56) die
                First performance of *Das Rheingold* (Wagner)
                Suez Canal opened
                Mendelyev devises the periodic table

1870   Florent Schmitt born
                Charles Dickens (58) dies
                First performance of *Die Walküre* (Wagner)
                Franco-Prussian War
                Negro suffrage enforced in USA
                Papal infallibility asserted by First Vatican Council
                Education Act makes primary education open to all in Great
                Britain

1871   Achille visits Cannes, has piano lessons with Jean Cerutti

        March Manuel joins National Guard

        December On defeat of Commune Manuel is sentenced to four
        years' imprisonment

1871   Proust, Rouault born
                Auber (89) dics
                Société nationale de musique founded

First performances of *Aida* (Verdi), *Rouet d'Omphale* (Saint-Saëns)
Paris Commune
Trades unions legalized in Britain

1872   *October* Achille enters Paris Conservatoire, in classes of Lavignac and Marmontel

1872   Diaghilev, Mondrian, Skryabin, Vaughan Williams born
Théophile Gautier (61) dies
Tolstoy completes *War and Peace*
First performances of *L'arlésienne*, *Djamileh* (Bizet), *The Stone Guest* (Dargomizhsky)
Secret ballot introduced in Britain

1873   Rakhmaninov, Reger, de Séverac born
John Stuart Mill (67) dies
First performances of *Jeux d'enfants* (Bizet), *Rédemption* (Franck), *Ivan the Terrible* (Rimsky-Korsakov), Symphony No. 2 (Bruckner), Cello Concerto No. 1 (Saint-Saëns), Symphony No. 2 (Tchaikovsky)
Ashanti War

1874   Wins third prize for *solfège*
Plays Chopin's F minor Concerto in Conservatoire concert

1874   Holst, Ives, Schoenberg born
Monet's *Impression, Sunrise* exhibited
First performances of *Boris Godunov* (Mussorgsky), *La danse macabre* (Saint-Saëns), *Die Fledermaus* (Strauss)
Bourbons recalled in Spain
Disraeli begins last term of office

1875   Wins second medal for *solfège* and first certificate of merit for performance of Chopin's Second Ballade

1875   Ravel, Rilke, Robert Frost, Thomas Mann, Roger-Ducasse, Hann born
Bizet (37), Corot (79), Sterndale Bennett (59) die
First performances of *Carmen* (Bizet), *Symphonie espagnole* (Lalo), Piano Concerto No. 4 (Saint-Saëns)
Third Republic founded in France
Disraeli wins control of Suez Canal for Britain

1876   Wins first medal for *solfège*

1876   Casals, Falla, Monteux, Vlaminck born
                First performances of *Der Ring des Nibelung* (Wagner), *Sylvia*
                (Delibes), *La Gioconda* (Ponchielli), *The Kiss* (Smetana), *Peer*
                Gynt (Grieg's music to Ibsen's play), Symphony No. 1
                (Brahms)
                Purcell Society founded
                End of the Second Carlist War in Spain
                Alexander Graham Bell patents the telephone
                Custer's last stand

1877   Wins second prize for piano

1877   Dohnányi, Cortot, Dufy, van Dongen born
                First performances of *L'étoile* (Chabrier), *Samson et Dalila*
                (Saint-Saëns), Symphony No. 2 (Brahms), Symphony No. 2
                (Borodin), Symphony No. 3 (Bruckner)
                Queen Victoria proclaimed Empress of India
                Russia declares war on the Turks
                Edison invents the phonograph

1878   Schreker, Masefield, Augustus John, Caplet born
                First performances of Symphony No. 4 (Tchaikovsky)
                Exposition Universelle in Paris
                Bulgaria established as separate principality under Turkey

1879   *October* Enters Bazille's class of accompaniment and practical
        harmony
        First surviving compositions date from around this year

1879   Beecham, Bridge, Delage, E. M. Forster, Ireland, Klee,
                Respighi born
                Viollet-le-Duc (65) dies
                First performances of *Eugene Onegin* (Tchaikovsky), *Une édu-*
                cation manquée (Chabrier)
                Jules Grévy elected President of the French Republic

1880   *July* First prize in practical harmony
        Mme von Meck engages him as pianist, travelling to Switzer-
        land and Italy

        December Enters Guiraud's composition class

1880   Bloch, Derain, Epstein, Medtner, Pizzetti, Thibaud born
                George Eliot (61), Flaubert (59), Offenbach (61), Wieniaw-
                ski (45) die
                First performances of *A May Night* (Rimsky-Korsakov),
                Pirates of Penzance (Sullivan)
                Gladstone becomes Prime Minister for the second time

1881   *July* Returns to Mme von Meck, this time in Moscow
          Accompanist for Mme Moreau-Sainti's singing class
          Meets Blanche Vasnier and dedicates a number of songs to
          her

1881   Bartók, Enescu, Léger, Miaskovsky, Picasso born
                Carlyle (86), Dostoevsky (60), Mussorgsky (42), Vieuxtemps
                (61) die
                First performances of *Les contes d'Hoffmann* (Offenbach),
                Piano Concerto No. 2 (Brahms), Symphony No. 4 (Bruck-
                ner)
                Boers defeat British at Majuba Hill
                First Irish Home Rule Bill
                In Egypt the Mahdi announces his aim of world domination
                Canadian Pacific Railway formed
                First electric tram runs in Berlin

1882   *May* Plays own music for first time in public

          July Second certificate for counterpoint and fugue

          August Returns to Mme von Meck in Russia, then to Vienna
          First versions of 'En sourdine' and 'Clair de lune', *Mandoline*
          First work published (*Nuit d'étoiles*)

1882   Braque, Joyce, Kodály, Malipiero, Stravinsky, Szymanow-
                ski, Virginia Woolf born
                First performances of *The Snow Maiden* (Rimsky-Korsakov),
                Parsifal (Wagner)
                Britain fighting in Egypt; Cairo occupied

1883   *June* Wins second Prix de Rome with setting of *Le gladiateur*

1883   Ansermet, Bax, Casella, Kafka, Webern born
                Manet (51), Wagner (70) die
                First performances of *Lakmé* (Delibes), Symphony No. 3
                (Brahms)

1884   *June* Wins first Prix de Rome with setting of *L'enfant prodigue*

1884   Modigliani born
               Smetana (60) dies
               First performances of *Manon* (Massenet), *Le villi* (Puccini),
               Symphony No. 4 (Brahms), Symphony No. 7 (Bruckner),
               Symphony No. 6 (Dvořák)
               Fabian Society founded
               Invention of Maxim machine-gun
               Third Reform Bill

1885   *January* Leaves for Villa Medici in Rome

       November Hears Liszt, who encourages him to listen to works
       of Palestrina and Lassus
       'L'ombre des arbres', 'Chevaux de bois'

1885   Berg, Klemperer, D. H. Lawrence, Pound, Varèse, Wellesz
               born
               Victor Hugo (83) dies
               First performances of Symphony No. 7 (Dvořák), *The
               Mikado* (Sullivan), *Der Zigeunerbaron* (Strauss)
               Khartoum captured: General Gordon killed
               Canadian Pacific Railway completed

1886   Finishes symphonic ode *Zuléima*, first envoi from Rome;
       severely criticized by the Académie
       'Green'

1886   Alain-Fournier born
               Liszt (75) dies
               First performances of *Khovanshchina* (Mussorgsky), *Vari-
               ations symphoniques* (Franck)
               Daimler produces his first motor-car

1887   *February* Returns to Paris
       Printemps, 'C'est l'extase', 'Il pleure dans mon cœur', 'Spleen',
       'La mort des amants'
       Begins *La damoiselle élue*

1887   Rupert Brooke, Chagall, Le Corbusier, Artur Rubinstein,
               Edith Sitwell, Villa-Lobos born
               Borodin (53) dies
               First performances of *Otello* (Verdi)
               Queen Victoria's Jubilee

1888   Hears *Parsifal* and *Die Meistersinger* at Bayreuth
        'Le balcon'
        Begins *Petite suite*, finishes *La damoiselle élue*

1888   Durey, T. S. Eliot, T. E. Lawrence born
            Alkan (75) dies
            First performances of *The Yeomen of the Guard* (Sullivan),
            Symphony No. 5 (Tchaikovsky), *Le roi d'Ys* (Lalo)
            Pasteur Institute established in Paris
            Pneumatic tyre invented

1889   Hears *Parsifal, Die Meistersinger* and *Tristan* at Bayreuth
        Visits Exposition Universelle in Paris
        'Harmonie du soir', 'Le jet d'eau', 'Recueillement'
        Petite suite performed and published, begins *Fantaisie* for
        piano and orchestra

1889   Chaplin, Cocteau born
            Gerard Manley Hopkins (45) dies
            First performances of *Don Juan* (R. Strauss)
            Exposition Universelle in Paris: Eiffel Tower completed
            Death of Crown Prince Rudolf of Austria at Mayerling near
            Vienna

1890   Begins opera *Rodrigue et Chimène* and *Suite bergamasque*,
        finishes *Fantaisie*

1890   Ibert, Frank Martin, Martinů, Nijinsky, Pasternak born
            Van Gogh (37), César Franck (68) die
            First performances of *Prince Igor* (Borodin), *Cavalleria
            rusticana* (Mascagni), *The Queen of Spades* (Tchaikovsky)
            Frazer begins to publish *The Golden Bough*
            Parnell's divorce scandal splits Irish Nationalists
            Charles de Gaulle born

1891   Meets Satie
        First set of *Fêtes galantes*

1891   Bliss, Ernst, Prokofiev born
            Delibes (55), Seurat (32) die
            Hardy's *Tess of the D'Urbervilles* published

1892   *January* Abandons *Rodrigue et Chimène*
        Begins liaison with Gabrielle Dupont

'De rêve', 'De grève'
Begins *Prélude, interludes et paraphrase finale pour l'après-midi d'un faune*

1892   Honegger, Milhaud born
            Lalo (69) dies
            First performances of *I pagliacci* (Leoncavallo), *Werther* (Massenet), Symphony No. 8 (Bruckner)

1893   *February* Meets Oscar Wilde

            April La damoiselle élue performed

            May Sees Maeterlinck's *Pelléas et Mélisande* and begins to set it to music
            Meets Pierre Louÿs

            December String Quartet performed
            'De fleurs', 'De soir'

1893   Mayakovsky, Wilfred Owen born
            Gounod (75), Tchaikovsky (53), Maupassant (43) die
            First performances of *Hänsel und Gretel* (Humperdinck), *Manon Lescaut* (Puccini), *Falstaff* (Verdi), Symphony No. 6 (Tchaikovsky)
            Foundation of Independent Labour Party in Britain

1894   *February* Engaged to singer Thérèse Roger

            March Ysaÿe gives first all-Debussy concert in Brussels
            Engagement broken off

            December Prélude à l'après-midi d'un faune performed

1894   e. e. cummings, Aldous Huxley, Piston, James Thurber born
            Chabrier (53) dies
            First performances of Symphony No. 1 (Mahler), *Thaïs* (Massenet), Symphony No. 5 (Bruckner)
            Dreyfus convicted of treason
            Japan declares war against China

1895   *August* Finishes first version of *Pelléas*

1895   Eluard, Robert Graves, Hindemith born
            Promenade Concerts inaugurated in London by Henry Wood
            Oscar Wilde sent to prison

First performances of *Till Eulenspiegel* (R. Strauss), Symphony No. 2 (Mahler)
First commercial showing of moving pictures by Lumière brothers
Freud publishes his first work on psychoanalysis
Röntgen discovers X-rays
Gillette invents the safety razor

1896   *February* First version of 'Sarabande' published

1896   Gerhard, Massine, Scott Fitzgerald, Sessions born
Bruckner (72) dies
First performances of *Andrea Chenier* (Giordano), *La bohème* (Puccini), *Der Corregidor* (Wolf)
French annex Madagascar
Gold discovered in Klondike

1897   *February* Orchestration of two of Satie's *Gymnopédies* performed

      June Begins *Chansons de Bilitis*

      December Begins final version of *Nocturnes*

1897   William Faulkner, Thornton Wilder born
Brahms (64) dies
Queen Victoria's Diamond Jubilee

1898   *June* Prosecuted for debts
Liaison with Gabrielle Dupont ends
'Dieu, qu'il la fait bon regarder', 'Yver, vous n'estes qu'un villain'

1898   Brecht, Eisenstein, Gershwin, Hemingway, Henry Moore born
Aubrey Beardsley (26) dies
Ballad of Reading Gaol (Wilde) published
First performances of *Véronique* (Messager), *Sadko* (Rimsky-Korsakov)
The Curies discover radium
Zeppelin invents rigid airship

1899   *October* Marries Rosalie (Lily) Texier

      December Finishes *Nocturnes*

1899   Auric, Noël Coward, Alfred Hitchcock, Lorca, Vladimir
       Nabokov, Poulenc born
       Chausson (44), Johann Strauss (74) die
       First performances of *The Tsar's Bride* (Rimsky-Korsakov),
       Enigma Variations (Elgar)
       Boer War
       Aspirin first marketed
       Dreyfus retried and again convicted

1900   *December* 'Nuages' and 'Fêtes' performed

1900   Antheil, Copland, Křenek, Kurt Weill born
       Sullivan (59) dies
       First performances of *Louise* (Charpentier), *Tosca* (Puccini),
       The Tale of Tsar Saltan (Rimsky-Korsakov), *The Dream of
       Gerontius* (Elgar)
       Opening of Paris Métro
       Boer War: relief of Kimberley and of Mafeking
       Boxer Rebellion in China
       Publication of Freud's *The Interpretation of Dreams*
       Gamma rays discovered

1901   *April* Becomes music critic for *La Revue Blanche*

       May Receives written assurance that *Pelléas* will be per-
       formed the following season

       October Nocturnes performed complete

1901   Giacometti, Malraux, Rubbra, Sauguet born
       Verdi (88), Toulouse-Lautrec (37) die
       First performances of *Rusalka* (Dvořák), *Feuersnot* (R.
       Strauss), Piano Concerto No. 2 (Rakhmaninov), Symphony
       No. 4 (Mahler), Symphony No. 6 (Bruckner)
       Death of Queen Victoria
       Marconi transmit radio signals across the Atlantic
       Nobel Prizes inaugurated

1902   *January Pour le piano* performed

       30 April Première of opera *Pelléas et Mélisande*

1902   Marlene Dietrich, Ogden Nash, Walton born
       Samuel Butler (67) dies
       First performances of *Adriana Lecouvreur* (Cilea), *Merrie*

England (Edward German), Symphony No. 2 (Sibelius), Symphony No. 3 (Mahler)
End of Boer War

1903   *February* Appointed Chevalier of the Legion of Honour
Estampes
Begins *La mer*

1903   Blacher, Khachaturian, Nicholas Nabokov, Simenon, Waugh born
Gauguin (55), Hugo Wolf (43) die
First performances of *The Apostles* (Elgar), Symphony No. 9 (Bruckner)
First controlled flight in heavier-than-air machine by Wright brothers

1904   *June* Abandons Lily for Emma Bardac
Danse sacrée et danse profane, *Masques*, *L'isle joyeuse*, *Trois chansons de France*, second set of *Fêtes galantes*

1904   Balanchine, Dali, Dallapiccola, Graham Greene, Kabalevsky, Skalkottas born
Chekhov (44), Dvořák (63) die
First performances of *Madama Butterfly* (Puccini), String Quartet (Ravel), Symphony No. 5 (Mahler)
Russo-Japanese War (1904–5)
Entente Cordiale between France and Britain

1905   *March* Finishes piano score of *La mer*

August Divorced from Lily

October Daughter Claude-Emma (Chouchou) born
La mer performed

1905   Greta Garbo, Jolivet, Koestler, Constant Lambert, Sartre, Rawsthorne, Tippett born
First performances of *The Merry Widow* (Lehár), *Salome* (R. Strauss)
Law of Separation of Church and State passed in France
Einstein publishes his *Special Theory of Relativity*
Revolution in Russia

1906   *March* Has dinner with Richard Strauss
First set of piano *Images* performed

1906   Samuel Beckett, Betjeman, Shostakovich born
            Arensky (44), Cézanne (67), Ibsen (78) die
            First performances of *The Kingdom* (Elgar), *The Wreckers*
            (Smyth), Symphony No. 6 (Mahler)
            San Francisco earthquake
            Vitamins discovered

1907   *January/April Pelléas* performed in Brussels and Frankfurt

1907   Auden, Moravia born
            Grieg (64) dies
            First performances of *A Village Romeo and Juliet* (Delius),
            Ariane et Barbe-bleue (Dukas)
            Picasso paints *Les demoiselles d'Avignon*
            Publication of Bergson's *Creative Evolution*
            First helicopter flies

1908   *January* Marries Emma Bardac

        February Conducts in London
        Pelléas performed in New York, second set of piano *Images*
        performed

        March Pelléas performed in Milan, conducted by Toscanini

        December Children's Corner performed

1908   Elliott Carter, Messiaen born
            Rimsky-Korsakov (64) dies
            First performances of Symphony No. 1 (Elgar), Symphony
            No. 7 (Mahler)
            Belgium annexes Congo
            First Model T Ford

1909   *February* Appointed member of the advisory board of the
        Conservatoire
        Conducts again in London

        May Supervises Covent Garden première of *Pelléas*
        'Rondes de printemps'
        Begins Clarinet Rhapsody and first book of *Préludes*

1909   Proust begins *A la recherche du temps perdu*
            Marinetti and Futurists publish manifesto in Milan
            First performances of *The Golden Cockerel* (Rimsky-

Korsakov), *Elektra* (R. Strauss), *Il segreto di Susanna* (Wolf-
Ferrari), Piano Concerto No. 3 (Rakhmaninov)
Joan of Arc beatified
Blériot flies across the English Channel
Bakelite invented

1910   *February Ibéria* performed

April Has dinner with Mahler

June Hears Stravinsky's *The Firebird* and meets the composer

October Father dies

November Travels to Vienna and Budapest
Trois ballades de François Villon
First book of *Préludes* published

1910   Anouilh, Samuel Barber, Jean Genet born
Balakirev (74), Tolstoy (82) die
First performances of *La fanciulla del West* (Puccini), *The
Firebird* (Stravinsky), Violin Concerto (Elgar), *A Sea Sym-
phony* and *Fantasia on a Theme by Tallis* (Vaughan Williams),
Symphony No. 8 (Mahler)
Union of South Africa

1911   *May Le martyre de Saint Sébastien* performed

June Travels to Turin

1911   Mahler (51) dies
Thomas Mann writes *Death in Venice*
Bruno Walter conducts posthumous first performance of *Das
Lied von der Erde* in Vienna
First performances of *Der Rosenkavalier* (R. Strauss), *Petru-
shka* (Stravinsky), Symphony No. 2 (Elgar), *L'heure espagnole*
(Ravel)
Nationalist Republic set up in China under Sun Yat-sen
Vitamins classified
Amundsen reaches South Pole

1912   *May* Ballet on *Prélude à l'après-midi d'un faune* performed by
Ballets Russes

September Finishes first version of *Jeux*

27 *December* 100th performance of *Pelléas* at Opéra-Comique

1912   Cage, Ionesco born
        Massenet (70) dies
        First performances of *Der ferne Klang* (Schreker), *Ariadne auf Naxos*, first version (R. Strauss), *Pierrot lunaire* (Schoenberg), *Daphnis et Chloé* (Ravel)
        China becomes a republic
        Titanic sinks
        Scott's last expedition to the South Pole

1913   *January* Orchestral *Images* performed complete

        May Jeux performed by Ballets Russes, Loie Fuller gives choreographic version of 'Nuages' and 'Sirènes'

        December Visits Moscow and St Petersburg at invitation of Koussevitsky
        Second book of *Préludes* published

1913   Britten, Camus, Lutoslawski born
        First performances of *La vida breve* (Falla), *Pénélope* (Fauré), *Le sacre du printemps* (Stravinsky), Piano Concerto No. 2 (Prokofiev)
        Treaty of Bucharest

1914   *February* Visits Rome, The Hague and Amsterdam

        July Last visit to London

1914   Panufnik, Dylan Thomas, Tennessee Williams born
        Alain-Fournier (28), Liadov (59) die
        First performances of *The Immortal Hour* (Rutland Boughton), *A London Symphony* (Vaughan Williams)
        Ezra Pound begins work on his *Cantos*
        Opening of Panama Canal
        Archduke Franz Ferdinand of Austria assassinated at Sarajevo
        Outbreak of First World War

1915   *March* Mother dies

        December Undergoes operation for cancer
        En blanc et noir, Cello Sonata, *Etudes*, Sonata for Flute, Viola and Harp

1915   Saul Bellow, Arthur Miller, Orson Welles born
        Rupert Brooke (28), Skryabin (43) die
        Chaplin's film *The Tramp*
        Henry Ford develops the first farm tractor
        Einstein publishes his *General Theory of Relativity*
        Lusitania sunk

1916   *October* Begins Violin Sonata

        December Etudes performed

1916   Babbitt born
        Granados (49), Henry James (73), Reger (43) die
        First performances of *Savîtri* (Holst)
        Battles of Verdun, the Somme, Jutland

1917   *September* Last appearance on concert platform, accompanying
        Violin Sonata

1917   Robert Lowell, Sidney Nolan born
        Degas (83) dies
        First performances of *Turandot* and *Arlecchino* (Busoni), *Pales-
        trina* (Pfitzner), *La rondine* (Puccini), *Parade* (Satie)
        Bolshevik Revolution in Russia
        Balfour Declaration

1918   *25 March* Debussy dies, aged 55

1918   Apollinaire (38), Klimt (56), Wilfred Owen (25), Parry (70)
        die
        First performances of *The Miraculous Mandarin* (Bartók), *Il
        trittico* (Puccini), *Histoire du soldat* (Stravinsky), Classical
        Symphony (Prokofiev)
        End of First World War
        Publication of Spengler's *The Decline of the West*

I
Youth and student years

Achille-Claude Debussy was born on 22 August 1862 in Saint-Germain-en-Laye, just to the west of Paris, the son of Victorine Manoury and Manuel Debussy, who at that time was keeping a small china shop. Achille was the eldest of five children. His musical gifts were fostered by Mme Mauté de Fleurville, Verlaine's mother-in-law, and in October 1872 he entered the Conservatoire to study *solfège* with Albert Lavignac and piano with Antoine Marmontel. In 1884 he won the Prix de Rome at the second attempt and took up residence at the Villa Medici the following year. He returned to Paris in 1887.

GABRIEL PIERNE

(1863–1937)

Gabriel Pierné was a pupil of Franck and Massenet at the Conservatoire. He won the Prix de Rome in 1882 and succeeded Franck as organist of Ste Clotilde in 1890. From 1910 to 1934 he was chief conductor of the Concerts Colonne. He conducted the first performance of *Ibéria* in 1910, the first concert performance of *Jeux* in 1914 and the first performance of *Khamma*, also in concert, in 1924.

I got to know Debussy around 1873 in Lavignac's *solfège* class at the Conservatoire. He was a fat boy of ten or so, short, thickset, wearing a black coat enlivened by a loose, spotted tie and short, velvet trousers. He lived on the fourth floor in the rue Clapeyron. His clumsiness and awkwardness were extraordinary, in addition to which he was shy and even unsociable.

In Marmontel's piano class he used to astound us with his bizarre playing. Whether it was through natural maladroitness or through shyness I don't know, but he literally used to charge at the piano and force all his effects. He seemed to be in a rage with the instrument, rushing up and down it with impulsive gestures and breathing noisily during the difficult bits. These faults gradually receded and occasionally he would obtain effects of an astonishing softness. With all its faults and virtues, his playing remained something highly individual.

He was a gourmet, not a gourmand. He liked nice things and quantity didn't matter to him. I can still remember clearly the way he used to savour the cup of chocolate which my mother would buy him at Prévost's, when he came out of the Conservatoire, or the way at Borbonneux's, where there was a window reserved for de luxe items, he would choose a tiny sandwich or a little dish of macaroni, instead of gorging himself on more substantial cakes, like his colleagues. Poor as he was, and from the humblest of origins, he had aristocratic tastes in everything.

He showed a particular predilection for minuscule objects and for things that were fragile and delicate. My father had a collection of the *Monde Illustré*, expensively bound. When Achille (as he was then called) came to the house, we used to love looking at the pictures in it. Debussy preferred the ones which didn't take up much room and had a huge margin left round them. One day he persuaded me to join him in cutting out these illustrations to decorate our bedrooms. The crime was soon committed and I remember Debussy taking away reproductions of well-known pictures, by Meissonier especially, surrounded by immense margins. I need not dwell on my parents' angry response!

I lost sight of him in the senior classes. I was studying with Massenet, he with Guiraud, but I was still in Rome when he arrived at the Villa Medici in 1885. Although he lived side by side with his fellow students, there was no real intimacy between them. He went out a lot, spent his time with antique dealers and made a clean sweep of tiny Japanese objects which entranced him. He was never to be seen except at meals.

Gabriel Pierné, 'Souvenirs d'Achille Debussy', *ReM*, 7, 1 May 1926, pp. 10–11

REVIEW

(concert of 16 January 1876)

Debussy (or rather de Bussy) appeared at Chauny (Aisne) with a singer, Mlle Mendès, a violinist, M. Mansart and a cellist, M. Samary.

Mlle Mendès and M. Samary will return to Chauny . . . And so, even more decidedly, will De Bussy, who carries so much courage inside such a small body. What verve! What enthusiasm! What real spirit! Never again can it be said that the piano is a cold instrument, that the finger which strikes the key is such a long way from the string that vibrates, that its life is lost along the way or that the sound is dead! This little budding Mosart [*sic*] is a veritable tearaway. When he takes over the piano, he imbues the strings with his whole soul. MM. Mansart and Samary needed all their considerable skill to keep up with him in the Haydn Trio, in which he was carried away by a charming frenzy; he is still not fourteen years old!

'Claude Debussy (1862–1962)', *Revue de Musicologie*, numéro spécial, 1962, p. 97

PAUL VIDAL

(1863–1931)

Paul Vidal studied at the Conservatoire and won the Prix de Rome in 1883, the year before Debussy. As well as composing, Vidal occupied a succession of posts at the Opéra, being made chief conductor in 1906. From 1914 to 1919 he was director of music at the Opéra-Comique.

I met Achille Debussy in October 1878 in Marmontel *père*'s piano class. I was immediately struck by his singular appearance, his burning eyes and the fierce, concentrated expression on his face; there was something of the savage about him. I succeeded in taming him and we soon became close friends.

Debussy had won the second prize for piano two years earlier and hoped to win the first prize in the summer of 1879, but he failed – a great disappointment for him and especially for his family, who wanted him to have a brilliant career as a pianist. His playing was very interesting but not without its defects: he had difficulty with trills, but his left hand was extremely agile and had an extraordinary capacity for extension. His gifts as a pianist showed themselves to particular effect during the years that followed in Bazille's accompaniment class, where he distinguished himself.

Our close friendship really began in Emile Durand's harmony class, during that same year of 1878/9. Debussy was not the poor pupil that some people had claimed. He did not see eye to eye with his teacher in the sense that, instead of coming up with the harmonic realizations which the latter was expecting, he always went one step further, inventing solutions that were ingenious, elegant and delightful but totally unacademic; and Durand, who was a good teacher but rather inflexible, had harsh words to say on the subject. Debussy, Pierné and I formed an inseparable trio in this class and once a week, when the weather was fine, we used to go and do our counterpoint in the Parc Monceau looking over the lake, where Debussy used to take great delight in the antics of the ducks.

I was a great admirer of Debussy's songs and never got tired of listening to *Madrid, princesse des Espagnes* and *Ballade à la lune*. As I was always bullying him to play me his latest pieces, and as he didn't necessarily have the time or the inclination to compose, he played a joke on me, getting me to learn by heart a volume of songs by Pessard and singing me *Les joueusetés de bonne compagnie* as though he himself had written it.

Mme Debussy was passionately attached to her son and a very excitable person: every letter she received from him when he was away was a real event in her life. She was very kind and spoilt me thoroughly; she was an excellent cook and was fond of preparing delicious side-dishes, which also appealed to Debussy's highly developed gastronomic tastes. She and her husband came from a very modest class, but could not be labelled as belonging to the masses because they were interested in everything and well informed. They went to all the latest theatre productions and liked discussing them.

During the years before his journeys to Russia and Vienna in 1881 and 1882, which revealed new horizons to him, Debussy's tastes were largely formed by the repertoire of Marmontel's class. There was considerable emphasis on the music of Chopin and Schumann, for whom Debussy had a special affection, and a great deal of Heller and Alkan was also played. These composers aside, Debussy professed warm admiration for Berlioz and particularly for Lalo: he could play off by heart passages of *Namouna*, which was as yet unpublished. He was a fervent supporter of Saint-Saëns's *Samson et Dalila* and enjoyed other theatre music by Delibes, Guiraud and even Pessard, whose *Capitaine Fracasse* delighted him.

He pretended to loathe Beethoven, but when we were in Rome together I twice saw him display enthusiasm for the German master, at performances of the Fifth Piano Concerto and of the Second Symphony. He was fond of 'Père Franck' and possessed a score of his *Béatitudes*. Like me, Debussy spent some time in Franck's organ class at the Conservatoire, and we both used to enjoy the old *maître*'s original behaviour and the way he would exclaim to his pupils, as they got near the end of an improvisation: 'Modulate . . . modulate . . . , further . . . further.' And then, alarmed by some eccentricity: 'Not too far . . . not too far.' These little ways of his did not diminish the affectionate respect in which we held him.

In 1880 Debussy joined Guiraud's class in his first year as a composition teacher, while I had been studying for two years already under Massenet. But we still continued to meet, and it was through me that he became the accompanist for Mme Moreau-Sainti's singing classes. In the summer of 1883 I won the Prix de Rome and Debussy came second, with the cantata *Le gladiateur*. This event was celebrated in the Debussy household by a meal which I still remember with pleasure. I was treated absolutely as one of the family and Ernest Guiraud presided over the festivities.

When I left for Rome, Debussy succeeded me as accompanist to the choral society La Concordia, directed by Mme Henriette Fuchs, with Gounod as president. As Gounod used to come to the society's rehearsals every Saturday, on his way back from the Institut, he got to know Debussy and took a keen interest in him. He backed him forcefully in 1884 in his successful attempt at the Prix de Rome with the cantata *L'enfant prodigue*. Gounod appreciated Debussy's extraordinary gifts and did not hesitate to proclaim that he was a 'genius'.

At the end of January 1885, I had the pleasure of seeing Debussy arrive at the Villa Medici. He was not the solitary figure that he liked to make out in his letters. Even though he complained from time to time of the lack of camaraderie in the Villa, he used to appear at the soirées given by the director, M. Hébert, playing piano duets and singing his songs, which everyone adored: there were continual demands in particular for *Chevaux de bois*, *Mandoline* and *Fantoches* (which he later altered – in my opinion, to its detriment). He and I spent most of our time together, playing piano duet arrangements of Bach's organ works, which he was passionate about. We also studied closely the two-piano arrangement of Beethoven's Ninth Symphony, Chabrier's *Valses romantiques*, etc. It was around this time that we met Liszt at a dinner given by M. Hébert. With Xavier Leroux's arrival in Rome, the three of us would spend our evenings giving readings. We read most of Shakespeare out loud, each of us taking a different role. Debussy had a marked predilection for the Goncourt brothers, Flaubert, Banville and Verlaine, at a time when the last was known only to a small circle. He was also very fond of the poetry of Paul Bourget.

Paul Vidal, 'Souvenirs d'Achille Debussy', *ReM*, 7, 1 May 1926, pp. 11–16

RAYMOND BONHEUR
(1861–1939)

Raymond Bonheur became a composer in a small way. One of his songs, *Avec les pistolets aux fontes* to words by Francis Jammes, was orchestrated by Debussy, though the score is now lost. He wrote one opera, *Mavra*, and planned another, *Le retour*, in collaboration with Gide.

It must have been in 1878, one gloomy morning when the Conservatoire classes were restarting after the summer holidays, that I saw Debussy for the first time; his mother had come to introduce him to our harmony professor, Emile Durand, and I remember that even though he was beyond the age of such things, he was dressed that day like a student in the junior piano classes, with short trousers and a velvet smock.

His exceptional gifts became clear from his earliest exercises: whether he was given a tune or a bass line to work from, he rarely failed to produce an ingenious realization, enlivening its banality with some subtle and unexpected harmony (a young composer who had already made his mark by winning the Prix de Rome visited our class one day and, as sometimes occurred, set us an exercise – a theme which we had to harmonize in four parts; came the day for him to correct them, and he was so disconcerted by the charming spontaneity of the young beginner's solution that, in a rare and elegant gesture, he took his own realization and tore it up in front of us).

Debussy and I became friends through a volume of Banville which I found in his hands, a rather surprising discovery in that milieu. He normally arrived at the last minute, coming across the courtyard of the old Conservatoire with the short, hurried steps which always characterized him. When the class was over we would often leave together and just as often I would go and see him at his parents' house and he would play me his earliest compositions on an old piano (I can see it still) with its keys covered in cigarette burns. Most of his settings of Bourget date from those long distant days, together with a number of small pieces which I recall only indistinctly, some of them later reworked under various titles; then a little later came his settings of Verlaine, full of exquisite feeling and already recognizably by him; I seem to remember also a rhapsody in the manner of Liszt, and thoughts of setting Banville's *Florise*, which never got beyond the project stage.

He seemed then to be withdrawn and rather distant, with a marked predilection for everything that was rare and precious, but a singularly attractive person none the less, despite a certain brusqueness on first acquaintance; and he was exactly the same when I met him again a few years later on his return from Rome, when he used to enjoy passing the time in the Brasserie Pousset. One noticed his forehead, that powerful forehead with the strange faunlike cast, which he thrust ahead of him like the prow of a ship; his brown eyes, hidden away beneath the frowning eyebrows and obstinately fixed on a point far away directly in front of him, while his index finger in a characteristic gesture tapped the ash from his cigarette. As often happens with people who are not satisfied with clichés and think for themselves, his speech was hesitant and he generally expressed himself in a voice that lisped slightly, in short, incomplete phrases, in monosyllables sometimes, trying his hardest to find a word supple enough to get across the nuance of an impression or a point of view.

With his dark hair, sensual nose and pale face surrounded by a light fringe of beard, Debussy in those days made you think of one of those noble portraits painted by Titian, and you could easily imagine him in the lavish surroundings of some Venetian palace. Born poor, he entered life with the tastes, needs and carefree attitude of a great lord; nothing upset him more than to be taken for a professional man and the very phrase filled him with a secret horror (a piece of innocent mystification: at the wedding of one of our friends, for whom we were standing as witnesses, Debussy signed the register in the usual way; then, having to say what his profession was, he thought for a moment before solemnly putting down 'gardener').

His parents had dreamt of a brilliant career for him as a virtuoso, but the discipline and enthusiasm required of a performer soon discouraged him. Certainly his extreme facility and the rare quality of his gifts could have made him a successful composer at an age when few people can resist such a lure; but his ambitions aimed higher than that, and he would more readily have agreed to forge banknotes than write three bars without feeling the imperious need to do so. There was in him no trace of that somewhat fatuous vulgarity so common among artists, nor of that tone of amiable camaraderie which often masks underhand intentions. He was extremely sensitive to the opinions of one or two people and had an extraordinary capacity for enthusiasm if a new work gave him grounds for it – he was in the thick of that stormy first performance of Lalo's *Namouna*, where his furious clapping and provocative attitude created such a scandal that the regular subscribers successfully insisted on the Conservatoire box being forbidden to students of the composition classes for several months. But at the same time he showed as great an indifference as I have ever known to the opinions of the masses, and above all a fine pride which was no more than his consciousness of living in some sense on a superior plane. He was, what is more, so totally devoid of any spirit of intrigue, of 'arrivisme' as they say, that one may wonder what would have become of *Pelléas* if the publisher Georges Hartmann had not appeared on the scene.

It is well known what an incomparable player he was of his own works, providing not only the illusion of an orchestra, but an extraordinary impression of life and movement. His hollow voice was rich in emphasis and expression, and those who have not heard him in the terrible scene with the hair in the fourth act of *Pelléas* can have no suspicion of its real tragic power. But it was when he played from a still uncertain sketch, with the fever of improvisation still more or less upon him, that he was truly prodigious – 'How I envy painters', he used to say, 'who can embody their dreams in the freshness of a sketch.' I shall always remember how dazzled I was when he showed me *L'après-midi d'un faune* in its original state, rippling with light, aflame with all the heat of summer, giving off a blinding radiance which was to be resisted in certain quarters for many a year.

It was a glorious late afternoon – he was living then on the rue de Londres, almost on the corner with the rue d'Amsterdam – and through the large open window the setting sun reached right to the back of the room . . . I have often heard *L'après-midi d'un faune* since, but no performance, however perfect, could make me forget those few minutes. In the same way, when I think of *Pelléas*, I like to remember the various episodes not in the dusty scenery of the Opéra-Comique, but in the charming atmosphere of that apartment on the rue Gustave-Doré where I saw them being born and transformed, one after the other. It was usually on Saturday afternoons that I would climb the four storeys and I could be almost certain of meeting some friendly face there; Satie, in any case, would be sure to heed the summons and would come from Arcueil, always on foot, and would be particularly punctual that day because he would have the use of the piano in the house until the evening. Debussy would begin by preparing tea with minute care, then, between a joke and a morsel of gossip, would sometimes let fall a brief, penetrating remark about the art he was then aiming at – but undogmatically, since he had no leanings towards the solemn, professorial tone. This art was one free of all formalism or any building-up of empty complexities, an art made of perpetual sacrifice, everything being subordinated to the single-minded search for expressivity. If he was particularly pleased with what he had been doing, he might show us the most recent pages, jumping, as the mood took him, from one act to another of the opera which then held him totally in its thrall; because, when he was first attracted by Maeterlinck's drama, he had no preconceived idea of turning it into a theatrical work. Idly, simply for the pleasure it gave him, he began to set to music the long scene by the well in Act IV, so different in its original version from what it was to become; another followed, and then another, and in this way the score found itself finished, almost without his realizing it.

If we now ask ourselves what were the most powerful influences on Debussy at the start of his career, we need to imagine the milieu in which he grew up and to be aware that all through his childhood the only music he got to know was what he was able to hear when his parents took him to the theatre (he retained fond memories of these occasions, and one day when we were discussing *Falstaff*, which he rated very highly, he told me that he came out from a performance of *Il trovatore* literally overwhelmed). It was only when he had the opportunity to study their works in his piano classes that he came into contact with the great Romantics who were to be his real initiators into music: Schumann, Liszt and Chopin – and particularly Chopin, who left an indelible imprint on him. Like many others, it has to be said, he was unable to escape the Wagnerian fever, and *Tristan*, the score of which he always kept by him, filled him with an agitation for which time alone provided the cure.

A journey he made around this time to Russia was particularly important because it seems to have been the start of a new direction in his composing. But the only music he brought back with him was the score of an old opera by Rimsky-Korsakov and some Borodin songs. It was not until around 1893 at Luzancy, where Chausson was kind enough to offer us his hospitality, that Mussorgsky was revealed to us. We were burning to get to know *Boris*, but it was then almost impossible to get hold of a score. Chausson, however, managed to do so and for hours at a time, over entire evenings, Debussy would be at the piano, initiating us into this amazing work.

Raymond Bonheur, 'Souvenirs et impressions d'un compagnon de jeunesse', *ReM*, 7, 1 May 1926, pp. 99–104

CAMILLE BELLAIGUE
(1858–1930)

> Camille Bellaigue became a music critic for the *Revue des Deux Mondes*. In his view Debussy's *Pelléas et Mélisande* contained 'germs of decadence and death'. Antoine François Marmontel (1816–98) was one of the best piano teachers of his time, whose pupils included Bizet, d'Indy, Albéniz and Francis Planté. Under his tutelage Debussy won a second prize in 1877, playing the first movement of Schumann's G minor Sonata.

The least gifted pupils always found in Marmontel something more than indulgence: encouragement, and reasons to hope and believe in themselves, even if their lack of talent meant that this faith could be applied to no more than their goodwill. Among these mediocrities, there was one about whom his companions had few illusions. Or rather, they did have illusions, and plenty of them, but in the wrong direction. The passage of time was to prove them singularly wrong, and to his favour, glory even, rather than theirs. 'There you are at last, my boy!' Marmontel would say, and into the room, frequently late, would come a small, sickly-looking boy. His blouse was held in by a belt and he carried in his hand a sort of beret with braid around the outside and a woollen pompom in the middle, like the hats that sailors wear. Nothing about the young Debussy, neither his looks, nor his comments, nor his playing, suggested an artist, present or future. His face had nothing striking about it except his forehead. He was a pianist, and one of the youngest of us, but not, I repeat, one of the best. I particularly remember his idiosyncrasy, or rather a tic, of emphasizing the strong beats in the bar with a sort of hiccup or raucous gasp. This exaggeration of the rhythms was later to be the least of his faults, in the field of composition at least, if not perhaps in his piano playing. He was very withdrawn, not to say a little surly, and was not regarded sympathetically by his fellow students.

Camille Bellaigue, *Souvenirs de musique et de musiciens* (Paris, 1921), pp. 34–5

NADEZHDA VON MECK

(1831–94)

Nadezhda von Meck was the wife of a contractor for the Russian railways. On her husband's death in 1876 she developed a passion for the music of Tchaikovsky, and for most of his life allowed him a large allowance. Debussy was employed by her as house pianist, in Russia and elsewhere, for three successive summers beginning in 1880. The following extracts are taken from her letters to Tchaikovsky.

10 July 1880, Interlaken

The day before yesterday there arrived from Paris a young pianist who has just won a first prize in Marmontel's class at the Conservatoire. I've engaged him for the summer, to give lessons to the children, to accompany Julia's singing and to play piano duets with me. The young man plays well, his technique is brilliant, but he's lacking in sensibility. He's still too young. He says he's twenty, but looks sixteen.

7 August 1880, Arcachon

Yesterday was the first time I had the courage to play *our* symphony with my little Frenchman. He did not play it well, although he read marvellously at sight. That's his only merit, but a very important one. He can read a score, even one of yours, *like a book*. Another thing in his favour is that he is thrilled by your music. In theory, he is a pupil of Massenet, whom he naturally takes as his guiding star. But yesterday I also played your Suite with him. He was delighted by the fugue, saying: 'I haven't seen anything as good among contemporary fugues. M. Massenet wouldn't be able to do anything like it.' He has no interest in the Germans, because 'they don't have our temperament, they're so heavy and unclear'. Altogether he is a typical product of the Parisian boulevards. He composes very nicely as well, but in that too he's a perfect Frenchman.

13 October 1880, Florence

My little Frenchman is leaving us next week; in fact I have kept him on for an extra fortnight. I'm sorry he's going because his music gave me a lot of pleasure and, all in all, he has a good heart. He was spoilt by a friendship with a Russian student in my employ. For one reason or another this student began to give himself airs and Debussy, who's no more than a child, followed his example, which succeeded only in amusing us. But since the student left a month ago, Debussy has completely changed.

31 October 1880, Florence

Imagine, this boy wept bitter tears when he left. Naturally I was very moved, he has a heart capable of strong attachment. He would not have left if his teachers at the Conservatoire had not vetoed his idea of prolonging his stay.

28 August 1882, Pletchtchevo

Yesterday, to my great joy, Achille Debussy arrived. Now I shall gorge myself listening to music, and he'll bring the whole house to life. He's a Parisian to his fingertips, a real *gamin de Paris*, as witty as they come and a brilliant mimic. He takes Gounod and Ambroise Thomas off perfectly, he makes you die laughing. He has a good nature; everything pleases him and he affords us infinite amusement. In short, a charming boy.

Nadezhda von Meck, Letters to Tchaikovsky, in: Edward Lockspeiser, 'Debussy, Tchaikovsky et Mme von Meck'; and 'Claude Debussy dans la correspondance de Tchaikovsky et de Mme von Meck', *ReM*, 16, November 1935, pp. 246, 247, 249–50; 18, October 1937, p. 218

NICHOLAS VON MECK

Nicholas von Meck was one of Nadezhda's sons.

In the year 1879 my mother, Mme N. F. von Meck, addressed herself to the Paris Conservatoire, requesting them to recommend her a pupil from the piano class who could teach my sisters music during the summer, accompanying their singing, play four-hands with my mother and play in her trios and quartets.

The Conservatoire sent A. Debussy, who was then nineteen. The little Frenchman arrived, dark, thin, sarcastic, and gave everybody amusing nicknames. For instance, he called our plump teacher '*petit hippopotame en vacances*', and we in turn nicknamed him '*le bouillant Achille*'. He joined us in Switzerland, and from there we went to Italy and stopped in Rome. Once we walked past the Villa Medici, where the best students of the Conservatoire and the Academy of Arts [L'Ecole des Beaux Arts] reside for a year at the cost of the French Government. One of us, pointing to the villa, said to Debussy: 'This is your future home.' It was interesting to see how longingly he looked back on the Villa Medici.

From Rome we went to Florence, where we lived at the Villa Oppenheim, and from here, in October, Debussy returned to his studies in Paris. On leaving us he was very sad, and my mother had to comfort him, promising that in the spring of 1880 he would again return to us. He did join us the next year, in Moscow, and he spent the whole summer with us visiting various places and towns in Europe.

My mother considered Debussy a gifted musician, not only as a pianist but also as a composer. He was a pupil of Massenet, and at that time his professor exercised a strong influence on him.

My mother acquainted him with Russian music and with Wagner. Of the Russians he got to know Tchaikovsky and all the members of the 'Kutchka', Rimsky-Korsakov, Cui, Mussorgsky and Borodin. Both Wagner and the Russian composers produced an unfavourable impression on Debussy, which was quite natural, since French music at that time was too near the music of the classical composers, and Debussy, following this tradition, did not react to all innovations.

But as he became better acquainted with Russian music he appreciated it, though by his French nature he was inclined to interpret it in a superficial and elegant manner. No doubt his acquaintance not only with Russian music and Wagner, but also with his contemporaries in other countries, widened his outlook and influenced his development. Of his compositions at that time his song, 'Ici-bas tous les lilas meurent', was frequently sung and played in our house by my sister Julia Pachulska [née von Meck].

In conclusion I may add that as a companion Debussy was a very pleasant, lively and even-tempered man, and we were always sorry when he left us.

Nicholas von Meck, 'Achille-Claude Debussy', manuscript memoir, published in: Edward Lockspeiser, *Debussy* (London, 5/1980), pp. 290–92

MARGUERITE VASNIER

(1869–1935)

Marguerite Vasnier was the daughter of Marie-Blanche Vasnier, with whom Debussy fell deeply in love during the 1880s and for whom he wrote many of his early songs.

At eighteen Debussy was a large, beardless boy, with clearly defined features and thick, black, curly hair which he wore plastered down over his forehead. But when, at the end of the day, his hair became unruly (which suited him much better) he was, my parents said, the image of a Florentine from the Middle Ages. It was a very interesting face; the eyes, especially, attracted your attention; you felt that here was a personality. His hands were strong and bony, with square fingers; his touch on the piano was sonorous, rather percussive but also sometimes very gentle and cantabile.

As he came from a very ordinary, poor family, he had to earn a living and he acted as accompanist for Mme Moreau-Sainti's singing classes. It was there he met my mother, who had a lovely voice and sang superbly. He accompanied her when she sang at society concerts, and at one of them they performed a song of his called *Rondel chinois*.

I have kept two of the programmes for these concerts, and it appears that he had the idea of calling himself Ach. de Bussy. But this little exercise in vanity could not have lasted with someone of his mocking habits.

He was not happy in his family life, caught between a pretentious, rather stupid father and a mean, narrow-minded mother. Given little in the way of encouragement, support or understanding, he asked my parents if he could come and work in their house, and from that moment he was welcome to use the house as if he were a member of the family.

I can still just recall him in the little drawing room on the fifth floor above the rue de Constantinople, where he wrote most of what he produced over a period of five years. He used to arrive most evenings and often in the afternoon as well, leaving the manuscript paper on a little table until later. He composed at the piano, a curiously shaped old Blondel. At other times, he would compose walking about. He used to improvise at length, then walk up and down the room singing to himself, with his eternal cigarette in his mouth or rolling paper and tobacco in his fingers. Then, when he'd found the idea, he wrote it down. He never crossed out a great deal, but he searched a long time in his head before writing anything down and was highly critical of his own work.

In summer, my parents used to rent a little villa at Ville-d'Avray; the singing classes had finished, so Debussy used to arrive every day during the morning and go back on the last train at night. He used to work long hours, but sometimes we went for long walks in the park of Saint-Cloud or played interminable games of croquet. He was very good at it, but a bad loser. Out in the countryside, he would sometimes become as carefree and cheerful as a child. For our walks in the woods, he refused to wear a straw hat, preferring a large, blue, felt one which he wore to one side; one day, as the eternal cigarette had singed the rim slightly, someone covered up the hole by sewing a piece of blue velvet over it, and this sent him into ecstasies. Sometimes he would turn his stick into a guitar and pretend to be a Florentine singer, improvising ditties and serenades or parodying Italian music, which he didn't care for. One day some street singers stopped in front of the house. He started by accompanying them on the piano and with his voice, and then invited them in and made them play, adding a line in patter which had us all rocking with laughter. He had moments of extreme gaiety like that, but these would be followed by hours of gloom and discouragement.

In the evenings, my mother would sing and he would accompany her. For the most part they performed music by him, which they studied together, and as I would usually leave my toys to lean on the piano and listen to them, he used to say: 'This young lady will be a music-lover, later on I'll teach her,' but the results of that were disastrous. Sometimes, when it was raining, we played cards. Bad sport that he was, when he lost he was in a furious temper, all the more so as he needed his winnings to pay for the train which brought him to us every day. Then, to cheer him up, a packet of tobacco would be slipped under his napkin as we sat down to eat, and he would be overjoyed!

He had his own decided tastes in everything: he was very fond of blue and used to be very careful choosing the colours of everything he wore. He was very pleased if you asked his advice about anything and, when he read a volume of poetry, the choice of which poem to set to music was the subject of long debates. He was called Achille then, a name which he found utterly ridiculous.

He was moody, touchy and sensitive in the highest degree: the slightest thing could cheer him up, but could likewise send him into a rage. He was unsociable, and did not disguise his discontent when my parents entertained, because he usually refused to meet strangers and this meant he could not come to the house. If by chance he did meet them, and they were lucky enough to find favour in his eyes, he could be charming, playing and singing Wagner, imitating and caricaturing some modern composer; but when they did not find favour, he knew how to register the fact. He was an original and slightly unpolished individual, but utterly charming with those he liked.

Being extremely ignorant and too intelligent to be unaware of it, he used to read voraciously during the long summer days when he couldn't compose or go for a walk, and I often found him hunting among my schoolbooks for the dictionary, which he studied conscientiously. 'I'm very fond of reading the dictionary,' he used to say: 'you learn any number of interesting things from it.' He had an innate taste in judging any kind of art, even for pictures and engravings which, in those days at least, did not interest him at all. When my father, who was a great lover of painting, got Debussy talking on the subject, he found his judgement sure and his opinions completely personal and quite remarkable.

He was preparing to go in for the Prix de Rome. His heart was not in it; I don't know whether, but for my father, he would have refused to try, but I'm certain he would have resigned afterwards and that he was only prevented from doing so by the fear of incurring my father's displeasure. He went in for the prize twice, the first time with *Le gladiateur*. He only came second and certainly relief at staying in Paris more than compensated for any disappointment – the very idea of being shut up for weeks on end filled him with horror. We would often go and see him while he was immured in the Conservatoire for the prize. The contenders received their parents and friends in a courtyard in the garden, where we stayed as long as possible in order to comfort him. He pointed to the window of his room and, when I asked him why there were bars across it, replied: 'No doubt because they think we're wild beasts.'

The second time, he won the prize. But when, some months later, he had to leave for Rome, he was in despair and wrote letters of bitter desolation. He found it hard to stay the course, and even made one brief escape to Paris. But when he came back for good, the former intimacy was no longer there. He had changed, as we had. We had moved house, made new friends, and he, with his moody, unsociable character and unwillingness to alter his habits, no longer felt at home. Even so, he often used to come in the evenings and play us what he had written in Rome. On leaving Paris, he had deposited a large number of his manuscripts with us, but he had taken many of them back and made use of them. He used to come, then, and ask for suggestions and advice, and even material help, because, no longer living at home and not yet having any sort of reputation, he still had to live.

It was then that he put into practice the vague idea of giving me piano and harmony lessons, because he wanted to please my parents. What an appalling teacher! Not an ounce of patience and incapable of explaining anything in a way that could be understood by a young girl like myself; one had to have understood before he had finished explaining. We abandoned the enterprise . . . Then gradually, he too made new acquaintances; he stopped coming and we never saw him again.

Marguerite Vasnier, 'Debussy à dix-huit ans,' *ReM*, 7, 1 May 1926, pp. 17–22

MAURICE EMMANUEL
(1862–1938)

Maurice Emmanuel entered the Paris Conservatoire in 1880. When Delibes excluded him from the Prix de Rome for exhibiting modal tendencies, he entered Ernest Guiraud's class, where he met Debussy. From 1909 to 1936 he taught music history at the Conservatoire.

Delibes was happy to leave the job of correcting our fugues to one of the older members of the class, a distinguished contrapuntist, Charles René, who acquitted himself better in this task, I may say, than our official teacher – a delightful composer but not a man of musical learning. One morning in the spring of 1884, a few days before the preliminary examination for the Prix de Rome, Delibes had asked his assistant to stand in for him. Owing to a misunderstanding, neither of our teachers appeared. After waiting in vain, we were going to leave the dingy classroom, with its single window, next to the dirty flag, giving on to the noisy faubourg Poissonnière, when the door half opened, permitting the entrance of a tousled head which inspected the premises . . . Its owner appeared in full view: 'My dear orphans,' he said, 'in the absence of your parents, I shall provide nourishment for you!' And he sat down at the piano.

I can assure the reader that it was no longer the youthful Claude-Achille who mystified us that day, but Debussy from head to toe, Debussy unalloyed. He delivered himself of a welter of chords which, for all their wildness, we could only admire with open mouths. These were followed by a rustling of misshapen arpeggios, a gurgling of trills on three notes simultaneously, in both hands, and chains of harmonic progressions which could not be analysed according to the sacrosanct textbook, and which left us bemused. For more than an hour, gasping, we stood round the piano before which danced the unruly curls of the 'energumen'. This was the name given him by the janitor Ternusse – who now, roused by the unaccustomed din, smelt trouble. He burst in and put an end to the 'lesson'. We had to decamp. But we met up in the street, on the corner of the boulevard, and excitedly discussed what we had heard: 'If that's what his cantata's going to be like,' said the wisest head among us, 'he's heading for a fall!' Such was our excitement and curiosity, we decided to obtain at all costs a favour that was only reluctantly granted to Conservatoire pupils, namely entry to the Institut on Judgment Day, convinced as we were that the verdict would be an important one.

Judgment Day arrived. Nearly all of us had managed to get into the sanctuary. When Claude-Achille's turn came, and the air was filled with the opening chords of *L'enfant prodigue*, we exchanged delighted glances. But these soon faded. Instead of the scandal we were counting on, and despite occasional signs of agitation on the part of one or two elderly conductors who looked surprised and inclined to protest, compared with the outrageous harmonies which Debussy had served up to us Claude-Achille's cantata struck us as debonair! It triumphed, in spite of some opposition. And while we did not grudge its success, we felt seriously let down that the expected brouhaha had not materialized.

But the interesting thing is that one of our number, in congratulating the winner, could not resist adding: 'All the same, *patron*, you didn't learn anything useful from that excellent lesson you gave us the other day!' Claude-Achille opened his eyes wide, in genuine astonishment. It didn't occur to him to consider the music that he wrote down as being on the same level as that which his fingers, guided by an already mature intuition, produced from the Erard pianos of the Conservatoire, much to their surprise.

Throughout his life, this composer who shook the world of music defended himself from the charge of wanting to dominate it. When his teachers at the Conservatoire came upon him harmonizing the given melodies after his own fashion or unleashing cascades of curious chords on the piano, they would exclaim, in a greater or lesser state of amazement: 'So . . . you claim . . . ?' – 'I claim nothing,' Achille would reply boldly, 'just listen!'

'What rules do you follow, then?' Guiraud asked him one day. 'My own predilection!' was the reply. 'That's all very well if you're a genius!' murmured that good-natured teacher. I don't know whether he thought that his pupil was one, because he died in 1892 before Claude-Achille had written his String Quartet. But Guiraud liked and stuck up for *La damoiselle élue*; he thought the *Ariettes oubliées* and the *Poèmes de Baudelaire* had great charm, and spoke of his pupil with the most affectionate admiration.

It might be of interest for me to relate some of the opinions aired by master and pupil on arts other than music. When Debussy came back from Rome, he was questioned by Guiraud who wanted to know what memories he had brought back with him. A divergence in their impressions then manifested itself in the most spirited manner. It was not that Guiraud's enthusiasms were adopted mindlessly or out of deference to received opinion: he was not at all keen on museums, an opinion with which his pupil agreed. But he retained an affection for large pictorial compositions *in situ* in the monuments for which they had been conceived, such as the frescoes of the Sistine Chapel and the stanze of the Vatican. Debussy preferred the loggie; he found more to please him in the details and variety of the decoration, in the familiar touch of so many scenes, along the curves of the arcades, than in looking at *The School of Athens* or *The Sibyls*. Guiraud reminded him of *The Pact of God with Mankind* on the ceiling of the Sistine Chapel; Debussy countered with Sassoferrato's *Madonna* at Santa-Sabina. He loathed Michelangelo's *Last Judgment*. On the other hand, Luca Signorelli's *Resurrection of the Dead* in Orvieto Cathedral had 'knocked him sideways'. 'And,' he added, 'not only because the angels in it are playing trumpets!'

He was unmoved by Roman monuments and the colossal constructions of the Renaissance left him cold: 'St Peter's is a covered market for giants, with reason but without taste.' And he finished off by saying: 'I prefer S. Severina.' 'Even so, you must have found one building in Rome that you liked! . . .' 'The Villa Pia,' replied the young composer, 'you can't live in it, it's no good for anything; it's just decorative, made of porticoes, balustrades, bas-reliefs and fountains, but the greenery round it is heavenly!'

Maurice Emmanuel, 'Les ambitions de Claude-Achille,' *ReM*, 7, 1 May 1926, pp. 44–50

PAUL VIDAL

Letter to Henriette Fuchs.*

So our friend Achille has won the prize despite himself! This sinister tale of adultery has been played out over a long period. Last year I had to persuade him to compete in the final round, against his wishes. Then during the winter he told me he wouldn't leave for Rome even if he won, that he was prevented from doing so. I can't say I was surprised, but even so I was angry for the moment and sorry I'd put him forward as accompanist for La Concordia. Another time his mother accused me of being his accomplice in that affair; he'd used me as an excuse for a whole heap of escapades and I had a job restoring her confidence in me. The tears I saw her shedding because of her son's misbehaviour are not designed to make me side with him when he turns on the charm. Everything you've seen me do for him, I've done for his mother, who's an excellent woman and treats me as a son. I don't know whether anyone will manage to overcome his egoism. He's incapable of any sacrifice. Nothing has any hold over him. His parents aren't rich, but instead of using the money from his teaching to support them, he buys new books for himself, knicknacks, etchings etc. His mother has shown me drawers full of them. His education has been badly handled. His father wanted to exploit him, make an infant prodigy out of him, and for a time it worked; but when the composer in him awoke, he sent the piano and the harmony books to the devil and did only what he wanted to, treating his father with ill-disguised rancour. His father has found it practically impossible to forgive the abandonment of the lucrative virtuoso career he'd dreamt of and has only just begun to recognize him as a composer, and that only from the time he started winning prizes for it. His mother loves him too much, she wants him with her all the time, wants to see him working hard etc., and that exasperates him. So his parents have no control over him. That leaves only Guiraud; he's always treated Debussy like a spoilt child and Debussy has paid him back by never turning up on time – I know, because he sometimes came to see me when he should have been at the class! But if anyone can influence him, it's Guiraud.

His succubus is battening on to all his little weaknesses. She's pretty and much pursued by admirers, which pleases her jealous vanity; it appears she's a talented singer (I haven't heard her) and sings his songs extremely well; everything he writes is for her and owes its existence to her. How can one expect him in the circumstances to exile himself for two years in Rome, which he already knows and abhors?

Personally, I feel I'm powerless to make him see reason. He treats me with a mixture of respect and disdain – the inevitable lot of people who do their duty. I've always been gentle with him and I've never attacked his wild passion head on. I thought for a moment, last year, that art had recovered its hold over him; which was why, wanting him to succeed, I introduced him to you and warmly supported his appointment with La Concordia. But his present behaviour fills me with remorse. Massenet won't find it easy to pardon the support I've given him, if he ever does! I've betrayed the flag to no good purpose and truly I'm sorry to have got mixed up in it all, and not to have let things take their course. His moral sense is undeveloped, he's nothing but a sensualist. I'm furious. I've acted like an imbecile. But, with all that, he has such talent and such a personality!

What can I possibly write to him? Rome is intolerable, life in the Villa is odious, there's no stimulus to compose anything . . . His is not a responsive character, he won't be able to benefit from the several good fellows there are here, I really feel powerless . . . To think I love an animal who doesn't love his mother!

Paul Vidal, letter of 12 July 1884, from Rome, to Henriette Fuchs, *Revue de Musicologie*, numéro spécial, 1962, pp. 99–100

II
The bohemian

On his return to Paris from Rome in February 1887, Debussy was faced with the unwelcome prospect of making a living. What little he did manage to earn seems to have come from private piano lessons. None the less he managed to visit Bayreuth in 1888 and again the following year. In 1892 he read Maeterlinck's play *Pelléas et Mélisande* which was to occupy him on and off for the next decade, while in December 1894 the first performance of his *Prélude à l'après-midi d'un faune* brought him to the attention of discerning music lovers. From 1892 to 1898 he was living with Gabrielle Dupont ('Gaby of the green eyes'), a liaison which, on his side at least, seems to have been fairly 'open'. In October 1899 he married his first wife, Rosalie (Lily) Texier, a mannequin.

JACQUES DURAND
(1865–1928)

Jacques Durand took over the management of the publishing house, founded by his father, on the latter's death in 1909. He was himself a composer, if without renown. In 1927 he produced a volume of letters written to him by Debussy, whose music was published by Durand from 1905 onwards.

(1889) In an attempt to do something to persuade music lovers of the charm of the *Petite suite*, it was agreed with Debussy that the two of us should give a performance of it at a Paris salon frequented by the élite among the dictators of aesthetic fashion. The performance took place and the reception was kind, but no more than that; I was well aware that we had not broken through.

Debussy was very nervous before sitting down at the piano with me, and had urged me not to go too fast. I promised. But hardly had we begun when Debussy began to hurry; and despite all my efforts, I was unable to hold him back. He was in haste to put this public trial behind him. So I followed the somewhat hectic tempi as best I could, and the work finished with a brio that was, probably, an important factor in the polite sympathy with which the work was finally greeted.

Jacques Durand, *Quelques souvenirs d'un éditeur de musique*, 2 vols (Paris, 1924/1925), I, p. 59

GABRIEL MOUREY

Gabriel Mourey was an art critic and also translated the poetry of Swinburne and Poe.

I had known Claude Debussy – in those days he signed his music 'Claude Achille Debussy' – since about 1889.

Where did we meet? I no longer remember. Debussy then lived with his family in the rue de Berlin – now rue de Liège – in a fairly small flat, but it was not there that I first found myself in the presence of

the future composer of *Pelléas et Mélisande*. In a café, then? Perhaps. Perhaps at that *brasserie* at the Chateaudun corner, which was well known
to all the artists and all the literary men of that period, which was called
Le Petit Pousset, and whither came Villiers de l'Isle-Adam, Léon Dierx,
Catulle Mendès, Emile Goudeau, Forain, and so many others. If it was
not there, in any case, that I met Debussy for the first time, we passed
there later on many delightful hours. What I do know for certain, is
that so soon as the first courtesies were exchanged, we started to talk
of Jules Laforgue, Verlaine, Mallarmé, and of Rossetti, for by that
time I had learnt to know them, and I had read the 'Blessed Damozel'.
And a cordial intimacy grew rapidly between Debussy and me.

I was working then on a collection of prose poems, partly in
dialogue, which I had named – and which is still named – 'L'Embar-
quement pour Ailleurs', and it was arranged with Debussy, to whom
I had shown the manuscript, that he should write, for the frontispiece,
a tone-poem, which we termed a *glose symphonique*, as the other word
seemed to us inadequate.

I also remember well Debussy's extraordinary charm at this time,
a charm made up of a thousand things difficult to analyse, but which
few men failed to feel. One must add that Debussy, although he knew
well how to be disagreeable and unpleasant to those whom we then
called 'muffs', and in whose number we included everyone who did
not share our literary and artistic tastes, knew how to be delicately
kind and cordial with his friends. Uncommunicative, certainly, always
reserved, silent, and rather mysterious, sometimes keeping silent for
a long time as if not particularly interested in the conversation, then,
suddenly, with a short, incisive phrase, or a precise but comprehensive
word, summing up his thought in a striking perspective.

In his words, as in his life, and as also in his music, Debussy never
abandoned his love of conciseness. He had, in all things, a hatred of
superfluous development, or useless ornament; none practised better
than he the art of finding just the correct phrase, the rightly placed
word, or the expressive gesture. Debussy was a concentrated being
who lived an intense inner life. He was not of those who talk a lot
but say nothing.

Gabriel Mourey, 'Memories of Claude Debussy', *Musical News and Herald*,
11 June 1921, pp. 747–8

CATHERINE STEVENS

(1865–1942)

Catherine Stevens was the daughter of the Anglo-Belgian painter Alfred Stevens. Debussy proposed marriage to her in the early 1890s; perhaps in 1892, since the manuscript of the first set of *Fêtes galantes*, dated May 1892, is dedicated to her.

Like me, he loved Javanese music; one day he liked Russian music, the next not. That was part of his paradox.

One day I came home to find Debussy with Mama. He had come to dinner. I had triumphantly brought back a book by Maurice de Fleury, charmingly inscribed by the author. Debussy took it and said to Mama: 'Madame Stevens, will you allow me to tear out this inscription and throw it on the fire? I cannot understand how anyone dares offer such an incestuous book to a young girl with an inscription.' And he ripped out the inscription, grinding his teeth the while.

Catherine Stevens, notes, quoted in: Marcel Dietschy, *La passion de Claude Debussy* (Neuchâtel, 1962), pp. 77, 87

RENE PETER

(1872–1947)

René Peter was the son of Dr Michel Peter, an adversary and cousin of Pasteur. Debussy got to know him in the mid-1880s, and advised Peter as he embarked on a career as a playwright. The two friends made a start together on at least three plays: *L'herbe tendre* and *L'utile aventure*, in addition to *F.E.A.* (*Les Frères en Art*), mentioned in the second extract below. In fact, this last was nearly completed and three acts of it, in Debussy's handwriting, were discovered after his death.

More than any man I have ever known, Debussy was a combination of two sharply opposed personalities, and I am convinced that it was this very opposition which gave his genius such an extraordinary breadth. Many times I have thought that there was in him a little of

that strange Dr Jekyll, whose dangerous duality is described by Robert
Louis Stevenson, and that the contrast between the man and the artist
was due to this innate psychological split. As a man, Debussy has often
been criticized, and perhaps too severely, for leading his life without
troubling himself overmuch about moral convention; but no one has
ever dreamt of denying that as an artist he remained ever proud and
pure, on a plane above money-making concessions or accommodations
to popular taste.

From there it is natural to go on and see this great composer's work
as a superior form of escapism towards an ideal all the more eagerly
sought as his real, daily life removed him ever further from it. This
explains the role, at the same time considerable and unimportant, that
women played in his life.

Our friendship had been interrupted for some time through no
wish of our own, and when we met again Debussy had just finished
Pelléas. He had traded in his real first name, Achille, for the more
modern one of Claude and was living under the sway of Gaby. She
was a blonde with catlike eyes, a powerful chin and firm opinions.
She looked after the domestic side − there was not much Mélisande
in her − and that was quite a big undertaking, first of all because they
were poor and secondly because Claude, being a large, spoilt child
who refused to allow himself to be manhandled by life, indulged all
his whims and was impervious to reason.

Was he suddenly struck with the desire for that brown Japanese
engraving which he later gave me for my birthday? He emptied his
purse without stopping to think where the next day's dinner would
come from. And while he was lost in thought in company with his
genius, Gaby would be out raising money on knicknacks at some
sordid pawnshop.

One of the most radiant and charming figures to whom Debussy
ever succumbed was undoubtedly the daughter of another fine artist,
a painter of Flemish origin who pictures conjure up all the feminine
graces of the Second Empire. Claude told me later a little of what
took place. Later still I met the heroine of this sentimental episode.
There can be no doubt of the mutual attraction that soon grew up
between the composer and the young girl. In other circumstances
Debussy would probably have tried to lead matters to some less than
idealistic conclusion, but here he was dealing with a young woman of

honour with whom there could be no question of love-making without marriage. And why not marry? I quote a passage from a letter she wrote to me shortly after we met: 'He gave me proof of such *disinterested* love during the worst moments of a family crisis, he whom people have called "grasping", and he was so intelligent and he played me *Pelléas*, which he was working on. I would have married him, despite everything that was being said about him at the time . . . if I hadn't met Henry!' The end of the story can be guessed at. Henry was a brilliant young doctor, sincere and charming. The happiness of Catherine (ah! I've mentioned her name without meaning to!) was in his keeping. Claude was dismissed gently, to spare his feelings, but for some days he was inconsolable. Then he returned to *Pelléas* . . . and to Gaby, whose triumph was, as always, to be only temporary.

When he met Lily Texier, this pale, delicate young woman had been some years earlier the companion of a cheerful young man of means, but she had been physically afraid of him. Now she wanted the guarantee of marriage and Debussy, even if her past life was not exactly bourgeois, was happy to regularize their liaison. There followed perhaps the happiest period of his life – 'a time of spring', he used to call it – and a flowering of rare but marvellous works, including the 'Toccata' and the *Estampes*. But then came fame!

René Peter, 'Debussy et l'amour', *Comoedia*, 4 July 1942

ROBERT GODET

(1866–1950)

Robert Godet was a Swiss journalist, man of letters and composer, who translated *Boris Godunov* into French. He was a friend of Debussy for the last thirty years of the composer's life. Jean Moréas (1856–1910), real name Papadiamantopoulos, was a French poet born in Greece.

The mention of Moréas brings to mind an aspect of Debussy which he showed only seldom, and which was all the more striking for that reason. He was never seen in the Latin quarter, but when this did happen, as in the case of his visit to the translator of Keats, one could only be grateful to fate for putting in his path the poet of the 'pale girls of clay', because the verbosity of the one contrasted in the most hilarious way with the reserve of the other. The mutual irritation was such that they ended up being entertained by it themselves and, as one followed the progress of their reciprocal mystification, one was soon no longer sure which of them was being doctrinaire and which ironical. At all events only one of them was amused on the evening when Debussy, forewarned of Moréas's recent infatuation with the second part of *Faust*, had taken defensive measures. He allowed Moréas to exhaust his stock of quotations without reacting, then said: 'That's very fine, but there's something better.' – 'Better? What do you mean, better? Better than the Mothers, better than Helen, better than Euphorion, better than . . .' – 'There's the Keeper of the Tower,' enunciated Debussy bluntly.' – 'The . . .?' – 'I said, the Keeper of the Tower, the watchman whose job is to signal the dawn and who, at the appearance of Helen, thinks it has broken in the South and drops his trumpet in amazement. That's an image worthy of your famous ancestors, Monsieur Jean Moréas, and I'm astonished it should have escaped your notice . . .' Consternation of the dumbfounded Greek! But he soon recovered from his stupor and, as though understanding had suddenly broken through, shouted in a voice to make the archipelagos tremble: 'Jokker! Beefore 'e comes to see me, 'e does 'is 'ommwork!' – 'Is that not in accordance with one of your best lines, which from the point of view of syntax is worthy of an old campaigner like yourself: *Et toi, son cou, qui pour la fête tu te pares?* (And what of you, her neck, who are adorning yourself for the festival?)' After which Debussy, having deliberately isolated the cacophonic alliterations of this alexandrine, continued with a kind of da capo which he seemed to enjoy hugely: *kou-ki . . . te-tu-te . . .* Moréas, mortally offended, but pretending to ignore Debussy's malicious intentions, then hurled at him the wounding term 'Mousician!' – 'And I believe you're a flautist too . . .' And so on, while Alphonse Allais murmured '*Arcades ambo . . .*' which he translated for the ladies present as 'Let's try and see the Greeks in a good light . . .' The nice part about all this was that, meeting Moréas some time later in a state of extreme agitation (he had been involved in several duels one after the other and, brave and honourable as he was, found himself threatened with disqualification for an involuntary gesture), we were quick to suggest a topic that might encourage him to relax: his beloved second part of *Faust*. He took the bait, went

through his stock of quotations yet again and, arriving at what had
been the last one, added: 'But there's one that surpasses all the rest.
Do you remember the Keeper of the Tower?'

*

It was the day of Ernest Guiraud's funeral – Debussy's old teacher,
to whom he remained grateful for never having impeded his development. He had the flu and a temperature, and while he got dressed he
had a more or less incoherent conversation with himself, muttering,
exclaiming and grumbling, along the lines of: 'Ah well, my dear
Guiraud . . . now where's the other boot? . . . As it's you, it has to
be done . . . Detachable collars really are the worst things I know . . .
My dear Guiraud, there'll never be anyone like you . . . Brrr, it's
cold! And where's the tie . . . But there's no way I'm going to stay at
home . . . Now then, is that everything? . . . No question about
it . . . what revolting weather! . . . no way I shall miss your funeral.'
Why, at that point, did an imprudent voice, delivered with all a
mother's authority, say: 'And then, it's important that you be seen
there!' – 'That I be seen there?!!!' retorted the unruly son, giving an
indignant start. Then, suppressing his anger, he went very pale and
said tonelessly, with a glacial calm: 'A fine reason to give a child. Ah
well, my dear Guiraud, some other time . . .' His overcoat, into
which he had already inserted an arm, went back immediately on to
its peg; and Debussy, as white as a sheet, turned on his heel, went
back to his bedroom and closed the door.

*

Did he spend much time with the Symbolists? Was he enthusiastic
about Impressionism? The Debussy we knew never mentioned a word
about such things, any more than he did about his visits to Mallarmé's
salon, which were perhaps not as frequent or as fruitful as is generally
made out. One remembers only the respectful but amused look in his
eye when he used to see the poet concentrating on the exploits of the
Lamoureux Orchestra, and noting them down instantly in a little book
whose pages were black with pencilled jottings. The only painter who
was constantly on his lips at this time was one whom, we can be sure,
he never met: Degas, and even Degas the infrequent painter of pastel
landscapes. He fascinated Debussy and, at the same time, gave an

example of discipline to his imaginative promptings. Talking of which, we may note in passing that he was always unhappy about what he called Rodin's 'romanticism'. On the other hand he was one of the first (and the few) to discern in Camille Claudel 'the genius to achieve a style without owing anything to the Academy', and to consider the works of this splendid artist as 'the most perfect examples of intimate lyricism' in the history of sculpture. Her 'Valse' had a place on his mantelpiece; and her 'Petite Princesse' sometimes smiled at him in his dreams.

Robert Godet, 'En marge de la marge', *ReM*, 7, 1 May 1926, pp. 63–4, 70–72

Debussy had a painter friend who, in the era of open-air painting, insisted on preferring the artificial lighting in his studio and who would conclude discussions by saying: 'Nature is something people have invented to gossip about!' One day this friend arrived bursting with a piece of information, accurate information too, which he thought would clinch the argument: he told us that the Japanese didn't even have a word for Nature. 'That must prevent them from making a lot of stupid remarks,' said Debussy, 'but also from making some useful distinctions. And they don't have a word for art, either.'

Another friend from around that time endeared himself to us with a brief unpublished work called 'The poet and the bird'. It was a subject which one of his teachers had asked him to treat in verse. He was not given to being prolix and had no trouble containing his Lucretian muse within the space of two, summatory hexameters:

> *Pour chanter, cher oiseau, dis-moi, comment fais-tu?*
> *Eh bien, j'ouvre le bec et je fais* tu tu tu.
>
> (When you sing, dear bird, tell me, what do you do?
> Well, I open my beak and go *tu tu tu*.)

Debussy was enchanted by this *tu tu tu*. He would have liked to submit it to the learned Benedictine Dom Caffiaux who tells us that Adam, the father of us all, took singing lessons from the birds – and he should know, having left us a history of music from the creation to the fall of Troy. He would have liked to submit it too to the poet Gresset, on whose authority we learn about our mother Eve that: 'As soon as she heard the pretty songs of the birds, she opened her mouth in rivalry . . .' *Tu tu tu*, how simple it seems! 'Yes,' said Debussy, 'and if on top of everything else it was actually true, you'd know why your daughter was ill: vocal exhaustion! But it's not true. The disease which prompts young ladies to sing, when they've a mind to, and even their fathers, is not the desire to imitate this *tu tu tu*, which in any case is inimitable. And if we have a fancy to ask the birds for lessons, that's as far as they can go: 'open your beak and go *tu tu tu*' – something we can't do, and all the time we're so impatient to get to know our own music . . .' In saying this, Debussy was on the way to the conclusion of the Chinese sage whom he was to meet later: 'The music of mankind comes from within.'

Robert Godet, 'Le lyrisme intime de Claude Debussy', *ReM*, 2, 1 December 1920, pp. 188–9

PRINCE ANDRE PONIATOWSKI

(1864–1955)

Prince Poniatowski was, at different times in his life, an industrialist, a banker and a planter, as well as frequenting literary milieux.

The first Tuesday evening on which Debussy took me to Mallarmé's, I found there Pierre Louÿs and Marcel Schwob, whom I already knew, Henri de Régnier, Georges Rodenbach, the author of *Bruges la morte*, and some others who were unknown to me.

Our arrival was greeted by a silence in which there was some element of ill humour, firstly because every arrival was an interruption, but also for another reason: how had Debussy come to make the acquaintance of this 'clubman'? And having done so, why bring him to such a gathering as this?

Mallarmé, being the soul of urbanity, set the situation to rights in a couple of words. He tilted his head back and took stock of me . . . then, with half-closed eyes, as though summoning up memories, he said:

'Yes, that's it! . . . When I saw you at the top of the stairs, I thought I recognized your face from our friend's pastels!' And holding out his hand, he asked me if I had seen Degas recently.

I attended these Tuesday meetings only rarely. I felt awkward there, occupying a place merely out of curiosity, among those young people who came in the spirit of apostles. But I continued to see Mallarmé outside his salon, at my house on the rue Balzac. The first time he came there was on a Sunday morning, after a mass at Saint-Gervais where Debussy had taken us to hear Gregorian chant. Very soon these Sunday morning sessions at Saint-Gervais became extremely popular. Indeed, the numbers of our group grew to such an extent that the parishioners complained to their curé, because their seats were taken every Sunday by crowds of people who, it had to be said, listened to the sacred chants in exemplary silence, but usually with their backs to the main altar.

During the summer of 1892 I had been in touch with Anton Seidl, and also with Walter Damrosch, whose orchestra had financial backing from Andrew Carnegie. I spoke to both of them about Debussy, extolling his abilities, and I thought Seidl was interested in putting on a fantasy for piano and orchestra which I knew Debussy had completed.

My idea was that, if this work was successfully performed in New York, I might persuade someone like Carnegie to take an interest in Debussy's career and to offer him over a period of two or three years the material and spiritual tranquillity which he lacked entirely in Paris. None of his works had reached the general public and the piano lessons at five francs an hour, which provided his bread and butter, exasperated him – even before I left Paris he was heading for a nervous collapse, as can be seen from the letters he wrote to me.

As early as July, I'd informed him of Seidl's good intentions, but the conductor needed to see the manuscript before putting the work into his autumn programme. I'd addressed my letters to Bailly, whose tiny bookshop on the chaussée d'Antin served as Debussy's headquarters. I was beginning to despair of receiving any reply when, too late alas, he explained the source of the mystery.*

André Poniatowski, *D'un siècle à l'autre* (Paris, 1948), pp. 241, 243, 304

---

*Debussy's answering letter had gone astray.

NARCISSE LEBEAU

(1865–1931)

Narcisse Lebeau, whose real name was Vital Hocquet, was
a contributor to the literary productions of the cabaret Le
Chat Noir. Debussy said he had 'painter's eyes', and he is
believed to have introduced Debussy to Satie. The memories recorded below date from the early 1890s.

A time of destitution and youthful enthusiasm . . . Debussy, who then
lived at 42 rue de Londres, couldn't afford to eat or clothe himself.
Lunch consisted mostly of a small bar of chocolate, such as schoolboys
eat, and what was, in those days, the classic *petit pain* costing a sou.
Dinner was, sometimes, more solid: Lebeau, who earned 500 francs
a month as a plumber, would come and fetch his friend and the
young woman who then shared his life and take them to some modest
neighbourhood dive: Boilesve's place on the rue Monthyon, near the
Folies-Bergère or, when 'the stars were touching' – that's to say when
their pockets were practically empty – to the Cabaret du Clou on the
rue Trudaine.

At the Clou the food was far from being as appetizing or as copious
as at Boilesve's! The 'ratatouilles' – which is the best word to describe
the stews they served up there – were sometimes so uninviting that
Debussy asked for the *plat du jour* to be replaced by 'omelettes with
sugar and jam', because he was keen on his food and incredibly keen
on sweet things of all sorts. Often Claude Achille's charming companion would bring some sweets, which the three of them would
divide up as *un*equally as they could.

Debussy adored watching games of billiards and going to the circus;
he was particularly fond, too, of Guignol. We used to spend hours at
the Guignol on the Champs-Elysées or at the Folies-Bergère, where
there were often billiard matches.

The room on the rue de Londres was a sort of panelled garret,
untidily filled with a rickety table, three cane chairs, a sort of bed and
a splendid Pleyel, on loan naturally . . .

In this room, where everything had to be done, Achille wrote
masterpieces. He was collaborating then with the poet Catulle Mendès,
for whom he felt a profound antipathy, on the confection of a *Cid*, in

a style far removed from that of *Pelléas:* a romantic work, full of concessions. At the end of one act, a group of storehouses collapse, accompanied by vertiginous arpeggios, and Debussy in performance would yell out the final verse in a voice which defies description: '*Et la croix de Jésus luira sur les mosqué . . . e . . . es!*' [and the Cross of Jesus will shine out upon the mosques].

The material difficulties under which Debussy laboured had no impact on his artistic intransigence. He refused to give piano lessons at twenty francs an hour on the pretext that the pupil was untalented. I mean! . . . Twenty francs! . . .

Lebeau permits himself to steal from Debussy's room a piece of Japanese silk, representing a stream with tree stumps and carp. Lebeau admits his theft and, after a discussion, it's agreed that in exchange for the Japanese silk he will hand over an umbrella. Delighted to have an umbrella, Debussy presents Lebeau into the bargain with a copy of the *Cinq poèmes de Baudelaire* on Holland paper, with this inscription: 'To Vital Hocquet, who stole my fish, but for whom I feel a special affection.'

Even if he refused to give lessons to untalented pupils for twenty francs, for the same sum he sold the music he had written on a poem by Verlaine to a society gentleman, who then passed it off as his own:

> *Mais je trouve encore meilleur*
> *Le baiser de sa bouche en fleur*
> *Depuis qu'elle est morte à mon coeur.*
> *Dansons la gigue . . .*

> (But I find still lovelier
> The kiss of her young mouth
> Since she has lost her hold on my heart.
> Let's dance the jig . . .)

There was a tailor called Hugo, like Victor, who had a shop on the rue Vivienne and had already fitted Debussy out on his return from Rome: the bill remained to be paid. Learning that his 'customer' had nothing to wear, he went to see him in his room and, pointing out that an artist like him couldn't go round looking like a tramp, measured him for a veritable wardrobe: evening dress, dinner jacket, frock coat, lounge suit, overcoat . . . 'You can pay me when you're famous.'

To be honest, it has to be said that when Debussy did become famous he did not pay the tailor: genius has its blind spots and, even, its ungrateful corners.

Wearing his new clothes, Debussy was able to be best man at the wedding of his friend Narcisse Lebeau, together with his colleague Charles Levadé and Alphonse Allais. Jacques Hébert, a Paris solicitor and fine musician – he was a pupil of César Franck – asked Lebeau to introduce him to Debussy. Lebeau invited him to join them at La Cigale, where Achille liked going to hear the singer Jeanne Bloch. The solicitor duly turned up, but Debussy, who was in a bad temper, did not deign to honour him with a look, still less a word.

Narcisse Lebeau, 'Souvenirs sur Debussy confiés à Marius Richard,' *La Liberté*, 11 and 13 December 1931

PAUL DUKAS
(1865–1935)

> Paul Dukas entered the Conservatoire in 1881, and Gui-raud's composition class four years later, when he began his long friendship with Debussy. Apart from his activities as a composer, he became an influential critic. Of Debussy's *Nocturnes* he preferred 'Nuages' to 'Fêtes', as being more characteristic of its composer, hailed *Pelléas* as a masterpiece, and defended *La mer* as being Debussy's personal view of the sea, so that whether or not the work conjured up the sea for others was beside the point.

Talking of Wagner reminds me of the friends whose news you asked me for: Debussy in fact has had advance notice put in *L'Idée Libre* of an article called 'On the uselessness of Wagnerism'. I've no idea what that might be, but when it comes out I'll get hold of it: it could well turn out to be profound, and it can't be denied that 'truth comes from the mouths of children'. It's a good title, isn't it? And you can tell it's Debussy a mile away.

This summer he also played me the first three movements of a string quartet which must be finished by now. Charming from beginning to end. He's got real musical talent, that lad! And an *angelic* facility, even though he denies it out of mistaken Baudelairianism and artistic perversity. He played me his opera too, which must also be nearly finished. I think you'll be very surprised by the dramatic breadth of certain scenes: it wasn't at all what I was expecting. What's more it's perfectly *natural*. Added to which, the short scenes are delightful and have a harmonic finesse which recalls his early songs. So the work has everything that's needed to fail! Let's hope he succeeds! Mind you, the libretto is totally devoid of interest. A mishmash of Parnassian bric-à-brac and Spanish barbarism. Did you know it's a version of *Le Cid* by Mendès?

Paul Dukas, letter of 1 October 1893 to Vincent d'Indy; published in George Favre: *Ecrits sur la musique et l'éducation musicale* (Paris, 1966), p. 97

ERNEST CHAUSSON and HENRI LEROLLE
(1855–99)   (1848–1929)

Ernest Chausson got to know Debussy in the early 1890s and soon became, in the latter's words, 'a big elder brother' to him, giving him advice and, no less important, money. Henri Lerolle was a well-known painter and Chausson's brother-in-law.

Early in 1894 Debussy became engaged to the singer Thérèse Roger, but the engagement was broken off in the middle of March because of doubts about the composer's past and, in particular, about his liaison with Gaby Dupont. The following is an exchange of letters between Chausson and Lerolle.

HL to EC, 25 February 1894

You know Debussy's getting married. He told you the same day he told me and I haven't seen you since. He's in the seventh heaven. Thérèse is ravishing, young and all the rest. I had dinner with him last night after he'd played the first act of *Tristan* on the piano. And I went with him to arrange for him to play more Wagner, at 250 francs a month. He's very happy about it. He has to earn money and not live on Thérèse's. Before he spoke to me, Mme Roger had come to tell me they were in love with one another and to ask me what I thought about it. But I didn't realize it had been settled. I told her what I thought of him as a musician, but explained that as a man I hardly knew him, except that I'm very fond of him. An apartment has been rented for them on the rue Vaneau for 16 April. He's spending all his time with Thérèse and not working much.

He played through *Tristan* yesterday. Mme Escudier is now inviting a number of Jews, including M. Pereire, who's extraordinarily ugly and unpleasant. But they all enjoyed it enormously. Debussy finds it very tiring. He relaxes by singing his own music in a muted voice, with friendly ears leaning over him to catch the sounds.

EC to HL, 28 February 1894

The announcement of Debussy's marriage left me speechless. I wasn't able to talk to him at length about it because he left immediately after dinner, and at table we couldn't discuss it in front of Abel Desjardins and his sister. He's deeply in love; and I find lovers so utterly captivating, not to say a rarity in our refined intellectual circle. This announcement is certainly going to set tongues wagging interminably. I can hear them from here, and am happy to hear them only from here. Personally, I'm confident about the outcome; I think it'll be a very happy marriage, precisely because it's not one that the ultimate in common sense would approve. Common sense always lands you in it. They love each other, that's the important thing.

HL to EC, 13 March 1894

If Debussy deserves the reputation given him by his friends, then it seems to me he has changed. In any case, he's very nice to us and he adores Thérèse and her mother.

I met Mlle Taravant at Lenoir's and she too told me everything people are saying about him. Knowing she's something of a gossip, I told her how Mme Roger had asked me for my impressions and how she had responded to them by saying that they were going to rent the apartment; that I'd told her what I thought of Debussy, the good and the bad, but that, seeing her mind was made up, I was not sure enough of my own views to say more. So I'm certain Mlle Tar . . . will take it upon her tongue to spread the word that the marriage was none of my doing. If I go on about all this, it's because no one in Paris is talking about anything else.

Debussy told me there was only one painter who knew anything about music, and that was me. Perhaps he has his reasons for saying so, the sly dog.

EC to HL, 19 March 1894

I've just written a long letter to Mme Escudier about Debussy's Wagner sessions, because I think it will be difficult to let them continue. Probably you've already broached the question, but anyway that's what I think, and the only way I can suggest to bring matters to a close is to refund half the money paid by the audience, as there have been only five sessions instead of the ten that were promised.

I haven't been able to think of anything else except this sordid affair since this morning and I'm feeling more and more despondent about it. Let me know if there are any new developments. My first impulse was to write to Debussy. Jeanne prevented me, and she was right.

EC to HL, 6 April 1894

Naturally Mme Roger spoke to me about Debussy, and in considerable detail. She was anxious above all to prove to me that she hadn't been as unwise as is generally thought. Indeed, if poor Debussy had replied sincerely to all the questions she asked him, the whole unpleasant business would have been avoided. Truly, the more I learn, the less I understand. I can see how he might have told lies, watered down the truth or put a different slant on things, even though that's a stupid and pointless way of behaving, but to lie directly to her face, with indignant protests, about something so serious, that I cannot comprehend.

HL to EC, October 1894

I've written to Bonheur asking for news and inviting him to come to Paris to go out on the town with Debussy and myself. So far I've had no reply. I've been to see Debussy who's getting on slowly. He played again for me some passages of *Pelléas* which I know off by heart, and which I love. What a pity he should be what he is, because we have such good times together. With you being away, if I couldn't go and see him any more I should end up being very depressed.

Ernest Chausson/Henri Lerolle, quoted in: François Lesure, 'Claude Debussy, Ernest Chausson et Henri Lerolle', *Humanisme actif. Mélanges d'art et de littérature offerts à Julien Cain* (Paris, 1968), pp. 341–3

PIERRE LOUŸS

(1870–1925)

Pierre Louÿs was a poet and novelist and one of Debussy's closest friends following their meeting in 1893. Paul Valéry said that 'in every way and at all times Louÿs was of the greatest help to Debussy throughout his career'. Louÿs made his name with sexually free novels, such as *L'homme de pourpre*, *Une volupté nouvelle* and, particularly, *Aphrodite*. Mme de Saint-Marceaux was a prominent society hostess.

Madame,

The unfortunate telegram which finalized the break, and which has caused my poor friend so much suffering, has certainly been misunderstood: but I recognize that appearances condemned Debussy and I am not surprised that people have been scandalized.

But perhaps you will allow me to add that a young man cannot dismiss like a chambermaid a mistress who has lived with him for two years, who has shared his poverty without complaint and against whom he can level no reproaches, other than that he is tired of her and is getting married. In the ordinary way these matters are settled with a few banknotes; it may not be the height of delicacy, but it serves. As you know, this was not a course Debussy had open to him. He felt he had to act with circumspection. It was a question of kindness, and also of prudence, because if treated more harshly she might have sought revenge. So he proceeded slowly. If his engagement had been announced less precipitately, Debussy would have had the time to disengage himself completely, before the day when a formal engagement forced him to put his former liaison behind him. He did not do so, or, if you prefer, he did not know how to do so: and he has been cruelly punished for it.

As for the rumours that have reached you about his past life, I stand as a witness that they are monstrous calumnies, and I think that the honour of a man (I do not speak of Debussy the artist, whom we are not discussing) cannot be wounded by anonymous letters, which are usually the work of a liar and always of a coward.

I know from personal knowledge that Debussy is incapable of

having lived as it is claimed. I know it also from two people who have been friends of Debussy's for twelve years and who are as revolted as I am by the sinister intrigue which is being played out around him. And I can give you their names: they are MM. Raymond Bonheur and Etienne Dupin. Monsieur Lerolle and Monsieur Chausson will confirm the value of their testimony.

I write this in a state of profound sadness, and with an outspokenness which, Madame, I beg you to excuse. I know of nothing more distressing than to see thus dishonoured, in a matter of no more than a week, a man who is loved and greatly respected, who has been starved of good fortune for fifteen years and who sees all the doors closed against him at the moment when it is becoming apparent that he is a genius.

Pierre Louÿs, letter of 22 March 1894 to Madame de Saint-Marceaux, in: *Cahiers Debussy* a.s. 3, 1976, p. 6

GUSTAVE DORET
(1866–1943)

Gustave Doret studied the violin with Joachim in Berlin, before entering the Paris Conservatoire where he was taught by Marsick for violin and Dubois and Massenet for composition. In 1894 he conducted the first performance of *Prélude à l'après-midi d'un faune* and ten years later was appointed principal conductor of the Opéra-Comique.

The first concert I was to conduct at the Société Nationale was set for 22 December 1894 and, as I expected, it was to be a considerable test.

At this debut of mine, Claude Debussy was to entrust me with the first performance of his *Prélude à l'après-midi d'un faune*. He took me to his tiny apartment on the rue Gustave-Doré (a strange coincidence!), spread out the proofs of the orchestral score, which were already covered with corrections, and sat down at the piano; while I, open-mouthed and with eager ears, sat beside him. I was completely seduced, entranced, overwhelmed.

I promised him that we would take as much time preparing the score as was needed. And never, I believe, did rehearsals take place in such an atmosphere of intimate collaboration. Debussy was constantly modifying this or that sonority. We tried it out, repeated it, compared it. Once the players had come to understand this new style, they realized that we would have a serious battle on our hands. Of course, Debussy's name was familiar to the real connoisseurs, but to the general public it was still unknown. The hour of the great test duly arrived, Debussy pressing my hands and hiding his anxiety behind a grin that I had come to recognize. There was a vast silence in the hall as I ascended the podium and our splendid flautist, Barrère, unfolded his opening line. All at once I felt behind me, as some conductors can, an audience that was totally spellbound. It was a complete triumph, and I had no hesitation in breaking the rule forbidding encores. The orchestra were delighted to repeat this work, which it had come to love and which, thanks to them, the audience had now accepted.

Gustave Doret, *Temps et contretemps* (Fribourg, 1942), pp. 94–7

COLETTE
(1873–1954)

Colette (Sidonie-Gabrielle Colette) had a full life as a music-hall star, actress and writer. She is perhaps best remembered for her *Claudine* novels, written at the instigation of her first husband, the critic Willy (Henri Gauthier-Villars).

My memory goes back to an evening long ago, the evening of the first performance of *Sheherazade*. Even when the concert was over, Debussy had still not had his fill of Rimsky. He made humming noises with his lips and reedy ones through his nose to try and recapture a phrase on the oboe, and recreated the timpani's low taps by drumming on the lid of the boudoir grand . . . To imitate a pizzicato on the double-basses, he stood up, took hold of a cork and rubbed it against the window-pane . . . In the same way does a satyr get to his feet and, eyes flashing beneath his twisted horns, pull out of the hedge a thorn that takes his fancy. Debussy looked like one of the followers of Pan. I sang him the phrase he was looking for, at the same time supporting myself with a few notes on the piano. His haunted gaze became human and seemed to take me in for the first time: 'Well remembered! Well remembered!' he said. Flattered, I seemed to hear him saying: 'That was an unexpected treat! How do you do!'

Colette, *Mes apprentissages* (Paris, 1936), pp. 208–9

LEON-PAUL FARGUE
(1876–1947)

Léon-Paul Fargue was a poet, novelist and journalist. He was one of the 'Apaches', the group of artists centred round Ravel, who dedicated to Fargue his piano piece 'Noctuelles', the first of the five *Miroirs*.

I got to know Debussy through Pierre Louÿs in 1895, coming out of a Sunday concert where, as I remember, they'd been playing Bizet's *Patrie* and Charpentier's *Impressions d'Italie*. It was shortly before we started the magazine called *Le Centaure*, Henri Albert, the translator of Nietzsche, Régnier, Louÿs, Valéry, Gide, Hérold, Jacques-Emile Blanche, André Lebey, Jean de Tinan and myself.

We set up our office at 10 rue des Beaux-Arts, next to the school, on the first floor on the far side of a courtyard. Debussy used to come and see us from time to time and make a little music for us, either brought by Louÿs or on his own. We would see him arrive looking sombre, wearing a very narrow little felt hat, a loose bow tie and a large, gloomy-looking cape. When he had divested himself of all these, he looked extremely pale, with a dull kind of pallor, his hair very black, with a straggly beard, a sort of sprawling lichen which spread over his face up to his eyes, his forehead jutting out like Jupiter's, with heavy eyelids and a small nose that looked as though it had been shortened. A fine mouth, red and sensual, provided the only note of colour in the ensemble. All in all he resembled a faunlike version of Jean Richepin, or better still Solario's 'Head of St John' in the Louvre. (At this period, Pierre Louÿs was going through a bad time. It was shortly before the triumphant success of *Aphrodite*. As for Debussy, he hadn't a penny. Both of them struggled by on pâté de campagne and sheep's foot jelly.)

Debussy would sit himself down without speaking at the piano of

the little study-cum-library and start to improvise. Anyone who knew
him can remember what it was like. He would start by brushing the
keys, prodding the odd one here and there, making a pass over them
and then he would sink into velvet, sometimes accompanying himself,
his head down, in an attractive nasal voice, like a sung whisper. He
gave the impression of delivering the piano of its sound, like a mother
of her child. He cradled it, sang to it softly, like a rider to his horse,
like a shepherd to his flock, like a thresher to his oxen.

Léon-Paul Fargue, letter to Auguste Martin, in: A. Martin: *Claude Debussy.
Catalogue de l'Exposition organisée du 2 au 17 mai 1942 au Foyer de l'Opéra-Comique*
(Paris, 1942), pp. ix, x

RENE PETER

Claude loved Lily and Lily loved Claude. She had arrived from the
Yonne some years before. With her slender figure, pale complexion,
small mouth and dark chestnut hair, she had come to Paris to earn an
honest living in a fashion house. I was there when Debussy met her
for the first time, neither of them showing any obvious signs of
attraction. Claude found her quite pretty but 'spineless'; sometimes he
even used to amuse himself imitating her little habits which she, being
a nice girl, took with the best will in the world. Then one day we learnt
that Claude and Lily had got married. Who knows what happened in
the intervening eighteen months? Perhaps the fact that Claude no
longer appeared to love Gaby made Lily feel she was free to act?

René Peter, *Claude Debussy* (Paris, 1931), pp. 31–3

EMILE VUILLERMOZ
(1878–1960)

Emile Vuillermoz studied at the Conservatoire under
Fauré and went on to become a music critic. He also
wrote a number of books, including histories of music and
studies of Chopin, Fauré and Debussy.

Those who know Debussy only from amateur photographs can have no way of guessing that his presence was transfigured by a single attribute: his voice – his unique, unforgettable voice. You may be imagining one of those golden voices, with an engaging timbre and seductive inflexions, which cast a spell upon the listener. No, his voice was discreet and confidential. His vocal chords produced sounds that were strange, slightly veiled, articulated with a light staccato that separated the syllables, imperceptibly damped by an invisible mute. Debussy rarely removed this velvet mask which served him well throughout his life. The delicately sarcastic tone, the deep, incisive timbre of a woodwind instrument, the pitiless shaft loosed with a mocking gentleness, while an eager, rapid glance scanned the listener's face, furtively judging the degree of his comprehension or complicity . . . those were the traits that made an intimate conversation with Debussy as absorbing as a game of chess.

When he moved to the piano to sing one of his works, that soft voice become cavernous and mysterious, with a variety of surprising nuances. It is the haunting quality of that voice which I chiefly remember from my first contact with the composer of *Pelléas*, on the occasion when I had the good fortune to hear a fragment, not merely unpublished but barely written, sung by its creator. I was then a student at the Conservatoire and in connection with some avant-garde concert or other I was given the job of asking Debussy for his support. I had never met him but I knew that the hedgehog was his emblem. So it was with some trepidation that I climbed the stairs of the modest block of flats in which he lived on the rue Cardinet. I was in luck: the composer was in. I could hear him trying out bits of themes on the piano, while he sang a newborn melodic line in the subterranean voice I have just described. I was reassured by this omen, and timidly rang the bell. The door opened. A beautiful but stern-looking woman appeared, holding in her hands various menacing items of household apparatus. I can still see the long-handled broom on which she was leaning, like a Valkyrie on her spear! I asked politely to see Debussy. Brünnhilde listened to me with an outraged expression. My audacity seemed to take her breath away. I began to stammer out the reason for my request, but in a crisp voice the guardian angel replied: 'My husband is not at home.'

During all this, Debussy was playing and singing louder than ever, practically drowning our conversation. I ventured an unbelieving glance at the half-open door of the study from which this torrent of music was emanating. But the vigilant protectress of her husband's labours, accustomed to obeying orders without worrying whether they carried conviction or not, was unmoved and repeated more crisply than ever: 'I tell you, my husband is not at home!' And satisfied with the solidity of this statement, the daughter of Wotan closed the door in my face. It was under these less than heroic conditions that I was the first to hear an unpublished fragment of *Pelléas* – as Debussy later verified – a long time before the audience at the Opéra-Comique.

Emile Vuillermoz, *Claude Debussy* (Paris, 1962), pp. 54–7

MADAME GERARD DE ROMILLY

Madame de Romilly was one of Debussy's piano pupils.
He dedicated to her the 'Prélude' from the suite *Pour le
piano*. She wrote down these memories in 1933.

It was at Passy in 1898, at the house of the Fontaine's where we met to form an amateur choir, that I saw Claude Debussy for the first time. He was an excellent chorus-master, with the patience of a saint, taking us individually through the different parts; and he managed to turn a handful of vague and inexperienced amateurs into a musical and disciplined body of singers.

In this capacity he introduced us to Russian music, still unknown at that time, then to the music of Chabrier, a composer full of originality whom he admired and whose *Ode à la musique* he got us to sing. He also conducted us in two choruses of his own, 'Ah! qu'il fait bon la regarder' and 'Yver, vous n'êtes qu'un vilain'. They were not yet in print and they were quite different from the settings published by Durand some years later, lengthened and elaborated by the composer himself. I missed the lovely, simple lines and the naïve melodies of the earlier version, so closely wedded to Charles d'Orléeans' poetry.

But it was unusual for Debussy to change the form of any of his works. I asked him one day if, when he heard a work he'd written long before, he ever had the desire to alter anything. 'When I finally decide to write down a phrase,' he replied, 'I've turned it around so many times in my head that it's impossible to imagine it being any different.'

It was at this time that my mother, wanting me to study singing, had the idea of engaging Debussy as my teacher. The day of my first lesson arrived and, in a considerably intimidated state, I waited by the window, watching for his arrival. He came in a little covered carriage, called a 'governess cart', drawn by a nervous pony. He wore a soft hat with a wide brim, his sharp features surrounded by a small, curly black beard. A large cape was draped around him, a strange sight which made me think of a young Roman in his chariot . . . I rushed into the drawing room and waited next to the Pleyel, which was covered with scores of all kinds, including *Les pêcheurs de perles*, Massenet's *Marie Magdeleine*, and *Lakmé*, as well as the operas of Wagner.

Debussy came in wearing, as he always did on later occasions, a blue serge suit and a knotted tie, and looking very smart. He came up to the piano, read the titles of the scores with a disapproving air, and put them all aside except those by Wagner and Bach, which were the only ones that found grace in his eyes. The lesson began, and he made me work at the vowels 'a-a-a-a' and then 'u-u-u-u', so as to bring the sound forward, he said.

Alas! It was the beginning of winter, and after only a few lessons colds and sore throats kept me in bed, to the disappointment of the maître, who looked forward each time to the little envelope placed discreetly on the end of the keyboard, containing his fee.

One day, tired of waiting for my recovery, Debussy said to me: 'As your sore throat prevents you singing for the time being, next Friday I shall give you a piano lesson: you will work at Schumann's *Kreisleriana* for me.' He had no idea whatever whether I was capable of playing such a difficult piece, one of the most taxing Schumann ever wrote. The following week I more or less (and rather less than more) played *Kreisleriana* and, thinking I would give him a nice surprise, I had also studied his two *Arabesques*. As soon as he recognized the volume, he picked it up and threw it to one side, saying: 'Not those, they're dreadful.' Next time he brought me *L'après-midi d'un faune*, which we then played regularly, as well as Chabrier's *Valses romantiques* which he was very fond of.

In my singing lessons, Debussy made me study all his works, from the *Ariettes oubliées* to the *Proses lyriques*, and not forgetting the *Chansons de Bilitis*. Soon after that I began to tackle Wagner, and Isolde's 'Liebestod', including the final high A which had to be sung softly and which generally I never managed to make any sound on at all! Sometimes Debussy would sing the role of Kurwenal, which suited his voice perfectly.

It was a delight to hear him sing and play. No other virtuoso I have heard since has had that kind of sparkling wit which made his playing so individual. But he was moody, and it was enough to ask him to play for him to refuse. Another day he would sit down at the piano and play and sing to his heart's content. If some piece struck him as strange, he had a peculiar way of deciphering it, stopping from time to time and aiming an interrogatory 'What?' at the problematic passage. In lessons he never bothered about performing difficulties: fingering for him did not exist. He would control everything like a conductor, saying: 'Get round it as best you can, but try and make it good.' He would often add, not greatly to my reassurance: 'I really only enjoy giving piano lessons to people who play better than I do.' And when I played Liszt's *Rhapsodies*, he used to recall his memories of the great Nicolas Rubinstein, whose magnificent performances had remained with him.

Debussy had excellent natural taste and adored beautiful things. He loved antiques and would spend hours in an antique dealer's shop near our house, on the avenue Victor Hugo. He would also leave there on account the fee for my lessons, to the great despair of his wife who was anxiously awaiting his return to be able to go out and buy the dinner! In particular there was a certain Louis XV sofa which he often talked to me about and which he was desperate to acquire. My father had some fine collections of things and Debussy would admire them at his leisure. His eye was caught by a box dating from the Middle Ages and an engraved bronze platter: 'They'd look good in my apartment,' he murmured. To my great delight, my mother sent them to him.

Paintings had a great attraction for him. He liked visiting museums and picture exhibitions, and had a predilection for the landscapes by the Scandinavian painter Frits Thaulow and for the paintings of Monet. He was always sorry he hadn't taken up painting instead of music.

To come back to our lessons, he introduced me to the music of the 'Five'. We ordered from the Moscow publishers Belaief all the works of Mussorgsky, Rimsky-Korsakov, Borodin and Glazunov, and played them enthusiastically in piano duet arrangements, scratching each other with a will. I suffered the more, because Debussy had rather unusual nails, curved like claws. I could never understand how, with those curved nails, he was able to produce such soft, cushiony sounds.

One day he said to me: 'We should be able to say that I've made you study one sonata by Beethoven. Let's choose the least bor. . . .' And after flipping through the volume, he decided on the one known as 'L'aurore'. I have to admit that having been saturated in Beethoven's symphonies since the age of twelve, I suffered from indigestion where this composer was concerned. In a mood of resignation the following week, I began to play my sonata, but in such a tedious fashion that on the second page Debussy took the score away and said: 'Let's look at something else.' That was the end of that sonata and we went on to Balakirev's *Islamey*, which I never tired of studying.

Chopin's *Barcarolle* was one of his favourite pieces, and it was the cause of violent scenes between us! I played Chopin very badly, and particularly the *Barcarolle*, which I had taken a dislike to ever since Debussy insisted on my repeating it a considerable number of times: 'You will work at it until you can play it well,' he said, 'for years if necessary.' The way he explained and analysed the piece was admirable, not bothering about details, only about the overall performance. When we got to the passage where the tune is heard in force, accompanied by ever more powerful octaves in the left hand, Debussy would sing and puff: you'd think he was pushing the gondola himself, and this energetic interpretation would end, thanks to my clumsiness, in general despair.

For a change of air, we turned to *L'apprenti sorcier* and to Dukas' Symphony, in a piano duet arrangement, leading Debussy to comment that 'it was like a man who had put his coat on back to front'. His remarks were always original and ironic. Chausson's anxiety-laden music was for him 'prison music'. César Franck's 'celestial harmonies' finally got on our nerves rather, and Debussy said of him: 'Poor Franck has such an angelic nature that when he wants to depict wicked people he has to make a lot of noise.' As for Charpentier's *Louise*, which had just had its first performance, this work had the ability to excite him in the highest degree. Reading the libretto would make him roar with laughter and he claimed that, when he was feeling low, he only had to open a score of *Louise* and read it to see black butterflies come flying out! He was delighted by the singing policemen and by the lullaby about 'ladies of love who are not all bad'. 'After that,' he said, 'whenever I see a policeman in the street, I think he's going to launch into song.'

Debussy loved his food. Talking of a society lady who sang his songs, and wanted him to come and play for her when she gave musical soirées, he said: 'She sings like a locomotive in distress, but her buttered scones are marvellous!'

Of another lady whose voice was in decline and who was singing the 'Liebestod', he said she gave the impression of scooping up sounds with a spoon. And when asked to give his opinion of a celebrated star of the Opéra: 'She sounds as though she's singing inside a glass bulb.' He refused to have at any price, for the role of Mélisande, the mistress* of a man of letters whose dream it was to play this part: 'Not only does she sing out of tune,' he said, 'she speaks out of tune.'

Debussy was a tease. At tea, he had the habit of absentmindedly tracing imaginary patterns on the table with his knife while he was talking. My mother couldn't help anxiously following these movements which threatened her tablecloth. Debussy saw this and, greatly amused, continued to inflict his torture.

He had very firm ideas about comfort. None of the chairs put out for him found favour in his eyes: whether they were Louis XV, Louis XVI, Empire, upholstered or not! He would fidget about, turn to and fro and finally ask for another one (was this perhaps an early sign of the illness which was to carry him off?) So a new chair had to be bought for him which was quite simply a modern cane chair, and which was called from then on 'Monsieur Debussy's chair'.

We had the idea of giving a small, private party for a few friends, so that they could hear the *Chansons de Bilitis* which Debussy had just finished, but which had not yet been published. I organized some ensemble items with my friends and Debussy agreed to accompany everything.

I began the concert by playing the 'Prélude' from the piano suite

*Georgette Leblanc (see p. 64)

which Debussy had offered and dedicated to me. Among our audience there were always some people who, although they appreciated the eclectic choice of the pieces, did not understand them all. The duet from Lalo's *Le roi d'Ys* was applauded, as were duets and trios by Schumann. The problems began when we came to the modern works. Debussy's music had a galvanic effect on an old Argentinian gentleman who had for some time been containing himself with difficulty. His outburst came immediately after hearing the *Chansons de Bilitis*. Not imagining for a moment that the composer was present, he marched up and down the room, shouting: 'No, no, that's not music! How do people come to write stuff like that?'

We were all transfixed with embarrassment. I took him by the hand and led him up to Debussy, whom I introduced to him so as to put an end to his imprecations. Debussy was enchanted. He smiled and shook his hand and afterwards he would often ask me for news of this charming gentleman; and he would add, in his slightly nasal voice: 'I like that man, I should be delighted to see him again.'

One day, at the end of 1899, Debussy, who was exactitude person-ified, arrived extremely late to give me my lesson. My mother had been sitting in her usual place for an hour and was considerably put out. Finally the door opened and Debussy came in, very out of breath, and said simply: 'Madame, forgive me for this unintentional delay; it's not entirely my fault: I've just got married.' Immediately we exclaimed that it was ridiculous of him to have come, that he was to forget about the lesson on a day like this. But Debussy refused to leave, sat calmly down and wanted to hear my exercises.

He told us that the priest, whom he went to to get him to marry them, had asked for eighty francs: 'You can imagine,' he said indig-nantly, 'after that we went to the *mairie*.' A few years later I told this story to his wife, who laughed and claimed there had never been any question of their being married by a priest, and that Debussy had probably wanted to make a good impression on my mother. I also learnt that Lilo Debussy was waiting that day at the bottom of the staircase to our apartment, sitting on the bench, until the lesson was over, so they could take a wedding ride on the open top of a bus! They got out at the Jardin des Plantes, round which Debussy dragged himself – he hated walking. Then, with his parents who had turned up for the occasion, they went and had dinner at the Taverne Pousset.

The meal was paid for by the fee for my lesson, and everyone went home on foot because there wasn't enough money left to take the bus. Debussy had terrible trouble getting home; he was exhausted by the day and particularly by this 'forced footing'.

Since my marriage in 1901, I was living in Vincennes and it was my turn to travel and take my lessons at 58 rue Cardinet. The Debussys lived on the fourth floor in a block of flats (almost on the junction with the avenue de Villiers), in a meticulously clean and tidy little apartment. From the windows you could see a little greenery, and the peace and quiet were only troubled at certain times by the happy cries of children in a school courtyard.

There was an atmosphere of intimacy and calm in the two small rooms joined by a bay. One was Debussy's studio where, on the desk, manuscripts, inkwells and pencils were laid out in perfect order. There was also a divan, several Oriental carpets and, on the walls, pictures by Henri Lerolle, Jacques-Emile Blanche, Thaulow, and drawings representing Lilo Debussy, then at the height of her beauty. She had delicate features surrounded by fair hair; she appeared to be the very incarnation of Mélisande. In the other room there was a upright piano, books and scores.

If Lilo was not a musician (which her husband was glad of), she was an accomplished mistress of the household, always on the lookout for treats and cooking exquisite little meals for him which he appreciated greatly and consumed with relish. She allowed him to sleep on late into the day (because he worked at night and was awake until morning) and with the skill of a conjuror managed to keep the household going on a budget which was usually hovering around zero. The two cats, which Debussy cherished, occupied an important place in the family, and had all their whims respected. As silent as their master, they had the right to spend the day solemnly on the desk and, if they so wished, to sow disorder among the pencils.

Madame Gérard de Romilly, 'Debussy professeur', *Cahiers Debussy*, n.s. 2, 1978, pp. 3–10

BLANCHE MAROT

Blanche Marot gave the first performance of the *Chansons de Bilitis* on 17 March 1900. Some time before this, Debussy came to see Mlle Marot's mother and asked her:

'Tell me, Madame, your daughter is not yet twenty? Good. It's very important, because if she understands the second song, 'La chevelure', she won't sing it in the right way: she mustn't grasp the true brazenness of Bilitis's language . . . My mother set Debussy's anxieties at rest and everything went splendidly.

Blanche Marot, quoted in: Charles Oulmont, *Noces d'or avec mon passé* (Paris, 1964), p. 70

ANDRE SUARES

(1868–1948)

André Suarès was a writer and a close friend of Romain Rolland.

The first time I saw him was on the eve of *Pelléas*. He was not a particularly noticeable figure: not tall, no more robust or thin than normal, but with a certain solidity about him and a rather dull complexion. He was fleshy-looking, with all the lines rounded; a silky, sensual beard and abundant, crinkly hair. His ironical attitude was innate, as was his inclination towards pleasure; his teasing spirit was full of wit and he made no secret of his appetites. There was a droop about the corner of his lips, and a certain nonchalance in his speech was matched by the delicate charm of his gestures. His passion was tempered by disillusionment and experience. Strong and sensitive, he showed taste in everything as well as simplicity under an apparently complex surface. He was as much a bohemian of Montmartre as a man of the world. There was something catlike and solitary about him, and I think a fundamental melancholy always separated him somewhat from others.

His forehead was of the kind one finds in so many great creative artists. Geometricians too, those virtuosos of number, have the same protuberances over the eyebrows. To the careful observer, Debussy's gaze spoke rather of a man out of the ordinary than of a composer. His fine eyes, caressing and inclined to mockery, sad and full of languor, passionate and thoughtful, were like those of some accomplished and powerful woman, eyes such as artists sometimes have, as though they had themselves been women in some previous life. His gaze could also take on a strange heaviness, an extreme concentration – the gaze of some French poet who continues to analyse even in reverie and whose understanding is never at rest.

André Suarès, 'Debussy', *ReM*, 2, 1 December 1920, pp. 124–5

III

'Autour de *Pelléas*'

Debussy's only completed opera, *Pelléas et Mélisande*, closely based on Maeterlinck's play, received its première at the Opéra-Comique on 30 April 1902, conducted by André Messager. Mary Garden sang the role of Mélisande.

GEORGETTE LEBLANC

(1875–1941)

Georgette Leblanc was an actress and singer, and for many
years the mistress of Maeterlinck.

In August 1893, some time before Maeterlinck and I met, he had a
letter from the poet Henri de Régnier, from which I quote the
following extract:

*My friend Achille Debussy, a composer of the most refined and exceptional
talent, has begun a setting of* Pelléas et Mélisande *in which the music
weaves delightful garlands around the text while treating it with scrupulous
respect. Before continuing with the considerable labour involved in this
project, he would like to have your authorization to do so . . .*

We were living on the rue Raynouard in Passy when, at the end
of 1901, Debussy came to play us his work. I saw him come into the
room. His extraordinary head is known from his portraits. But in the
flesh various special traits became apparent, and from small details of
colouring, bearing and gesture, one could make a number of guesses
about his secret personality. His complexion was matt and as white as
wax, his fine, crinkly hair broke up the massive line of his formidable
skull. His eyes, sheltered beneath the prominent forehead, sparkled
discreetly. His gestures were few in number and he rarely smiled.

While he talked to Maeterlinck, I pondered on the difference
between these two who were both putting up defences against each
other. Debussy's restraint was physical. One felt in him a tendency
towards sadness and even something unhealthy which was biding its
time. With Maeterlinck, his physical and moral equilibrium declared
itself instantly. His shyness was the result of character and habit. The
composer suffered from the little things in life. The poet refused to
put up with them. In him the 'no entry' sign meant: 'Don't disturb
me!' In Debussy it seemed to say: 'Don't make me suffer!' Both
of them had an anxious look in the eye, but of a different kind: the
poet's was clear and briskly questioning, the composer's fixed and
intense, not provoking any reply. The most remarkable thing about
Debussy was that his body was built for strength, but to all appear-

ances did not contain it. His strength had been drained away by his genius.

Debussy played us his score. The position of the piano against the wall obliged him to turn his back to us and allowed Maeterlinck to make desperate signals to me: as he knew nothing about music, time seemed to him to be going slowly. Several times he wanted to leave the room; I held him back. Resignedly, he lit his pipe.

During this first hearing of *Pelléas*, many of its marvels escaped me; but at the prelude to Mélisande's death I felt that special, unique emotion which comes to us in the presence of a masterpiece: our life seems to detach itself from us, something comes to a stop; words, tears, emotion itself, everything that goes to make up our humanity, at the service of the great moments in life suddenly becomes inadequate. We are suspended in an unknown world where our utterances no longer make sense.

As Debussy was leaving, we talked about casting. I wanted the role passionately. Maeterlinck expressed his wish to have me as Mélisande, and Debussy declared himself delighted. It was decided that private rehearsals should begin right away, and we said goodbye.

There were two or three rehearsals at my house and two evening ones in the very modest apartment he shared with his first wife on the fifth floor in the rue Cardinet. Debussy was thrilled by my interpretation. He told me that, having seen me so violent in *Carmen*, he had at first had doubts as to whether I would be able to transform myself. We understood each other perfectly over the music, but during the pauses we didn't talk.

My rehearsals with Debussy were continuing, then, when one day Maeterlinck read in a newspaper that another artist had been engaged for the part of Mélisande and that she was rehearsing with the composer. Debussy's behaviour surprised me, because he was not a man to pay compliments insincerely. He continually said what pleasure he got from my diction. Was it not the poetry in *Pelléas* which had inspired him? Had he not followed the play word for word in a way that had never been done before? No, the quarrel was not between him and me. It emanated from the Opéra-Comique, from the time of *Carmen* when I repulsed certain advances . . . I had to pay the price of my intransigence.

Maeterlinck, considering that he had been injured by Debussy, referred the matter to the Société des Auteurs, thinking all the rights belonged to him. He was mistaken, first of all because the law gives composers rights superior to those of writers; and secondly because in his initial authorization he had added the generous phrase: 'The piece will be played where, how and when you wish.'

Justly irritated to find himself powerless before the law, Maeterlinck brandished his stick and told me was going to 'give Debussy several whacks . . . to teach him how to behave . . .' I waited anxiously, certain that a drama was going to follow. I did not see Debussy, with his tragic mask, receiving correction kindly! . . . I kept looking up the road to see if I could see Maeterlinck. At last he appeared at the top of the hill, waving his stick at the sky with crazy gestures.

It was a pitiful story. As soon as he got into the drawing-room, Maeterlinck had threatened Debussy, who was sitting peacefully in a chair, while Madame Debussy ran desperately to her husband clutching a bottle of salts. She begged Maeterlinck to leave, and indeed there was nothing else he could do.

Maeterlinck, who didn't like composers any more than he did music, used to laugh and say: 'Those composers, they're all insane, all sick in the head!'

Georgette Leblanc, *Souvenirs* (Paris, 1931), pp. 166–72

ANDRE MESSAGER

(1853–1929)

André Messager studied at the Ecole Niedermeyer, his first success as a composer coming with the ballet *Les deux pigeons* in 1886. He wrote no less than eight light operas in the 1890s, including *Les p'tites Michu* and *Véronique*, and as conductor at the Opéra-Comique was largely responsible for persuading the director, Albert Carré, of the value of *Pelléas*. Messager conducted the première of the opera on 30 April 1902.

The singers read through *Pelléas* at my house, with no one else present. Debussy played his score on the piano, singing all the roles in that deep, cavernous voice of his which often meant transposing lines an octave down, but whose delivery gradually became irresistible. The impression produced by that music on that occasion was, I believe, unique. To begin with there was a kind of mistrust, a resistance, then an ever closer attention, with the emotional temperature rising until the last notes of 'Mélisande's death', which fell amid silence and tears. At the end all of us were carried away with excitement, burning to get down to work as soon as possible.

During the weeks that followed, rehearsals took place amid growing enthusiasm; each scene was gone over twenty times without any of the singers showing the least sign of temper in the face of the composer's demands – and he was very difficult to satisfy. With the first orchestral read-through began a series of gloomy days and discouraging rehearsals. Debussy had had the generous but unfortunate idea of getting the orchestral material copied by a friend who was hard up, but who was a mediocre copyist and a somewhat rudimentary musician, and it took three or four rehearsals simply to get the corrections sorted out. In the meantime a new difficulty had arisen, of some seriousness, to do with the changes of scene. Although the stage of the Opéra-Comique looks fairly large, it has such small exits and such narrow wings that it is impossible to manoeuvre even a flat through them, and we were having to make on average three rapid changes per act! Debussy, imagining that these changes would be more or less instantaneous, had linked the different scenes with music that was far too short. He had to return to work, grumbling and raving, and I went to see him every day to snatch away the notes he had written between one rehearsal and another; that is how he wrote the wonderful interludes which provide such a moving commentary on the action.

André Messager, 'Les premières représentations de *Pelléas*,' *ReM*, 7, 1 May 1926, pp. 110–12

MARY GARDEN

(1874–1967)

Mary Garden was born in Aberdeen and spent her youth in the United States. She then studied in Paris with Lucien Fugère and made her début at the Opéra-Comique in

1900. She later returned to the USA, both as a singer and
as Director of the Chicago Opera.

There was a piano in that salon, and while I sat down before it and
idled over the keys Messager strode over to a table upon which was
lying a copy of the French magazine, *L'Illustration*. Opening it, he
came upon some music that immediately excited him, for he shouted
out:

'My God, Mary, here's a composition by Claude Debussy, and it's
perfectly beautiful.'

I came over to look at it, and it was the song 'Extase', and the more
I examined it the more it seemed to be mine, so near were its mood
and idiom to me.

'Oh, how I want to possess that song!' I cried out to Messager.

'Perhaps you shall some day – and its composer, too,' said Messager.

'André, you're jealous!' I laughed. 'Of a few bars of music!'

Later, after we produced *Pelléas et Mélisande*, I told Debussy that
it was the song 'Extase' that had first brought us together, which
explains why he then dedicated the song to me. It wasn't until some
years later that I discovered that the same song had also brought
Debussy and his first wife Lily, together. She, too, had seen the song
in *L'Illustration* and said to herself: 'I'd like to know the man who
wrote this song – I've *got* to know him.' Lily would say to me, 'Mary,
I fell in love with Claude through that song, didn't you?' and I would
answer, 'Only with his music, Lily.'

One day M. Carré let us all know about this new opera, and after
he had finished talking about *Pelléas et Mélisande* and its composer,
he began assigning roles to each of us. Then one afternoon we were
all invited to M. Messager's home. We were there only a short while
when the door opened and in came Debussy. We were all presented
to him, and he spoke the usual words of greeting. Without another
word, he sat at the piano and played and sang the whole thing from
beginning to end.

There we sat in the drawing-room – M. Carré, and M. and Mme
Messager, and the whole cast – each of us with a score, heads bowed
as if we were all at prayer. While Debussy played I had the most
extraordinary emotions I have ever experienced in my life. Listening
to that music I seemed to become someone else, someone inside of me

whose language and soul were akin to mine. When Debussy got to the fourth act I could no longer look at my score for the tears. It was all very strange and unbearable. I closed my book and just listened to him, and as he played the death of Mélisande, I burst into the most awful sobbing, and Mme Messager began to sob along with me, and both of us fled into the next room. I shall never forget it. There we were crying as if we had just lost our best friend, crying as if nothing would console us again.

Mme Messager and I returned to the drawing-room just as Debussy stopped. Before anyone could say or do anything, he faced us all and said:

'*Mesdames et messieurs*, that is my *Pelléas et Mélisande*. Everyone must forget that he is a singer before he can sing the music of Debussy. *Oubliez, je vous prie, que vous êtes chanteurs!*'

Then he murmured a quick '*Au revoir*' and, without another word, was gone.

We all went home and began studying our roles.

After we had all studied our parts, we were called into M. Carré's office.

'I assume you have all mastered every note and word of your roles,' he said.

'We have,' we assured him.

'We are going to modify our procedure this time,' he went on. 'As the next step there will be individual rehearsals with M. Debussy. Each of you will have an afternoon with him. Remember that when you go into that rehearsal room you are expected to know your parts to perfection. Whether you sing them or not will rest entirely with him.'

I suppose I should say something about the structure of the Opéra-Comique building. There are the main stage and the opera house itself, and then up on the fifth floor there is a theatre with another huge stage. When anything was going on downstairs, a rehearsal or a performance, we could still rehearse, all of us, on the fifth floor. It was an enormous hall. When necessary, even the orchestra could come up and rehearse with us.

Besides that big auditorium, there are about ten small rehearsal rooms. It was in one of these smaller chambers that Debussy was to conduct the rehearsals. He took one of us at a time, and the rehearsals lasted from about one-fifteen to six. I remember very clearly going up that first afternoon. I knew, as everyone knew, that this production had to be perfection itself, and I was fully prepared.

Debussy was already in the small rehearsal room when I arrived. Without any preliminary chatter, except a quick exchange of 'How do you do's?' we began. I opened my score, and Debussy sat down at the piano. We did the first act, Debussy singing the role of Golaud. His voice was very small and husky . . . I never knew a composer who could sing and few who could play the piano well. Charpentier couldn't play a note. But Debussy was a magnificent pianist. So there he sat, singing the part of Golaud, playing the piano, and never saying a single word. When we came to Pelléas, he sang that too, and all the other roles as well, except mine. Then we came to the scene of the Tower. I was singing my lines when, without a word, he got up abruptly and left the room. I stayed there a little while and waited, quite bewildered. I had a feeling I had offended him in some mysterious way and I began to prepare myself for the shock of not singing Mélisande. I put on my hat and was about to leave the rehearsal room when a boy came in and said: 'Miss Garden, M. Carré would like to see you in the office.' When I walked in, there sat Debussy with M. Carré. Rising from his chair, he came right up to me and took both my hands in his.

'Where were you born?' he asked.

'Aberdeen, Scotland.'

'To think that you had to come from the cold far North to create my Mélisande – because that's what you're going to do, Mademoiselle.'

Then he turned to M. Carré, and I remember he put up his hands, and said: '*Je n'ai rien à lui dire*. I have nothing to tell her.'

He paused, as if embarrassed, and, still looking at M. Carré, added: 'What a strange person, this child.'

With that, he fell silent, in that curious detached way of his, took his hat, and, mumbling a 'Goodbye,' walked out of M. Carré's office. Debussy was always doing that – suddenly walking out. He walked out of Lily Debussy's life that way, he walked out of mine, and he even walked out of Mélisande's. When he was finished, he was finished.

It was after the last rehearsal that Debussy did the very characteristic thing of walking out of the life of Mélisande. He never came to a single performance of *Pelléas*. Again and again I asked him to come to watch the complete fulfilment of his dream, and one night he tried to make me understand.

'Mary, I can't ever go,' he said. '*Pelléas* is my child. I had it in my hands for ten years. I gave it to the public, and now it doesn't interest me any longer.'

Debussy was as good as his word. I only remember his being present once again, and that, too, was at a rehearsal. I was creating Mélisande with another company, in Brussels, several years later, and Debussy, who was now married to his second wife, came into the dark house one afternoon. He sat there, silent and detached, and when he had anything to communicate to one of us on the stage, he would write it down on a slip of paper and send it up by a boy. But he never appeared on the stage and he never came over to greet me. Debussy lived in a world of his own, where no one, not even his first wife, Lily, with all her care and adoration, could reach him.

Shortly after the première of *Pelléas*, Debussy, his wife Lily, and I became inseparable friends. During question-and-answer period of a talk I gave in December of 1949, someone in the audience sent up a question that was not shown to me till the evening was over. I wish it had been read out, for I would have liked very much to answer it, and answer it truthfully and frankly. The question was, 'Were you ever the mistress of Claude Debussy?'

Debussy and his wife used to come for dinner at my house twice a week, and sometimes three times. Just before the première of *Pelléas* I had taken a tiny apartment on the rue Washington, a modest affair, but quite charming. I was then getting sixteen hundred francs a month, and that was a good deal of money – for me – and it would have been even more for Debussy, who never had any. Debussy loved good eating, and he adored everything that was rich and flavoursome. He also secretly loved sumptuous and luxurious things. In his craving for things, he had the most extravagant brain I have ever known. But he never could do what he wanted and he never could buy what he wanted because he hadn't the money. He had a deep longing for costly things which he could never satisfy, and which in the end destroyed his marriage with Lily, the only woman he ever loved, if, that is, he was at all capable of loving anything but his music. The two of them occupied a small apartment on the rue Cardinet, no. 58. I used to go up there later and study all those beautiful songs of his with him.

The day they came to dine with me, I would wait at the window, watching for them. One day I saw a carriage draw up to my house. There sat Debussy in all his glory, alone. When he came into the house, I asked, 'Where's Lily?' and he replied, 'Oh, she's walking.' And Lily arrived soon afterward, on foot. Why they separated that way I don't know, but Debussy must have loved that little show of solitary comfort.

After dinner we used to go into the drawing-room, and Lily and I would go into a corner and talk about things. Then Debussy would sit at the piano, and for an hour or so he would improvise. Those hours stay like jewels in my mind. I have never heard such music in my life, such music as came from the piano at those moments. How beautiful it was, and haunting, and nobody but Lily and I ever heard it! Debussy never put those improvisations down on paper; they went back to the strange place they had come from, never to return. That precious music, lost for ever, was so unlike anything Debussy ever published. There was a quality of its own about it, remote, other-worldly, always saying something on the verge of words.

At those moments Debussy was in that far-off world of his, inspired, as if in a trance. He just sat there and played. He never moved and he never said a word. What it was or what he was trying to say through his music, he never told us and we never knew – he just played. And then, with that suddenness of his, he would get up and come over to speak to us. And that was the end of it.

Later I worked with Debussy on the première of his *Damoiselle élue*, which I created at a Concert Colonne. As so often happened when I studied Debussy's music, my emotion got the best of me one day and I burst into tears. Debussy laughed and ridiculed me.

'*Ma petite* Mélisande,' he said, 'you are a sentimental dove.'

Debussy dedicated his *Ariettes* to me, and we studied them, along with the *Chansons de Bilitis*, in that little room of his on the rue Cardinet.

Debussy and I made two trips together to London, the first one on the invitation of André Messager, then directing at Covent Garden. Messager, who was Debussy's closest friend, was eager to have him see Forbes Robertson as Hamlet.

I knew Debussy was mad about Shakespeare, but I had no suspicion how far his madness went. I sat next to him at that performance, and he seemed like a child in a trance. So profoundly was he affected that it was some time before he could speak. I have never known anyone to lose himself so completely in the spectacle of great art.

Our second visit to London was less exhilarating. A special matinee was scheduled of Maeterlinck's *Pelléas et Mélisande*, with Sarah Bernhardt as Pelléas and Mrs Patrick Campbell as Mélisande. That was a combination both Debussy and I would have gone to St Petersburg to see, out of sheer curiosity.

We left Paris on the night train and arrived in London early the following morning. We went to the home of a friend of mine, ate a delicious lunch, and were soon seated in the theatre, where we arrived long before curtain time. We waited with mounting expectancy.

Then the play began, and it wasn't long before Debussy and I were looking at each other in great wonder. Not one member of the cast had the slightest comprehension of Maeterlinck's drama. Bernhardt, that supreme artist whom no one adored more than I, was utterly miscast.

'She is trying to impersonate Robin Hood,' I whispered to Debussy, who was getting very restless.

With the third act, the thing became painful beyond words. There, Mélisande, leaning from her bedroom window in the tower, lets fall her long, golden locks into the hands of Pelléas below. Debussy almost screamed when Mrs Patrick Campbell unloosed an avalanche of jet-black hair!

'When is the next train to Paris?' he asked, his nerves completely shattered.

We left the theatre at once and after a tiresome journey arrived in Paris at midnight.

It was in the third year of our great friendship that I went to live in Versailles. I invited Debussy and his wife to come out to stay with me for two weeks. That was in the month of June of 1904. And the three of us had such fun! We used to go all through Versailles, making such dreadful comments on people and things. What we said about them was the purest vitriol. And Debussy loathed most people – at any rate, people who were not simple and natural. I never met a more baffling man in my life. His friendships were few and his confidences were rare.

One day, in her husband's presence Lily said to me:

'Mary, I want you to scold Claude for me.'

'Why, what has he done, Lily?'

'Well, there's a lady in Paris by the name of Bardac,' she said. 'She has a great salon and she gives wonderful musicales where very important people come. The best pianists go there to play Claude's music, and she has invited Claude again and again, but he won't go.'

'Claude,' I turned to him, 'why don't you go to Mme Bardac's? It might be a good thing for you and your music.'

All he said was, '*Je ne sais pas.*'

Toward the end of the two weeks, Debussy and I were walking in the park at Versailles. Suddenly he stopped and faced me.

'Mary,' he said, 'I have an obsession, and I must tell you about it.'

'Please do, Claude.'

'Ten years I worked on that opera of mine, and then I was never satisfied,' he began.

'I know, Claude.'

'Ten years I lived with this Mélisande, and I never thought I would ever find anybody who could make her come to life as the woman I lived with. And you did that, Mary.'

'You've made me very happy saying that, Claude.'

Debussy looked as if he were under a strain of some kind, nervous with me for the first time since we had met.

'I am obsessed with love of you, Mary,' he said finally.

'That's a pity, Claude,' I said.

'But I'm very serious,' he went on. 'I can't live without you, and I must know if you have any feeling for me.'

'Not that kind, Claude,' I replied. 'I love and adore your genius, I like you as a friend, but Debussy the man means nothing to me.'

He took it as he took everything, without another word. But it bothered me very much, because, you see, it had never shown itself to me in any way before, and as we walked back to my villa I began to think of why he would say that to me, and suddenly it came to me.

'Claude,' I said, turning to look at him, 'it isn't *me* you love, much as you believe it.'

He made no comment.

'It is Mélisande you love. You've loved her for ten years, and you still do, and it is Mélisande that you love in me, not myself.'

Debussy showed no sign of having heard me. He had made his declaration, and that was the end of it. I am sure I was right. He had always addressed me as '*Ma chère* Mélisande' and his letters to me all opened that way. And I think I got the final proof that I was right later, when he left Lily for Mme Bardac. He couldn't have been in love with me in June and with Mme Bardac in September.

Later that afternoon, I saw Lily, and while we were alone I thought it best to tell her what Debussy had said to me in the park.

'Lily,' I said, 'I've got something to tell you. I've always been honest with you, and I think I should be frank now.'

'By all means, Mary,' she said, looking just a little frightened. 'What is it?'

'Claude has just told me he loved me, and I don't like that in our friendship at all. It would ruin it for all three of us.'

'What did you tell Claude?'

'I told him I loved him as a friend and a musician, but that was all, and that I hoped the friendship of all three of us would continue as before.'

Lily now looked at me with that sweet, serene look of hers – she was such a beautiful thing.

'I'm so glad you told me, Mary,' she said. 'I think you're the only woman in the world I would give Claude up for.'

I didn't know what to answer to that. I felt it made matters worse for me in a way, because I now knew she was perfectly willing to have it. But there was no continuation of the drama that might have been. It was finished as far as I was concerned. Just how Debussy went on feeling about me, I had no way of telling, but his leaving Lily for Mme Bardac convinced me he had been cured of his 'obsession'. Once, many years later, M. Carré did tell me that he had received a letter from Debussy in which he said, in reference to me, 'Her voice is a torment that I can't get out of my mind.' Only the three of us – Claude, Lily, and I – knew about his declaration to me in the *bois* at Versailles. You see, after that day at Versailles everything was finished between Debussy and me. I accompanied them to the station, and there Debussy took me in his arms and for the first and only time kissed me. 'Goodbye, Mary,' he said, and that was the last contact I had with him, except that one time in Brussels when he sent pencil notes to me from his seat in a dark auditorium.

I could never have loved Debussy. Never for a moment did he affect me that way, and he would have repelled me as a lover. But Lily was a dear, just a sweet, simple girl who didn't care for anything in God's green earth but that man. They had met in Montmartre when Debussy hadn't a sou to his name. Debussy had been living there with his mistress, a woman named Gaby, and he was said to be crazy about her because she had green eyes. It was through Gaby that Debussy met Lily one day, which was ironic, just as it was ironic that it was because of Lily's urging that he went off to Mme Bardac's musicales. Well, Debussy met Lily, fell in love with her, and she with him, and he left Gaby to marry her.

I honestly don't know if Debussy ever loved anybody really. He loved his music – and perhaps himself. I think he was wrapped up in his genius. People say that he married Mme Bardac for money, but I don't know. He was a very, very strange man. Perhaps he was unhappy at the end. Messager showed me a letter from him that might bear that out. 'Oh, how I wish I could recapture the happiness of the days of *Pelléas et Mélisande!*' he wrote. 'But it is hopeless. That joy has vanished for ever.' Debussy and I had one thing in common – we neither of us knew what the word jealousy meant.

That little drama had taken place in Versailles in the summer of 1904. When I returned to Paris in September, the first thing I did was to go to the rue Cardinet, no. 58, and tell Lily and Claude that I was back in town and waiting to have them come to dine with me again. They weren't in, either of them. I left word that they should come to see me, and returned to my apartment rather puzzled. Three hours later, my door opened and in came Lily – alone, and wild with sorrow.

'Lily,' I cried, 'what in heaven's name is wrong?'

'Claude has left me!'

And she burst into a frenzy of tears.

I took her in my arms and tried to comfort her.

'Tell me about it, Lily.'

It seems that Debussy had been in the habit of taking a walk every morning. Well, he went for his walk one morning and never came back. It was a very cruel thing, I suppose, but you can't help admiring people who make a decision like that and keep it – provided they keep it. It needs strength of character . . . Lily went on crying inconsolably. Finally, she calmed down a little.

'Where is Claude now?' I asked Lily.

'I have no idea, Mary.'

'Have you asked his father?'

'Not yet. He's coming to Paris tomorrow, and I'm going over to see if he can find out where Claude is.'

'Very well, Lily,' I said. 'Let me know the minute you find out, and I'll see if I can help in any way to bring Claude back to you.'

A week went by, and no word from Lily. Then one day a messenger boy brought me a note to come at once to a certain hospital in Paris – nothing more. Fearing the worst, I put on my hat and hurried down to the hospital. When I arrived I got hold of the head man there.

'Who is it?' I asked, breathless with fright.

'Mme Claude Debussy.'

They took me into a tiny room, and there lay Lily, with a bullet in her breast, wanting to die because her Claude had not come back to her. You must understand that this young girl never knew anything else in life but her love of Debussy. She took care of him like a child. They had worries and debts and disappointments, but nobody ever got into the little apartment of the rue Cardinet to interrupt Debussy at his music. Lily kept the world away, so her beloved Claude could work – and be hers alone . . . As Lily lay there, pale and bandaged, she told me the story.

She had seen Debussy's father, and he had told her that his son was in Dieppe, living with Mme Bardac.

'I knew then, Mary, that he would never come back to me,' she sobbed.

Lily must have known her husband very well to suspect that if ever he made a decision he would stick to it. So she went out and got a revolver, and this beautiful young creature who had never held a gun in her hand, and didn't know how to use it, went into her bedroom and shot it off against the wall to try it.

Then she sat down and wrote Debussy a letter and sent it off by messenger in care of his father. She wanted the letter to be on its way at three o'clock, because at three o'clock she planned to kill herself and she didn't want Claude to get the letter until she had done the fatal thing to herself. Then she turned the gun on herself . . .

'Oh, Mary,' Lily whimpered, 'I didn't aim right, and I don't know how long I lay on the floor. I never lost consciousness. I heard someone coming into the bedroom. It was Claude. And he came over and stooped down to look at me.

' "Claude," I said, "if you're coming back to me, take me to the hospital, and see if I can live. If you're not coming back to me, leave me here to die." '

Without saying a word, Debussy flew down the stairs and returned with an ambulance. He brought the men up with him and they carried Lily down those five flights of stairs. I found out from the surgeon that when they arrived at the hospital, Debussy asked:

'Can Mme Debussy's life be saved?'

'I don't know, yet, Monsieur,' the doctor replied. 'But you can wait here in the hospital, and in one or two hours we may be able to let you know.'

Debussy then took a seat in the corner of the waiting-room, and with his hat on waited, like a bad boy in school, for the verdict. After two hours the surgeon came out.

'M. Debussy, we are happy to tell you that your wife will live.'

Debussy looked up at the doctor and in his husky voice muttered just one word: '*Merci*.' And he walked out of the hospital and out of the lives of all of us. It was then that Lily called for me.

'Lily,' I asked, 'what did you put in that letter to Claude?'

'I said, "When you get this, Claude, I shall be dead. Please come to me. I want no hands to touch me but yours." '

When Lily had finished telling me the story, the surgeon came in to dress her wound.

'I'll step outside,' I said.

'You don't have to, if you wish to stay.'

I stayed. The surgeon went to Lily's side and opened her nightdress, and in my life I have never seen anything so beautiful as Lily Debussy from the waist up. It was just like a glorious marble statue, too divine for words! Debussy had always said to me, 'Mary, there's nothing in the world like Lily's body.' Now I knew what he meant.

And lying underneath Lily's left breast was a round dark hole where the bullet had gone in, without touching anything vital – and Lily didn't die. They never got the bullet out. That little token of her love for Claude Debussy stayed with her till she died.

Mary Garden (and Louis Biancolli), *Mary Garden's Story* (London, 1952), pp. 49, 63–8, 73–83

HENRI BUSSER
(1872–1973)

Henri Busser entered the Paris Conservatoire in 1889, studied the organ with Franck and Widor and composition with Guiraud, Gounod and Massenet. After winning the Prix de Rome in 1893, he became a conductor and then returned to the Conservatoire as a teacher first of vocal ensemble and then of composition. He conducted the off-stage chorus at the première of *Pelléas* on 30 April 1902 and took over the rostrum from Messager from the fourth performance on 8 May.

7/9 April 1902: Final rehearsals. Carré is asking Debussy to compose continuous orchestral interludes to connect the scenes. 'That's impossible,' Debussy says. 'I can't produce music in one continuous stream. I'll add them during the holidays.' Orchestral rehearsals will be suspended if the changes aren't ready!

12 April: I meet Massenet in the theatre corridors and persuade him to come and listen to *Pelléas* which is being rehearsed in the auditorium. He stays with me and listens to the last two scenes without saying anything. Debussy sees him and comes to greet him. Massenet says how moved he is by this new and unusual work!

17 April: At today's rehearsal Messager and Debussy are in a foul temper. They consider, and rightly, that Périer and Dufranne are singing at the tops of their voices; on the other hand they're very happy with Mary Garden and Mlle Gerville-Réache. But the scene-changing is dreadfully slow; there are black looks in plenty! . . .

28 April: The great day finally arrives! Public dress rehearsal of *Pelléas*. Success is assured with the fourth and fifth acts. Debussy takes refuge in Messager's office and nervously smokes one cigarette after another.

30 April [? 1 May]: The morning after the première I go to see Debussy in his modest apartment on the rue Cardinet: he's writing interludes to join some of the scenes together. While he goes to the piano and plays me what he has sketched out, his young wife wanders in and out, arranging the flowers I've brought them in a vase. This little room we're in, with oil paintings, watercolours and drawings on the walls, radiates happiness. The delightful Lily is its source. She's happy that *Pelléas* is being produced. 'It's my work too,' she says, 'because I gave Claude encouragement when he was despairing of ever seeing his work reach the stage!'

3 May: Third performance. Large audience, more responsive and sympathetic. At the end there are calls for Debussy, but he refuses to appear on stage.

A few days later, Debussy and his wife come to dinner, with Mary Garden, in my little apartment on the rue de Saint-Pétersbourg. We celebrate the success of *Pelléas*, which is now assured. Debussy is well aware that he has broken completely with the pernicious habits of opera composers. He tells us: 'I try and move the listener through the simplicity of the vocal line, through the discretion of the orchestra; I detest the brutal effects so greatly prized by my predecessors.'

8 May: Debussy and his wife come to see me and put me on my guard against the possible whims of the singers. Both of them seem quite exhausted.

23 May: *Le médecin malgré lui* by Gounod. I take Debussy and his wife to the performance, which they adore. Debussy particularly admires the wit of Gounod's writing and his style of orchestration. He calls it 'a little masterpiece'.

26 June: Fourteenth performance of *Pelléas* which, to my great regret, is the last one this season. The audience very enthusiastic. Three or four curtain calls after each act. Mme Debussy tells me that her husband is working hard at the interludes to connect the scenes.

7 July: For a long time I've been wanting to compose an opera based on Mérimée's novel *Columba*. I write the music for the prologue at high speed and play it to Debussy, who is encouraging and gives me some valuable advice, warning me to 'beware of facile effects!'

Henri Busser, *De Pelléas aux Indes Galantes* (Paris, 1955), pp. 112, 115, 116, 118, 119, 121

ROBERT GODET

On a memorable occasion, Claude Debussy uttered some remarks of a nature which are most appropriate to the margin of his article on Charles Marie Weber. As part of their interest is derived from the circumstances in which they were spoken, the events which they recall should first be recapitulated.

When the Paris Opéra-Comique decided in the beginning of the year 1902 to produce *Pelléas*, the author of this work, who for a long time had danced attendance, did not imagine that its performance would be immediate; learning during the month of March that it would take place before the end of April, he was taken by surprise. Undoubtedly he had already planned the score in his mind for some considerable time but he had written completely only the parts for voice and piano. However advanced this sketch may have been (excepting always the Interludes which developed only gradually in rehearsal), to transform it into an orchestral version within three or four weeks appeared a jest or wager. Debussy had no choice. He took up the challenge and won, but at what a price! Each scene was taken for study immediately it was delivered; the smallest delay in sending the following one would have compromised everything: a steeplechase ensued between composer and performers in which it was doubtful who would prove the victor. Fortunately he possessed many other resources than that of technical ability: notably, the secret of mental discipline which allowed him to erect partitions between his thoughts and any outside noises (more precisely, the trills of a singing student on the floor above, the scales of a piano pupil on the floor below), and to concentrate all his faculties towards one particular end as soon as he had taken up his pen, and that, as it were, by command, without hesitation or respite, from one act to the next until the last chord was written. I recollect him stooping hour after hour over staves ruled for him beforehand haphazardly from an imagined plan, and distributing over them arabesques of elegant design with equal calm and sureness, untouched by any revision. And this calm hardly threatened to abandon him even when the first orchestral parts arrived, on which an unskilled copyist had omitted to indicate in the pauses of each instrument the intervening changes of time or of signature. 'Splendid occasion for learning the art of scratching out,' groaned Debussy, appalled at the idea of the numberless erasures that these deplorable manuscripts would require. Fortunately, it was possible to deputize for him in this work, but not so quickly as desired. Urged on by the impatience of a management which accused him of the errors committed by his copyist, and seeing his overwhelming task further complicated by the stage trials through which he found himself obliged to develop the Interludes, he had, in addition, to settle affairs with the legatee of one of his patrons who died at the most inopportune moment, and this exposed him to daily summonses for debts he could not repay. During this period, no less insistent and soon no less threatening were the complaints followed by attacks from the poet Maeterlinck, who, having conceived his Mélisande in the person of an artist who was not given the role, accused the musician of distorting his intentions and began a campaign of protestations against the *Pélleas* of the Opéra-Comique, strengthening his arguments by articles bearing titles full of promise: 'Eloge de la Boxe . . . Eloge de l'Epée, etc . . .' It was under such conditions, harassed, overworked, betrayed by friends, even by fate, exposed to the worst anxieties, to the worst slanders, that Debussy spent his days on the stage, his nights at his work-table, and deprived by this of his habitual recourse against the torments of life, for all reading he was obliged to limit himself to deciphering the official papers which continued to accumulate, or the telegrams from M. Messager which unceasingly poured in.

Thus prepared, the dress rehearsal of his masterpiece was not of a nature to bring him comfort. The impression was that of a disaster, but probably the importance of the continuous ironic or hostile manifestations was exaggerated through nervous tension. For instance, at the moment when Golaud, the magnificent Golaud of M. Dufranne, represses a sob in a convulsive laugh and cries: 'See, already I laugh like an old man,' it only needed a good comrade of the composer to come out with this flash of wit, '*Oui, mon vieux, ris*

Golaud,'* to make the whole room gay, and merely thinking of diversion, it joyfully found revenge for the scandal caused by the scene of little Yniold in which the word 'bed' brought forth its virtuous indignation, the innocent child being apostrophized as *'Petit Ignoble'* . . . Debussy, however, was the picture of imperturbability. Were it not for his pallor, one would have sworn he was thinking of other things. He did not even tremble at the hilarious explosions which punctuated – Heaven alone knows under what petty pretext – the dying agony of Mélisande; and if, in the last interval, he reacted with a shrug of his shoulders to a certain censorious remark on 'the melody, the harmony, the rhythm – the Holy trinity' which he scoffed at, it was quite imperceptibly. The curtain down, one last surprise was reserved for him: the Under-Secretary of the Beaux Arts, friend of the poet Mendès whose anger Debussy had aroused on returning him a libretto, pointed out to the author of the new work the inconvenience in a theatre subsidized by the State, of offending the modesty of an elect public: listening only to his kindness, he advised him to decide immediately on the necessary sacrifice in view of the first performance taking place within two or three days (30 April 1902). That is how the Maeterlinckian 'bed' prevented Debussy from gaining his – there is no justice! – before taking steps for Golaud and little Yniold to unlearn part of their roles. I still remember having been with him to fetch, fresh from the press, a copy of the vocal score that I still possess (Fromont Edition), in which he marked the required cut without foreseeing that this mutilation of his masterpiece would be perpetuated (unfortunately it has been adhered to in the full score printed since then, and the scene of little Yniold is thus deprived of one of its chief moments).

Night was already falling when the author of *Pélleas* was accompanied back to his door. He insisted that I should go up for a cup of tea. It was then, in a quiet tête-à-tête, in which he did not make the slightest allusion to his work or the somewhat tumultuous reception it had received, that he began to praise, as he knew how to praise, with all his heart and all his soul, the 'horn' of Oberon. Probably too tired to play the homage to Bach which was one of his classic recreations, he chose the theme most suitable for relaxing his nerves without being obliged to raise his voice: Weber . . . It is still

*ris Golaud = rigolo

unknown today whether he realized that he had just given a decisive blow to romanticism in music, some forms of which remained so dear to him: that which is well known, is that he would have defended these forms before all and above all from 'Debussyism' if that monster had already existed! In recording a significant document of his state of mind on the most memorable occasion of his career, I disclaim – is it necessary to say so? – all pretensions to Debussyism as the word is generally understood: the remarks which follow are none the less exact as regards the ideas which the inimitable master expressed that evening, and they constituted the sincere evidence of his admiration for one whom he called – with congeneric sympathy – 'a prince among magicians'.

'Do you know who kept faithful company with me just now? No, you will not guess. This so-called visitor, Heaven be praised, has no part in the 'event of the day'. I am even embarrassed to introduce him to you, he so detests ceremonies. Let us call him, if you will, Oberon's horn. Fascinated at all times by its melancholy call, perhaps I would have ignored its real power of evocation if the echo of its three distant notes, awakening at the moment I least expected it, had not most opportunely revived in me the emotion of that magic word with which Weber was pleased to enrich our art, and which he opened so wide with so sober a gesture. What a refuge for an artist of this world, especially when he is engaged on parting from his dream and exposing it to reality's revenge! Let us not insist. We know the reserve of Oberon's horn, and how much it forbids any emphasis. And yet, as one thing follows upon another, Weber, while preserving me from my personal vicissitudes, made me think of the multifarious revelations of music: serious, lively, passionate, mystic, of those which refresh the style, of those which unsettle the expression, and I asked myself if his music, above all, were not pre-eminently the 'revealer' in a certain sense and a certain domain, it being well understood that neither its effect nor (I imagine) its motive is to found an undiscovered æsthetic order or to determine an unknown type of passion. That which it inaugurates without any pretension to innovation, is the musical reign of a kind of poetry that hitherto had only spoken, or, if you prefer it, had merely hummed between its lips. Weber lends it his magnificent voice, and then, as if by the phenomenon of spontaneous combustion (I had this chemical metaphor from Dickens's Bleak House), a truth which nothing had announced bursts

forth, a truth whose discovery appears to me more important than that of the most ingenious rhetoric. Weber sings and thereupon the voice of this Orpheus renews the harmony of nature with the human soul in a visionary kingdom which has no difficulty in persuading us of its reality, since the law which governs it secures for art a life of its own, far better balanced than ours. In this accord which he constructs so harmoniously, note that Weber begins by instinctively transposing its two terms: it is in the measure, when matter unloads its weight, that it impresses him so that he succeeds in animating it with his breath when he sets it down. And if, for example, he turns his landscapes into living beings, one might even say individualized in their characters, and if he transforms his characters, even those that are supernatural, into elementary types of innocence and malice akin to the tree and the flower, it is the genius in him, in spite of himself, that transfigures them until they are knit one within the other. Do you not admire in that a delightful miracle? Certainly in Oberon, *the ground was prepared for the music by the fable: still, for the miracle to take place a special magic was necessary, the bewitching enchantment of Ariel 'more rapid than thought', of Puck, equally apt at suddenly descending to the ground as in vanishing into space with a flap of his wings. But look at* Freischütz: *between his forest vibrating with the terrors and rather heavy and childish joys of the Germanic legend and, for example, this forest in the Ardennes, so resolutely fictitious, where burst forth like rockets the concetti of* As you like it, *there is certainly an insuperable distance. Now, is it not all the more strange that, barely touched by the wand of the magician Weber, the realistic and natural scene for the most German of melodramas assumes a grace and freshness, a mystery even worthy of Shakespearian fantasy? Any manufacturer of the picturesque would have deemed it shrewder and more expeditious simply to imitate the given surroundings. But Weber is a poet: he recreates his surroundings, and he recreates them (as for instance his Max, his Agatha, very human, with flesh nourished by his blood but rendered volatile by his dream) by exercising a sovereign independence which is the privilege of masters in transposition.*

In order to understand well the kind of quality I mean, remember the passages of Wagner (of the first period and even the second) when that other sorcerer, but Klingsorian (a Klingsor whose digestion would be equal to his appetite) borrows inspiration from our sober magician: it immediately loses its airy grace, its innocent freshness, and as regards mystery this is injured by excessive emphasis. Adorned beyond measure in order better to attract, it adapts its gestures which had expressed an ethereal nostalgia, to the expression of the most violent desires; perverted in that fashion, one is pained to recognize it under its luxurious trappings, even without considering that they defend it badly against the caprice of fashion. One must go as far as Parsifal *– to the perfect 'enchantment' which, in its essential being owes nothing but to itself – to find again among much that is unequalled, that simplicity of harmony and especially that pureness of tone with which we associate in our dreams the eternal youth of* Oberon *or* Freischütz, *in contrast to the wear and tear of the too-usual Wagnerian idiom.*

Now, supposing a visitor from Mars were to come this evening to pay us a musical call – all the stars having fallen, as you know. I willingly leave to you the controversial subjects: theory of sound, scales, chords, form, the whole group. But let us take note of the word 'timbre' which just escaped me. I would take charge of this chapter 'orchestra' and it would hardly give me any trouble: Weber alone would undertake the whole. Barring one or two postscripts, his work is the best of instrumental treatises. What is a clarinet? I would not know how to instruct the Martian better than by referring him to Agatha to learn the virginity, not of that young girl, but of the instrument which would reveal to him in the Concertstück one of the most beautiful secrets of its deep register. The flute? There I should be embarrassed in my choice, but there is a duo which would reveal to the Martian one of its latest possibilities – notwithstanding the period – the thirds accompanying the 'casting of the bullets' or those not less nocturnal but so different in shade, which are introduced in the adorable air of the said Agatha in the second act of Freischütz; *and in this same act he would hear in the 'hunting scene' the piccolos which have lost nothing of their fierceness. He would hear in addition, a quartette of horns which remains a model of wildness, whilst that of the overture has not been surpassed for sylvan charm and birdlike sweetness. As foreshadowing our modern brass, I could find nothing better, off-hand, than the song of the trumpet to the sunrise in* Oberon, *and those breathless exclamations of the trombones in the overture of* Freischütz. *Now if the Martian had not had enough of the wind instruments, well! we would have to abandon all hope of going to bed early . . . Who has made better use of the strings than Weber, of associating them, contrasting them, choosing amongst them the most expressive, entrusting an E string with a 'cantilena', making the most*

of the bowing, varying the attack and the style of the tremolo? He has
resplendency, he has delicacy, and I think he is without a rival in the art
of subduing – that is to say, notably in the use of the mutes: think of those
with which he tempers the violins in the prelude of Oberon *in order better*
to illuminate the answer of the violas and violoncellos; think of the ethereal-
ity of the different violins in the air already mentioned of Agatha, and in
the octet of Euryanthe *so mysteriously darkened for the appearance of the*
ghost . . . It is not sufficient to say that the instrumental resources are
familiar to him to a rare degree: it would be necessary to say that he
scrutinizes the soul of each instrument and exposes it with a gentle hand.
Deferential to his resources they yield him more than he appears to demand.
Also, the most daring combinations of his orchestra, when he makes himself
most deliberately symphonic, have in particular the tone colour preserved
in its original quality: such as colours superimposed without mingling, the
mutual reactions of which enhance rather than abolish their individuality.
A predilection for the voluminous, if not corrected by aversion to neutral
tone, is fatal. Weber, when he gathered together his forces, knows well
how to be formidable, but as a colourist he has too great a sense of values
and as a musician too much taste, for quantity ever to matter more with
him than quality. Only one example more, not of the first but of the second,
a quite minute example but a very delectable one, and then goodnight
(already the Martian has vanished), re-read the four or five introductory
bars to Max's air in G, after the waltz in Freischütz, *and listen intently*
for the hammering of the clarinet which insinuates itself into the frail
sonorous edifice between the tone colours of the flutes which crown it and
the tones of the oboe which support it. Then you will tell me what you
think of it. . . . but not on the evening of a dress rehearsal!

On leaving the composer of *Pélleas*, I remembered his recent meeting with a lady who had thought to be agreeable to him in condensing
the history of music into terms inspired by the snobbishness of the
moment: 'Palestrina . . . Schumann . . . Mussorgsky . . . Do you
see anyone else?' To which he had answered as gravely as possible: 'I
will think it over.' This comic incident returning to my mind, 'Well,'
I said, 'you have kept your word, you have thought it over.' – 'Oh,
so little . . . Well, however little it may be let us add Weber.' – 'And
Debussy?' – 'Since we have been fortunate enough to forget him, let

us continue doing so. Besides he is falling asleep. Let us hope that the night will bring him good counsel.'

Robert Godet, 'Weber and Debussy', *The Chesterian*, June 1926, pp. 220–26

MAGGIE TEYTE

(1888–1976)

Maggie Teyte was born in Wolverhampton and studied in Paris with Jean de Reszke. She took over the role of Mélisande from Mary Garden in 1908.

My first meeting with Debussy had taken place soon after my début at the Opéra-Comique. One day I was told to present myself at his house, which was 80 avenue de Bois de Boulogne, now called the avenue Foch. It was a beautiful little house at the end of a cul-de-sac, and it bordered on the Ceinture, a local railway line that encircles Paris. I remember a young Frenchman once asking me where Debussy lived, and on being told that it was near the Ceinture, he remarked that that was no doubt the reason why Debussy wrote such awful music! I don't remember ever being disturbed by trains passing under the composer's windows, but that may have been because I was too enthralled by his music.

How well I remember that first visit! First, I was fascinated by the collection of china cats up on the mantelpiece – cats of all sizes and colours. I had plenty of time to examine them, for it was quite a while before Debussy came in. Time is difficult to judge so many years later, but I may have waited anything from ten to twenty minutes. When the composer did come in, he walked straight across the room, without looking at me, and seated himself at the piano. Then he turned and looked at me, and I don't know what he expected to see – if it was a twelve-stone prima donna, he must have been very disappointed, for in fact I was so small and thin that he evidently didn't think I should be able to sing at all. After a pause, the following conversation took place.

DEBUSSY: Vous êtes Mademoiselle Teyte?
MAGGIE: Oui, monsieur.

Debussy looked at the piano again for several seconds, and then back at me. He seemed puzzled.

DEBUSSY: Vous êtes Mademoiselle *Maggie* Teyte?

(He pronounced Maggie with the g's soft, like those Italian soup cubes.)

MAGGIE: Oui, monsieur.

After this there was complete silence for many, many seconds. Evidently he couldn't believe his ears, for with a penetrating glance from his black eyes he finally said in rather a fierce voice:

DEBUSSY: Mais, êtes-vous Mademoiselle Maggie Teyte de l'Opéra-Comique?

MAGGIE: Oui, monsieur!

I heard later that when he was told of my nationality, he exclaimed: '*Quoi? Encore une écossaise?*' This may account for his next remark, which was 'I will have Mélisande as *I* want her!'

Naturally, as I had come to study the role especially with him, I had nothing against that. As Jean de Reszke and Reynaldo Hahn had taught me Mozart, so now I was taught the pedantic and precise method of approach to the idiom of this new chromatic music. Debussy really stands alone in this idiom – other composers of the same genre have done their best to weave different patterns in his colour scheme, but they have all been captured in his web, devoured – and forgotten!

I never heard Debussy play any music but his own – but how wonderfully he played that! Composers are notorious for not being able to interpret their own compositions – I think this is fairly true of a great many of them – but Debussy's gifts as pianist and conductor were always sufficient to express the essence of his own music – pedantic, poetic and savage in turn, as the score of *Pelléas et Mélisande* shows to those who know and understand it.

For nine months I studied the role of Mélisande with the composer. Debussy was a man of very few words, and thank goodness he didn't find much to criticize. This was probably due to my Mozartian upbringing, for I have always approached the interpretation of Debussy as though he were a modern Mozart.

He was reticent – often silent – and yet, according to his

biographers, he seems to have been the centre of a lively group of musicians and artists. This has always surprised me, as during the nine months of my studies on *Pelléas et Mélisande*, and when we were associated at a number of concerts later on, he spoke very little.

Only once or twice during my studies with him do I remember this habit of silence being broken – one occasion was one morning after a rehearsal, when we were joined by André Caplet in Debussy's salon. The master suddenly let forth on the subject of Wagner and Mozart – they had spoiled a lot of paper! One would dismiss a statement like that coming from most people as so much hot air, but when the speaker was Debussy one had to take notice – to find out, if one could, what was behind his words, for of course they could not be taken entirely at their face value. But it was not until several years later that I was able to get from Debussy any really clear impression of his views on himself in relation to other composers.

I began by asking Debussy what he intended to compose next, and this first reply was an astonishing one.

'I shall produce nothing more of the kind I have been writing,' he said.

When I suggested that this might be because his style of music was not sufficiently appreciated, he assured me that the contrary was the case. He *was* appreciated by the *cognoscenti*, and about the rest of the world he cared little. In ten years' time, he prophesied, the general intelligence of the public would have caught up with him and everyone would be singing and playing his music. He was right there, though he didn't live to prove it. But if it wasn't lack of appreciation, what was it, I asked?

Debussy told me that it was simply that he had reached the limit of the idiom in which he had been writing. He was afraid of repeating himself. His idiom was not a system that he had deliberately invented – it had forced itself upon him, and when he had reached its limit, he was forced to turn to something else. He went on to explain that he had not repeated himself so far, but that the imitation of his style by other composers had made much of his work seem uninspired and monotonous. He thought the plagiarism by other composers had done him harm without doing them any good, and he denied all responsibility for the so-called Debussyisms of modern composers. I concluded that he was not impressed with the originality of the modern school of music.

'No,' he said, 'not deeply. In France it is largely superficial. In Italy they are still bound fast by traditions. In Germany there is not a single composer of original genius.'

'What about Richard Strauss?' I demanded in some surprise.

'He is a marvellous technician,' said Debussy, 'nothing else. He chose to concentrate on orchestration and to become a musical scholar instead of an original creator.'

'And there is no one else?' I inquired tentatively.

'There is no one else,' answered Debussy shortly. 'The rest are not even worth mentioning.'

I chose this moment to raise the question of Wagner.

'Wagner was a great literary and dramatic genius,' answered Debussy, 'but no musician.'

Maggie Teyte, *Star on the Door* (London, 1958), pp. 64–9

HENRY MALHERBE

(1887–1958)

Henry Malherbe was a writer who won the Prix Goncourt in 1917. He was also on the administrative staff of the Opéra-Comique and was its director from 1946 to 1948.

Some months before the war, when Debussy came to performances of *Pelléas*, he only stayed in the auditorium for one or two scenes. He would run down the corridor to my office without talking to anybody and sit down in front of me, to make feverish notes. Every time, he made changes to the orchestral score. Then we would have a long chat until the end of the performance.

Debussy ended up being utterly disenchanted with the stage presentation of *Pelléas* at the Opéra-Comique. He dreamt of different decors and a new interpretation. By an extraordinary stroke of luck a true artist had been appointed as director of the municipal theatre in Rouen. He was called Masselon. He had red hair, bright, slit eyes and a long, rough-looking nose – all the traits of a sly Norman peasant. But his character showed a rare delicacy and generosity. He had the idea of putting *Pelléas* on at Rouen according to Debussy's wishes. I was a little nervous about introducing my rustic impresario to our most aristocratic composer. But the bucolic director and Debussy, normally so frosty, hit it off splendidly. We met frequently to prepare for the performances. Debussy had approved the models of the set, designed by a young painter, and it was agreed that we would leave for Rouen, he to conduct the orchestra, I to superintend the production. The war broke out shortly afterwards.

Henry Malherbe, 'Deux maîtres que j'ai connus', *Candide*, 717, 9 December 1937, p. 19

IV
Friend and companion

EMILE VUILLERMOZ

Debussy lived in a kind of haughty misanthropy, behind a rampart of irony, protecting himself fiercely from bores and fools. A triple, barbed ring of defensive paradoxes, biting persiflage and acute mockery kept intruders at a distance, so that they could never be sure whether the spikes with which he armed his volatile sensibility were activated by a savage *pudeur* or by the 'holy egoism of genius'! His admirers admired him from afar, without daring to tell him of the pleasure he gave them, or to thank him for it. You were aware that expressions of admiration were as ridiculous as if you had taken it upon you to offer effusive thanks to a lilac for bursting into flower in springtime: and you knew that Debussy was quite likely to answer, in that gentle, sarcastic voice of his which underlined every word with a quiet, straightforward irony: 'I did not, I promise you, do it specially for you!'

Emile Vuillermoz, 'Claude Debussy', *Le Ménestrel*, 11 June 1920, pp. 241–2

ALFREDO CASELLA
(1883–1947)

Alfredo Casella, born in Turin, came to the Paris Conservatoire in 1896, and studied the piano with Louis Diémer and composition with Fauré. He later taught the piano there and, in 1912, began his conducting career at the popular concerts in the Trocadéro. In 1915 he played the piano in the first performance of Ravel's Piano Trio, shortly before returning to Italy.

Physically Debussy was very unlike the willowy and soulful-looking æsthete fondly imagined by so many of the young women who with all too faulty fingers were wont to essay the first *Arabesque* and the 'Jardins sous la pluie'. He was of middle height, and was thick-set and sturdy. The head was a strange one: the enormous forehead bulged forwards, while there seemed something missing at the back of the huge skull. His colour was sallow; the eyes were small and seemed half-sunk in the fat face; the straight short nose was of the purest classical Roman type; in the thick and jet-black hair and beard fifty years had here and there sown a silver thread. As always with artists of the finer sort, the hands were most beautiful. Debussy's voice was unprepossessing, being hoarse (and this was aggravated by the abuse of tobacco), and he spoke in an abnormal, nervous, jumpy way. His dress was scrupulously cared-for in every detail. His walk was curious, like that of all men who have a weakness for wearing womanish footgear.

He was something of a glutton. When he and I, in his later years, lived in the same quarter of Paris, I not seldom, on a fine day about noon, would come upon the composer of *Pelléas* before some display of comestibles in the avenue Victor Hugo, accompanied by his favourite dogs and much engaged in selecting some choice fruit and superfine cheese to take home for luncheon.

He was extremely difficult to approach. He was hardly ever seen at the theatre or at concerts; he shrank with loathing from any public display of himself. His friends were very few. To his wife and little daughter he was greatly attached; he adored them both.

He worked hard. He told me once that he could only create when in the midst of intense light, and his little studio in the avenue du Bois was lighted by three very large windows which bathed with sunshine all the various precious objects of art – chiefly Asiatic – which were cunningly arranged in the beautiful room.

He did not teach, and had no disciples. He hated conducting, and had for that matter no gift in that way. He once confessed to me, 'When I have to conduct I am ill before, during and after!' He played the pianoforte admirably. No words can give an idea of the way in which he played certain of his own *Préludes*. Not that he had actual virtuosity, but his sensibility of touch was incomparable; he made the impression of playing directly on the strings of the instrument with no intermediate mechanism; the effect was a miracle of poetry. Moreover, he used the pedals in a way all his own. He played, in a word, like no other living composer or pianist.

Not only was he a unique interpreter of his own works, but also in some of the older music, particularly Mozart's, he was wonderful. It is one of the most happy and lively memories of my artistic life to have heard him play a number of Chopin's pieces, Chopin being a composer of his particular predilection and one whose every secret he marvellously divined. Until he informed me of this fact one day I was utterly unaware that in his youth he had worked long at the pianoforte with a pupil of Chopin's (the name escapes me),* and he explained to me how considerable a part this instruction had played in his musical formation, not only as pianist, but also as creator.

Himself so incomparable an executant, Debussy was extremely exacting of the interpreters of his works. Rarely indeed have I ever seen him fully satisfied with a performance. He detested almost all the greatly celebrated 'virtuosi', who are so generally quite unmusical; on the other hand, he was well disposed towards certain cultivated and intelligent interpreters who enjoyed no clamorous reputation, but who loved music with the same disinterested, sacred love as he.

Debussy was extremely cultivated, particularly in literature and the plastic arts. He had little use for latter-day painting. In music, too, he felt aversion for the new anti-Impressionist tendencies. Thus, while he was very fond of Stravinsky's *Petrushka* he cordially abhorred the same composer's *Rite of Spring*. Once when we had been together hearing Ravel play his *Valses nobles et sentimentales* Debussy made this surprising remark to me: 'A good deal more can be done with that music!' And I remember how, in February 1917, I played to him my own Sonatina and how he said to me: 'My dear fellow, I am really fond of you, and I sincerely wish you may compose many more works of the sort, since you are made that way. But I confess to not understanding how such music can have come into anyone's mind!'

His character was extraordinarily nervous, impulsive and impressionable, and he was easily irritated. The oddity of his appearance, his unprepossessing voice, a strong dose of *gaucherie*, and finally an almost incredible shyness which he disguised under a show of paradox and often sarcastic and unkind irony, all this naturally made for a certain awkwardness in one's first relations with him. But then he was capable of deep and loyal friendship, and his affection for a few persons was boundless. He was generous, and he delighted to aid the needy – not seldom anonymously and with exquisite delicacy.

To the end he remained what the French call *grand enfant*. That same wonderful innocence and limpidity of feeling which is the fundamental characteristic of his art transpired in all his deeds and words. At fifty

*Mme Mauté de Fleurville

he amused himself more than did his little daughter Chouchou with the toys brought home for her by her mother. And he teased the household animals with the ferocious selfishness of a nasty little boy.

He much preferred – and how rightly! – the music hall of the English type to the majority of theatres and concerts. He had a craze for the sea (and how he glorified it in music all know), but he did not care for mountains. When I asked him one day the reason of this antipathy, he answered childishly: 'It's all too high!' He loved Italy, and especially Rome, and he cherished the idea of seeing Italy once more, when the war was over . . .

Alfredo Casella, 'Claude Debussy', *The Monthly Musical Record*, January 1933, pp. 1–2

PAUL DUKAS

People have said – though no one, praise be, has yet committed it to paper – that he was heartless, an egoist, a trifler with the feelings of others, and Heaven knows what else! That he was capable of disaffection is to say that he was capable of affection, as the last years of his life were to prove, alas. Those who knew and loved him will never be able to read the tragic letters he wrote at that time without feelings of anguish.

When he was angry – which was rare with him – his eyes would flash; as a friend he showed an exquisite delicacy. A certain wilfulness, born of his reading, sometimes gave his attitude a considered, deliberate air. It was in fact the way his mind naturally expressed itself. You had to have known him in his adolescence really to understand him and, indeed, really to love him. From the beginning of his life as an artist he was deeply involved in the literary movement of the time. Verlaine, Mallarmé and Laforgue introduced us to new tonalities and new sonorities. The most powerful influence on Debussy was that of writers, not of composers.·

If you were to ask me what is the link between the works of Debussy's youth – of which *L'après-midi d'un faune* is the most characteristic example – and the more determined-sounding ones of his maturity, I would say they are joined less by their spirit than by their shared habits of speech. He was well aware of it and, at the end of his life, wanted to divest himself of this technical mastery. During those last serious, heartfelt conversations I had with him, he often stressed the need he felt to simplify and purify his music, to remove from it all the marks of professional virtuosity. He was talking one day about *La chute de la maison Usher*, and I asked him whether the form would be the same as that of *Pelléas*. 'Oh, much simpler,' he replied. And he would, I'm sure, have reached the goal that he set himself.

Paul Dukas, quoted in Robert Brussel: 'Claude Debussy et Paul Dukas', *ReM*, 7, 1 May 1926, pp, 101, 105

CHARLES KOECHLIN
(1867–1950)

Charles Koechlin was a pupil of Massenet and Fauré at the Conservatoire, where he was an older contemporary of Ravel. He became a composer and teacher, whose open-mindedness attracted the young, including some of *Les Six*: Poulenc had composition lessons from him.

My first memory of Debussy goes back to the time, rather distant now, when I could not accept without some demur his musical character and the independence of his technique. Having dinner with him at the house of one of my friends, I listened to him pronouncing severe judgment on Grieg, then at the height of his celebrity – and even on the first movement of César Franck's Violin Sonata: he spoke of its 'facile sentimentality', and if one thinks about it there are some bars of the piece which might support his claim.

People have said he was lazy, or at least unreliable, and only sat down to compose every now and then. That would have been his right; he paid posterity in royal coinage. But – as far as I can judge – this reproach smacks of philistine injustice, and Debussy certainly did not deserve it. It was simply that he belonged to a generation which had a horror of hustle and making do. Finishing a song took him a long time. And living in Paris – especially in the grip of celebrity – time is something one never has enough of. In the past his music had been published by subscription, and one day he said to me: 'Durand is terrible; he always wants scores and more scores!'

Charles Koechlin, *Debussy* (Paris, 1926), pp. 20, 30

If someone now says or writes: 'Debussy was on very good terms with Vincent d'Indy, indeed with the Schola Cantorum', let us be clear about the facts.

There can be no doubt that, being not much of a socialite and loving music above everything else, Debussy would have particularly responded to the atmosphere of the Schola Cantorum concerts and of the hall where they were held, an atmosphere of reflection, intimacy, and seriousness, free of snobbery or social pretensions and imbued with enthusiasm for art. And if the relations between d'Indy and Debussy were cordial, as is quite possible, so much the better. At the Société Nationale they had fought the good fight for French music, together with Chausson, Chabrier, Fauré and others . . .

But whether Debussy *approved of the teaching of the Schola*, by which I take it is meant the teaching of composition, whether he liked the music of the pupils who worked according to the principles of d'Indy's *Traité* and whether he really *liked* d'Indy's music, that is another question. I don't dwell on the particular (and secondary) issue of what Debussy thought of d'Indy as a composer. At all events, I remember clearly one day when, in front of me, Debussy expressed himself in no laudatory fashion about one of d'Indy's scores – perhaps his best one!

What we are discussing is Debussy's opinion of the teaching of the Schola and its *results*. Claude-Achille's music exists freely, without theories, without dogmas, without a priori principles. The Schola of 1905 was on the contrary theory, complete dogmatism, the certainty afforded by d'Indy's *Traité de composition* through his laws on modulation, catalogues of musical forms, analyses full of *masculine and feminine themes, bridge passages, cells*, the regular ordering of a 'mandarin system': in short, everything Debussy loathed . . .

He reacted in his own fashion, through his articles and conversation. Who was it that made fun of the systematic use of folktunes, 'kept in order by bossy counterpoints' which was why they 'always looked slightly embarrassed'? Who fathomed the (unfathomable) tedium of 'those earnest, solid exercises called, out of habit, symphonies'? (It's clear that this was aimed at examples written by students of the Schola.) And who, talking about a highly respectable pupil of d'Indy's, the composer of a symphony indeed, nicknamed the Andante from it 'the laboratory of emptiness'? Debussy, who else? And we may observe finally that, whereas the Schola liked to make connections between architecture and music, Debussy insisted on keeping the two separate. When he found himself faced with the sort of cold musical development that people call 'well made' (what he termed 'mandarin labours') he could be heard to say: 'That's architecture, not music.'

Charles Koechlin, 'Souvenirs sur Debussy, la Schola et la S.M.I.', *ReM*, 15, November 1934, pp. 242–5

Debussy had a high esteem for Satie, and I remember, one evening when I was dining with Debussy as the guest of our mutual friend Jean Bellon, how the composer of *La damoiselle élue* (which he played to us that night) took up the cudgels on behalf of Satie against Willy.*

You have indicated very clearly the element of instability in the life of this great artist; but you are quite right to be, on the whole, 'on his side', and to stress the absolute probity of his art, whose sole aim was to produce beauty, with no thought of *arrivisme*. As to his marriage with Madame Bardac, I am certain that Debussy was attracted both by the woman and by the artist who had such a great admiration for him. People have said all sorts of things about Debussy – most of them, I believe, quite untrue. Nevertheless, he certainly did not have the same high moral standards as Dukas, for example, or Roussel. But that was perhaps due to his early education. In any case, he was not envious, and he was always very kind towards me.

Charles Koechlin, undated letters to Rollo H. Myers, in: Rollo H. Myers: 'Charles Koechlin – some recollections', *Music and Letters*, July 1965, pp. 222–4

I used to see Debussy from time to time at the publisher Baudoux's. He readily showed himself to be sarcastic and unsparing. But he was

*Willy: Colette's first husband – see p. 48

not as *exclusive* in his tastes as has been made out, nor an admirer only of his own compositions. 'Nobody these days knows how to write music any more,' he used to say, 'and that goes for me as well.'

I had met him in the corridors of the Opéra-Comique during the performances of *Pelléas*, but how could I express in a couple of words the effect that masterpiece had on me? I could offer only a few banal phrases. We saw each other from time to time and Debussy gradually came to the conclusion that, in fact, *I was on his side*. When three of my *Etudes antiques* were given at the Concerts Colonne, he came to a rehearsal and listened sympathetically. And when I complained of the heavy-handed percussion players, he said: 'I agree! Our percussion in Europe is an art of barbarians.'

When, in 1913, he was looking for a colleague to orchestrate his ballet *Khamma*, he conferred that honour on me. I therefore had the opportunity to see him regularly at close quarters. I went to him every week to show him my orchestral sketches, in his charming house near the avenue du Bois. We didn't chat; we concentrated on my orchestration, which he was happy with, although he warned me that it might be rather hard to perform. He described all the strange novelties that were going to be discovered in Stravinsky's *Sacre du printemps*, know that certain passages made hitherto unheard of use of bitonality. But he supported musical instinct and creative intuition, as against music that is laboriously fabricated. 'In Rome,' he said, 'when we used to tell one of our number that we didn't find such-and-such a passage convincing, he would invariably reply: *it's intentional*.' And then Debussy repeated in a sarcastic tone of voice: 'Intentional, intentional . . . that's not enough!' He knew himself to be impulsive and naturally impatient: 'So you're teaching your son? (I was grounding him in Latin and mathematics.) I could never do that − I'd never have the necessary patience . . .'

Charles Koechlin, 'Souvenirs sur Debussy', *Cahiers Debussy* n.s. 7, 1983, pp. 4−6

ERIK SATIE

(1866–1925)

Erik Satie studied at the Conservatoire in the early 1880s without distinction. He got to know Debussy in the early 1890s and the two saw each other regularly until just before Debussy's death. At the age of nearly forty, Satie went to study at the Schola Cantorum under d'Indy and Roussel. In 1911 Ravel's advocacy brought him some recognition and in 1917 his music for the ballet *Parade* marked him out as more than just an eccentric.

Being a Prix de Rome is highly significant. As an indicator, it's perfect. Faced with it, you know what you're letting yourself in for; because the Prix de Rome is real, it keeps its value in the market. If you're taken for a ride, there's nothing you can say.

When I think that Debussy himself was on 'dear colleague' terms with those people! . . . You could often come across souvenirs of the faubourg Poissonnière with him (even though I realize these souvenirs imposed themselves on his memory by pure intoxication). That's why he was weak enough to let himself be appointed a member of the Conseil Supérieur of the Conservatoire. He was truly a victim of his place of education, even though he put a lot of energy into correcting its faults as far as he could.

Debussy was far from having the same harsh tastes politically and socially as he had in music. This artistic revolutionary was very bourgeois in everyday life. He didn't approve of the 'eight-hour day' or other social modifications. I can tell you that for certain. The increase in salaries – except for him, you understand – was not something he favoured. He had his 'point of view'. A strange anomaly.

Among my memories as a guest, I cannot forget the delightful lunches I had, over several years, with him when he was living on the rue Cardinet. Eggs and lamb cutlets were the centre of these friendly occasions. But what eggs and what cutlets! I'm still licking my cheeks – on the inside, as you can guess.

Debussy – who prepared these eggs and these cutlets himself – had the secret (*the innermost secret*) of these preparations. The whole

ensemble was washed down with a delicious white Bordeaux whose
effects were touching, happily conducive to the joys of friendship and
of living far from 'lumpish fellows', 'desiccated mummies' and other
'old crows' – those pests of humanity and the 'poor in pocket'.

Physically, Debussy took after his mother. He was endowed with good
health and it was only a few years before his death that the fatal disease
took hold of him. His character was, basically, charming and his fits
of bad temper were entirely of the 'explosive' variety – there was never
the slightest animosity afterwards. He never held *his* outbursts against
you; proof of a naïve egotism which, I can assure you, had its attractive
side. Right from our first meeting I felt a sympathy towards him and
I wanted to be near him all the time. For thirty years I was lucky
enough to be able to fulfil this desire. We never had to explain things
to each other – half a sentence was enough, because we understood
each other and, it seemed, had always done so.

Erik Satie, *Ecrits*, ed. Ornella Volta (Paris, 1977), pp. 36–7, 50, 51, 67–8

CYRIL SCOTT

(1879–1970)

> Cyril Scott received his musical education mainly in Ger-
> many, and his music was popular both there and in Eng-
> land during the first decades of this century. He also wrote
> on occultism and food reform, among other topics.

My meeting with Debussy took place at the house of Mme Bardac,
the pale, fair-haired woman who eventually became his wife. At the
time of which I write he was married to the dark and beautiful girl
whose tragic death after her separation from Debussy was to throw
the whole musical world of Paris into a turmoil of indignation. The
story, in fact, is not a savoury one, and shows the French composer
in an unfavourable light, though there may have been mitigating
circumstances which gossip was careful to suppress.

   Mme Bardac had arranged our meeting for the afternoon, *not* the
evening; the reason being, she explained, that Debussy loved to come
in a hat nearly as big as a parasol: a curious reason, indeed, since one

does not, as a rule, wear one's hat in the house. But about twenty years ago in Paris there was an eccentric fashion connected with top hats which obliged their owners to bring them into the drawing-room instead of leaving them in the hall. How this illogical custom worked at a dinner party, I have forgotten: did we all take our top hats with us when we greeted our hostess and then hand them over to the butler to dispose of, or did we deposit them at our sides on the floor when we sat down, leaving them there to be collected by a domestic while we were at dinner? Be this as it may, it was unfortunate for the man who paid a call in a bowler or a squash hat, as my friend Ernesto Consolo once did; since he was shown up the back staircase, and had some difficulty in explaining that he was not a lackey sent on an errand!

Debussy, with his somewhat Christ-like face, marred by a slightly hydrocephalic forehead, was neither an unpleasant personality nor an impressive one. In manner he was, for a Frenchman, unusually quiet, both in the way and in the amount he talked – at any rate to strangers. Thus, when at Mme Bardac's request I had played him some of my works, he said very little at the time, and only in later years when I visited him at his house in the Bois de Boulogne did I obtain his true opinion.

If I were asked to describe Debussy's character, I should find it difficult; therefore I can only give my very brief *impressions* of him, and nothing further. I think he was one of those few Frenchmen who sacrificed French politeness to sincerity: to those he admired and liked, he was charming; to those he disadmired and disliked, he was the reverse. He once asked me rather naïvely if I consorted with the composers of my own country, and without waiting for an answer told me he did not consort with the composers of France. Certainly, even apart from *living* musicians, he had very pronounced dislikes, one of which was Beethoven, whom he described as *le vieux sourd*. On the other hand, he had an unusual admiration for Schumann's Piano Concerto, which struck me as rather strange, for without meaning to disparage that work, I should have thought it too unsubtle to appeal to his taste. As to Richard Strauss, although the orchestration seemed to him highly ingenious, he failed to recognize any intrinsic style in the works themselves, which offended him by their all too frequent banalities. But on this point we disagreed, for admitting these banalities, Strauss, when writing at his best, possesses so distinct a style that any failure on the part of a fellow composer to recognize it seems astonishing. With regard to Tchaikovsky, of whom we also spoke, our opinions were more in unison; Tchaikovsky, be it remembered, was having a great vogue in England at the time – so great, by the way, that Sir Henry Wood told me his directors wanted him to conduct the 'Pathétique' every night at nine o'clock at the Proms, which, thank God, he refused to do. That Debussy should ardently dislike this most popular of the Russian composers I could well understand, and I was not surprised when he deplored British taste which could set up such a vulgarian as an idol to be worshipped. According to *him*, the British had accepted the very worst 'Russian' and overlooked the truly admirable ones, Rimsky-Korsakov, Mussorgsky, and others.

In view of what Debussy has written about my own works, I ought to mention that he never saw my more popular compositions, but only those I thought worthy of his interest, namely, the more serious orchestral ones, and a few others such as the Piano Sonata, the Violin Sonata, the Second Suite for Piano (dedicated to him), and one or two short violin pieces. Of the orchestral compositions he admired most a rhapsody which has since been lost in Petrograd, and of the smaller works the Piano Sonata and the Second Suite. And I think these *were* my best efforts up till the time I last saw him in 1913. I had broken my journey in Paris on my way to Switzerland, in order to dine with him and his wife, and had spent a very enjoyable few hours in his studio, playing and talking. That studio, incidentally, struck me by its remarkable neatness – there was not a piece of music or music-paper to be seen anywhere, only a piano heavily covered with a silk cloth, a large and elegant desk, chairs, table, and bookshelves containing, among other volumes, several works of Kipling.

That evening, although Debussy was charming and affable to me as usual, he spoke despondently of his own work, and was, I gathered, in the midst of an unproductive period.

'My style', he said, 'is a limited one, and I seem to have reached the end of it.'

Cyril Scott, *My Years of Indiscretion* (London, 1924), pp. 100, 101, 103–5

IGOR STRAVINSKY

(1882–1971)

Igor Stravinsky studied with Rimsky-Korsakov and first came to Paris in 1910 when, on 25 June, *The Firebird* was given its première by Diaghilev's Ballets Russes.

I was called to the stage to bow at the conclusion, and was recalled several times. I was still on stage when the final curtain had come down, and I saw coming toward me Diaghilev and a dark man with a double forehead whom he introduced as Claude Debussy. The great composer spoke kindly about the music, ending his words with an invitation to dine with him. Some time later, when we were sitting together in his box at a performance of *Pelléas*, I asked him what he had really thought of *The Firebird*. He said: '*Que voulez-vous, il fallait bien commencer par quelque chose.*' Honest, but not extremely flattering. Yet shortly after *The Firebird* première he gave me his well-known photograph in profile with a dedication: '*à Igor Stravinsky en toute sympathie artistique*'. I was not so honest about the work we were then hearing. I thought *Pelléas* a great bore as a whole, and in spite of many wonderful pages. (Debussy once told me that he had composed a part of *Pelléas* in a room whose wallpaper pattern was made up of oval portraits of Sadi Carnot.)*

The great event in my life then was the performance of *Pierrot lunaire* I had heard in December 1912 in Berlin. Ravel was quickly contaminated with my enthusiasm for *Pierrot*, too, whereas Debussy, when I told him about it, merely stared at me and said nothing. Is this why Debussy later wrote his friend Godet that 'Stravinsky is inclining dangerously *du côté de Schoenberg*'?

I had talked with Debussy about Puccini's music, and I recall that Debussy respected it, as I did myself.

I also recall a luncheon at Debussy's shortly after the first performance of *Petrushka*, and with particular pleasure. We drank champagne and ate from a dainty *dentelle couvert*. Chouchou was there, and I

---

*President Sadi Carnot was assassinated in 1894.

noticed that her teeth were exactly like her father's, i.e., like tusks. Erik Satie joined us after lunch, and I photographed the two French composers together, and Satie photographed me with Debussy. Debussy gave me a walking-stick then, with our initials inscribed together on it in monogram. Later – during my recovery from typhus – he presented me with a handsome cigarette case. Debussy was only slightly taller than I am, but he was much heavier. He spoke in a low quiet voice, and the ends of his phrases were often inaudible – which was to the good, as they sometimes contained hidden stings and verbal booby traps. The first time I visited him in his house, after *The Firebird*, we talked about Mussorgsky's songs and agreed that they contained the best music of the whole Russian school. He said he had discovered Mussorgsky when he found some of the music lying untouched on Mme von Meck's piano. He did not like Rimsky, whom he called 'a voluntary academic, the worst kind'. Debussy was especially interested in Japanese art at that time. I received the impression, though, that he was *not* especially interested in new things in music; my own appearance on the musical scene seemed to be a shock to him.

Igor Stravinsky, *Expositions and Developments* (London, 1962), pp. 34, 67–8, 130–31, 138–9

GABRIEL ASTRUC
(1864–1938)

Gabriel Astruc began as a music publisher, before becoming an impresario. He handled several of the Paris appearances of Diaghilev's Ballets Russes, the two men running the gamut of relationships between amity and enmity. He was the moving spirit behind the building of the Théâtre des Champs-Elysées, but his inaugural season of opera there in 1913 made him bankrupt. The two souvenirs of Debussy that follow date from 1910 and the winter of 1914 respectively.

On the day of the dress rehearsal of *Aida* at the Châtelet, with Toscanini conducting, Debussy was in a box. During the interval, I went to find the composer of *Pelléas*, the Italian première of which Toscanini had given some time before; he was replacing the conductor of the Turin Opera who had fallen sick at the last minute, and had learnt the score in a single evening . . . before conducting the performance from memory! For this reason, although Debussy and Toscanini had never met, they adored each other. Toscanini was having a ten-minute rest, meditating with his head in his hands. I didn't warn him but arrived with Claude . . . When the door opened and he saw Debussy, Toscanini got up. The two men looked at each other for a long time and then, unable to speak for emotion, fell into each other's arms.

Debussy had run out of fuel and begged me to find some anthracite for him. The coal merchant had a pretty wife who was also an excellent musician, and she gave him some in return for an inscription on her copy of *Pelléas*.

Gabriel Astruc, *Le pavillon des fantômes* (Paris, 1929), pp. 301, 319

JACQUES-EMILE BLANCHE
(1861–1942)

Jacques-Emile Blanche was a fashionable painter, whose sitters included Oscar Wilde, Aubrey Beardsley, Thomas Hardy and Henry James. He also painted a portrait of Debussy's mistress Marie-Blanche Vasnier.

On the reverse side of the Debussy monument, the Martel brothers show the composer at the piano, surrounded by several of his friends. Debussy at the piano! One had to have seen it to appreciate its magic. No words could describe the mysterious enchantment of his playing, or of his way of humming while he *recited* his settings of poetry. During those late afternoons in Pierre Louÿs' bachelor flat, Claude would be seated at a harmonium of no great distinction, playing a reduction of newly composed pages from the orchestral score of *Pelléas*. Work on it was slow and we despaired of his ever finishing it. Having to give music lessons irked him. Indolent as he was – a dreamer, a sensualist, a voluptuary – a thousand outside amusements distracted him from an arduous task which meant his staying at home. His needs were imperious and frenetic. His friends did their best to satisfy his besetting sin: greed. How many times have I come across him leaving Cuvillier's with a bottle of port and caressing a pot of caviare, which he would then consume alone in his unheated apartment. After our meetings, someone would take him off to dinner at a restaurant; then we'd go on to the circus or the music hall – but under no circumstances the theatre – and he would finish his evening with a long walk until dawn.

By 1900, little remained of Debussy, the Prix de Rome winner. I had known him when he was at the Villa Medici – when he wore his hair like a helmet over his forehead in the Byzantine manner. Claude's sculptured face looked, at the time of *Pelléas*, like a fourteenth-century mask. We were struck by his extraordinary intellectual development, due in part to the books recommended to him by Pierre Louÿs, although his choice of Rossetti's *The Blessed Damozel* as a text for his obligatory cantata was an early indication of his tendencies; and these were indeed to be confirmed by every text that inspired him, from Baudelaire to Mallarmé.

When, after *Pelléas*, people encouraged him to write more operas, he tried unsuccessfully to make a fantastic comedy out of Poe's *The Devil in the Belfry*. Literature still fascinated him. Later on he spoke enthusiastically of a rather vague project for which he even asked me to provide an outline. His idea was for a cosmogonic drama, without words or plot, in which invisible singers, soloists and chorus would deliver onomatopoeic syllables, to the accompaniment of lighting effects on stage. The orchestra, who would be hidden behind the scenery, would symbolically represent clouds, the winds and the sea. From these dreams sprang the great symphonic masterpieces of Claude's maturity – what the Germans call 'musical tableaux', but without any storyline printed in the programme to help the ordinary music lover. Debussy's sensitivity to all the sounds of nature drew him ever closer to these attempts at 'equivalence' in orchestral timbre and even on the piano.

One day when we were in the garden, a storm broke; we all took refuge in the house but Claude refused to follow our example, determined to enjoy to the full the smell of the wet earth and the gentle patter of rain on the leaves. In memory of that June evening, he dedicated to me the marvellous set which contains 'Jardins sous la pluie'; and 'Pagodes', a transposition of the Javanese dances we heard together so often at the Universal Exhibition in 1900.

Jacques-Emile Blanche, 'Souvenirs sur Manet et sur Debussy', *Le Figaro*, 22 June 1932, p. 5

SYLVAIN BONMARIAGE

Sylvain Bonmariage was a prolific poet and novelist. From internal evidence, the following conversations must have taken place around 1903.

One Thursday Paul-Jean Toulet, I think at Debussy's request, took me to dine at 80 avenue du Bois de Boulogne, where I was given the most delightful welcome. Music touches the senses rather than the intelligence. That is why it conquers the masses and that is why musicians love good food and good wine. Madame Debussy excelled in providing an intimate atmosphere in which good conversation could flourish.

Debussy insisted on showing me the poems of mine which had attracted him and in the margin of which he had pencilled a few notes.

'My dear *maître*,' I said to him, 'your encouragement not only fills me with justifiable pride but gives me a determination to work. I shall confide this to my teacher and friend Pierre Louÿs, who is a good friend of yours and to whom I owe whatever talent you are kind enough to see in me.'

Toulet gave a start. 'Pierre Louÿs tries to measure his popularity in terms of the young. He speaks and writes nice things about them. But that's as far as it goes. If you go on following his advice, you'll be nothing but a fantasist.'

'But Toulet, isn't that the description you yourself give of your incomparable poetry? Fantasy is the real conscience of the artist.'

'I agree,' said Debussy, 'and I would add that French music is nothing but fantasy within sensibility.'

'That may or may not be true,' said Toulet, 'but Sylvain Bonmariage has no musical education. He knows only about painting and sculpture.'

Debussy interrupted at length to underline the total absurdity of discriminating between the rhythmic and plastic arts. They come together in poetry.

'That's true,' I said, 'but a poem has a message. Every poem is made up of writing. If you, my dear *maître*, set it to music, you change its message. If Fauré, or Dukas, or de Séverac do the same, each of them makes it say what they want it to say.'

Debussy replied: 'So you really think a poem has only one meaning! Aren't you aware that each one of your poems is transformed by each of its readers? And it's the same with every musical score. You only have to listen to experts talking about them. You write poems as you like. We can draw from them the music that we like. And the listener, or reader, finds in them the charm that he likes. Everything is relative. I know that every work of art contains elements that are praised and applauded without exception; and it is easy to see that these elements are the ones most readily understood by mediocre intelligences.'

'Which is to say, the critics,' murmured Toulet.

'Critics,' said Debussy, 'are people who trade on the authority and name of newspapers to talk about something of which they know nothing. Ernest Reyer, who knew what music was, became a music critic by accident. And as soon as he started writing for the *Journal des Débats* he began to write nonsense and to get other people to believe it. Pierre Lalo, whom Toulet and I are so fond of, manages to say interesting things about musical pieces, but he's no more than a scholar. Critics? I know only one, whose articles a composer can take seriously, and that's Willy. He knows nothing about music. He couldn't tell you what a semiquaver was, but he understands a work and, if he so chooses, can make it a success!'

'Miracles!' said Toulet, 'If Willy is God the Father, then I incline towards atheism.'

'Well, what I say is absolutely logical,' replied Debussy. 'Someone who is familiar with technique has his preconceived ideas. Before he listens to a score, his opinion is ready made up, according to his personal view of the composer. Who among the gentlemen of the press would dare to judge a work of Puccini or Massenet as it should be judged? For a man like Schneider,* Massenet's *Don Quichotte* is the work of the composer of *Manon*. The uninstructed man, on the

*Louis Schneider, Massenet's biographer

contrary, writes only what he thinks, what he feels. He is not impressed by compositional subtleties and technical sleights of hand of which he has no inkling and which are responsible for the tiniest portion of a work's merit. The best box on the ears the critics have had was the business of *Carmen*. The mandarins of the press totally failed to understand Bizet's score. But we know the pedestal on which it's been put by the public. I too have been slated and whistled at. You remember, Toulet, the Lamoureux concert at the end of October 1901? My *Nocturnes* were drowned by whistling, especially the third one. And that fine scandal was provoked, not by the audience, but by a campaign on the part of the all-holy critics. A year ago in London the *Nocturnes* had their revenge.'

I was at the Opéra-Comique with Madame de Givré during the interval. It was a matinee dress rehearsal of Mozart's *Don Giovanni*, superbly conducted by Reynaldo Hahn. Debussy, making his way quickly along the corridor, bumped into me. He turned round to apologize, shook me by the hand, and was very much taken with Madame de Givré to whom I introduced him. I met Debussy a few days later at an exhibition of Gauguin's paintings at Durand-Ruel's gallery. He was alone. We talked and he asked who was the delightful woman with me at *Don Giovanni*. I told him briefly who Madame de Givré was and explained how closely united we were.

He smiled: 'Toulet told me about it, but I didn't realize it was on such a level. So you're not married. What does it matter? Love is a sacrament. It is self-sufficient. The important thing is to float on the waters and not drown in them. Even in the giving of oneself there must be moderation. Apollo – it is to you as a poet that I am speaking – masks his rays and veils the flashes of his lightning. Whenever he fancies he is playing brilliantly on his lyre, he is wounding and consuming himself. And Apollo is the victim of no one but himself. You let your pen run on with fine phrases and you end up with a certain charm at your fingertips. It is that charm you must be wary of. I can sense the nature of your love affairs: vivacious, strongly individual, indispensable to both sides and enveloping the whole world in their joint shadow.'

I replied that my life belonged to Catherine as hers did to me, but that there was absolutely nothing of the sponger about her, that she was a friend of Pierre Louÿs and that on the latter's advice she was getting me to work. I went on to tell him how profoundly she admired his music and how delighted she would be if he would come and visit her. Knowing he had a total horror of what is called 'society', I told him that the company on the avenue Mozart would consist simply of Toulet and Pierre Louÿs.

Debussy turned up at the appointed time, Pierre Louÿs shortly afterwards, but Toulet three days later, having made a mistake over the date. After so many years, I cannot hope to recreate the atmosphere of that meeting with complete accuracy, even with the aid of my sketchy notes, so I shall merely record the most important elements of our conversation.

Catherine (talking about Wagner): 'There are some people who, in their manifestation of the Infinite, are surrounded with too much splendour. Their ideas carry them above our heads and they attract the plaudits of the crowd. Dare I say that my admiration for them is no more than lukewarm? Between them and me lies a secret discrepancy. Others, on the contrary, make less noise but move me more. Their thought penetrates the depth of my being, vibrates insistently in my heart. Monsieur Debussy, you belong to the latter.'

Debussy: 'Madame, the greatest satisfaction for an artist is to learn that he is the cause of such emotions. You have no need to be grateful to me. I am more grateful than you can imagine to you after what you have just said.'

*

Pierre Louÿs: 'Words have a plastic power which only poets take account of. Composers cannot tap it. The blessedness of music lies elsewhere. In the eighteenth century music was a pleasure for the élite. Nowadays it is escapism. It saves us from the worst aspect of the times: the certainty that writers evince in the face of their ignorance about life.'

Debussy: 'Life? You speak about life. We choose from possibilities. You all have a tendency to oppose life and exactitude. Nothing could be more mistaken. Life is a compromise between instinct and civilization. The nobility of the human condition consists in aspiring to the freedom which nature has given us.'

*

I speak of Mary Garden, of the charm she gave off as Mélisande and of the impression she made on me when I was introduced to her away from the theatre.

'It was the contrast. She was no longer in the first flush of youth, but youth surrounded her and she was lit up by it. Did this youth derive from my memories of Mélisande? Was it the artist shining out in her?'

Debussy: 'Some people, and they are the most attractive kind, have not exhausted the privileges of youth even though it is already a little way behind them. It was a period of which they did not take their full advantage, a form of capital secretly available to them, on which they can now draw at will. That is the secret of the attraction Mary Garden holds for you.'

*

Pierre Louÿs: 'Naturalism is life rendered more real than in nature, and so uglier and bereft of everything that comes from the soul. It has nothing to do with truth.'

Debussy: 'There's only one kind of truth: that which kills.'

*

At Catherine's request I go to fetch a bottle of old Armagnac, of the highest quality. Louÿs appreciates it and I know that Debussy will also.

Debussy: 'Vincent d'Indy can only work with a bottle of good champagne by his side. I don't go as far as that. But I believe in the capricious magic of alcohol and I'm not averse to feeling its effects. Sometimes it brings us strangely close to things we're familiar with and allows us to see them in a new light, sometimes it takes us far away so that we forget them. It can bring the past back to us with a terrifying precision and give the smallest details a significance which had escaped us . . . I would add that a little alcohol plunges us into a gentle melancholy and that it is a better preparation than loose talk for love-making . . . All the words in the world don't have the power of two glasses of this Armagnac, invented by God to prepare mankind for bliss.'

*

Pierre Louÿs: 'You ask me, Madame, if I believe in the occult? Every poet does to some extent, sometimes without wanting to. In the worst hours of a serious illness I have sensed, behind the screen of death, not the beginning of another life but the continuation of this one.'

Debussy: 'That's obvious. None of us, if he is worthy to be called a human being, is able to die. He simply changes his condition. He passes from one side of life to the other, as you leave bachelorhood for marriage or a military life for a civilian one.'

*

Catherine: 'Have you noticed the mysterious way love has of taking over our hearts?'

Debussy: 'And especially the hearts of artists. Burdened as we are by works and worries, we look for an ultimate realization in love. And we give ourselves with our eyes closed, without moderation, without calculation.'

*

Pierre Louÿs: 'In the kingdom of the spirit the most elevated things are the simplest. The most accurately reasoned seem the least reasonable. The world abounds in things which escape all logical explanation.'

Debussy: 'Poetry and music, these are never negations or affirmations. They are allusions to life.'

Pierre Louÿs: '. . . allusions which generate illusions.'

Debussy: 'People talk of musical adaptations. The word is badly chosen. It would be better to say "interpretations". Apart from advertisements and manuals of practical science, every text needs to be interpreted in a poetic or symbolic sense. A writer always means to say more than he does.'

Pierre Louÿs: 'I agree, to the extent that the poetic meaning of a text is the one which lies beyond logical analysis.'

Catherine: 'Is there then a sort of superior signification?'

Debussy: 'Our thoughts pass through our hearts and through our heads. Do you imagine, Madame, that in travelling upwards from one to the other they are not transformed? I will go further. There exist people, landscapes and works of art which form part of our sensibility and of our intelligence and which, for that reason, modify our ideas.'

Sylvain Bonmariage, *Catherine et ses amis* (Gap, 1949), pp. 160–75

M. D. CALVOCORESSI

(1877–1944)

M. D. Calvocoressi, Greek by birth and French by education, was a writer and critic and an early champion of Ravel.

Our acquaintance had not started under auspicious circumstances. At the end of 1902 – that is at a time when he was still smarting under the unfair onslaughts on his *Pelléas* – he had been invited to contribute articles to *La Renaissance Latine*. He accepted, and I was asked to write an article announcing the news (this article, entitled 'Claude Debussy, Critique', gave me a welcome opportunity to show again how much I regretted my obtuseness with regard to *Pelléas*). Then Debussy, who meanwhile had been offered, and had accepted, the post of musical critic of a daily paper, the *Gil Blas*, wrote to Binet-Valmer, the editor of *La Renaissance Latine*, that pressure of work would prevent his contributing to this periodical. Binet-Valmer, very much distressed, urged me to implore him to reconsider his decision. I, he said, as the musical critic of the *Renaissance*, was the only one to whom the task could be entrusted. Reluctantly, I accepted; and at last Debussy promised to do his best (a letter which he wrote to me on the matter is reproduced in Léon Vallas's book, *The Theories of Claude Debussy*, London, 1929). A few days later, he did send in an article – the one which is to be found under the title 'Considérations sur la Musique de Plein Air' in his collected essays, *Monsieur Croche, Anti-Dilettante*, in which he suggested, among other things, that since *I pagliacci* was being given at the Opéra, it was high time to manufacture barrel-organs capable of playing Wagner's *Ring* in the streets.

The article was duly set in type, and lay waiting, when suddenly *La Renaissance Latine* changed hands. The new proprietor and editor, coming across it, gave it a glance, exclaimed: '*Mais c'est idiot!*' and decreed, despite my expostulations, that it was not to be published. I called at once upon Debussy to explain and apologize. He assured me that he quite realized my helplessness; but I am certain that the episode left in his mind as unpleasant a memory as it did in mine.

For several years I did not see Debussy. In 1908, I met him in Durand's music shop. I heard him ask one of the staff whether he knew anything about Rimsky-Korsakov's new opera *Le coq d'or*. I, who had just received advance copies of the vocal score of this, with my French translation, went to him and asked leave to send him one. He accepted; and a few days later I received from him a long letter congratulating me on 'the skilful way in which I had dealt with the somewhat ponderous humour of the libretto' – which made me feel that far from deserving congratulations, I had achieved a translation which might convey wrong impressions. Anyhow, he had graciously accepted my diffidently offered olive-branch: and that was the main thing. To be quite candid, I do not know to this day whether there existed any reason for me to feel it needful to hold out an olive-branch to him: such was the atmosphere of Paris at that time.

In 1913 I was asked by the editor of the Philadelphia *Etude* to interview him on modern musical developments, and on that occasion I had a long and interesting talk with him. All told, he asked me more questions than I was able to ask him: for, as he confessed, he had not followed recent events very closely 'because he wished to concentrate and had made it a rule to hear as little music as possible'. He did not know a single bar of Schoenberg's music, which Ravel at that time had already begun to study eagerly, but he did know a few examples of Bartók's and Kodály's, and found these interesting in several respects. He praised Stravinsky's 'keen, fervid curiosity', and remarked that 'it was good for young artists to be alive to new possibilities and to cast about, but that no doubt Stravinsky would sober down in due time'. Then he started speaking feelingly of the evils of premature discussion of young composers. 'I consider it', he said, 'almost a crime. The former policy of allowing artists to ripen in peace was far sounder. It is unwise to unsettle young composers by making them the subjects of discussions that are, often, as shallow and prejudiced as they are premature. Hardly does a composer appear than people begin devoting essays to him and weighing his music down with ambitious definitions. They do far greater harm to young composers than even the fiercest detractors could do.'

As I listened, I could not help regretting that these words of warning should not have been uttered some twenty years earlier, when they might have helped to scotch the growth of the practice. Then, perhaps, there might have been less of that pitting one composer against another which was soon to become disgraceful when it was not purely and simply ludicrous. By 1913, however, most people – including the leaders of the little cliques – had practically ceased wasting their energies in guerrilla warfare. But for many years, starting from the moment when he first stepped into the limelight, Debussy himself had suffered at the hands of writers who did their utmost to deny him the peace for which he longed. And there was in the tone of his voice a wistfulness which made it clear that he was thinking of himself as much as of any of the younger composers he was referring to.

M. D. Calvocoressi, *Musicians Gallery* (London, 1933), pp. 118–19, 122–3

GEORGE COPELAND
(1882–1971)

George Copeland was born in Boston and was one of the first pianists to play Debussy's music regularly in the United States. He was also a champion of Spanish music, and in 1929 uttered the heretical words, 'Too much Beethoven never did anybody any good.'

One night *Pelléas et Mélisande* was to be given, and I proposed that we attend.

'Why?' he asked. 'Let us rather go to *Tosca*. They perform *Pelléas* in exactly the same manner as they play *Tosca*.'

George Copeland, 'The first – and last – times I saw Debussy', *Music*, November 1944, p. 8

JACQUES DURAND

(1906) Richard Strauss wrote to me one day to say he very much wanted to make Debussy's acquaintance. He was coming to conduct some concerts in Paris and asked me to arrange a meeting with the composer of *Pelléas* during his stay. I mentioned it to Debussy. Although he didn't enjoy seeing new faces, he agreed to have lunch with the composer of *Salome* at my house.

On the appointed day, the lunch took place with just the three of us. Strauss had just been responsible for founding the copyright society in Germany and spoke at length on the subject to Debussy who, wholly ignorant as he was of the workings of the parallel French society, got little pleasure out of this conversation, which was too commercial for his taste.

Debussy generally dealt with embarrassing situations by thinking of something else and losing himself in his dream world. Lunch therefore passed in active conversation on the part of Strauss and obstinate silence on that of Debussy. I have a feeling that the meeting Strauss had asked for did not exactly turn out as he expected.

Jacques Durand, *Quelques souvenirs d'un éditeur de musique*, 2 vols (Paris, 1924/1925), II, p. 30.

SIMON HARCOURT-SMITH

My acquaintance with Debussy and my subsequent friendship with him, in so far as a child can claim friendship with a genius, occurred when my father was head of the British School at Athens. Debussy was supposed to be an extremely satirical, crinkly person. I can only say that, possibly because of his tender love for Chouchou, his daughter, he seemed equally to be devoted to other children. My first experience of him was of this rather important, bearded figure who would explode suddenly in great indignation; and perhaps my first recollection of him is his seizing my arm when I was aged about six and saying: 'If you have any affection, my boy, for me, *never* play or even talk of Wagner or Beethoven to me, because it is like somebody dancing on my grave.'

Simon Harcourt-Smith, BBC talk, 25 January 1979

GEORGES JEAN-AUBRY
(1882–1949)

Georges Jean-Aubry was a French writer on music who
moved to London in 1915. As editor of *The Chesterian*
from 1919, he was a staunch supporter of contemporary
French composers.

When he requested me to call on him I was merely a young man
without any special reputation, with no great outlook, and without
influence. What is more, I was practically buried in a French provincial town. If I make mention of these personal details which reflect no
particular glory on myself, it is merely because they are calculated to
give an idea of Claude Debussy which does him greater justice than
that which has at times been spread abroad by superficial newspaper
men. The truth is that no one detested all that in any way, shape or
form, was akin to advertisement or lack of reticence more than Claude
Debussy. I do not know but that, during the first period of our
acquaintanceship, he imparted various confidences to me in order to
see whether I would hasten to transform them into 'echoes for the
press'. He had his own method of ridding himself of newspaper men.
It consisted in making those brusque and paradoxical statements with
which (often in the most ridiculous manner) the French press has been
nourished in the course of the last fifteen years.

Physically it has been said of him that in his youth he seemed like
an Assyrian prince. When I knew him he was in his forties, and his
features at times showed weariness; yet he retained his somewhat Asiatic
appearance. His eyes were slightly narrowed, his black hair curled
lightly, and he had the broadest forehead and the largest ears that I
had seen up to that time.

He spoke little, and then in brusque phrases; generally with a
mingling of indolent and decisive intonations of voice, in which one
could feel the ill-restrained wrath and irony he had for those who
did not understand, or who endeavoured to falsify that in which he
believed.

I do not believe that any man has ever been in his art and thought

more abidingly sincere than Claude Debussy. Neither his capricious
sallies nor his paradoxes should create an illusion as regards this fact.
No man appears to me to be more consistent, more coherent than he,
when I pass in mental review the sum total of his ideas on art, on
life, on people and things.

Among his cherished dreams had been that of writing a *Tristan*.
One day, in order to rid himself of an importunate, he told someone
who asked him at what he was working: 'I am creating a *Tristan*: it
is a subject which has not as yet been treated.' Newspaper men at once
gave rein to cheap witticisms in connection with this remark. Claude
Debussy once more had neglected to take the trouble to explain himself.
For him the world was divided into two classes of people: stupid
people, to whom it is useless to explain anything, since there is nothing
they ever understand; and intelligent people, for whom a mere hint
suffices without need of commentaries.

Georges Jean-Aubry, 'Claude Debussy', *Musical Quarterly*, October 1918,
pp. 543, 553

KARL LAHM

I saw Debussy at the time of the première of *Pelléas*. His appearance,
as I remember, was decidedly that of an aesthete, but extremely
powerful and open – his second name was after all Achille – he was
a smart Parisian, not affected or dreamy, not effeminate – in every
respect an artist who had his own world, a thinking man, and above
all a Frenchman.

My first encounter with him, in a fairly large gathering, was not
very fruitful, but characteristic. The art critic Louis Vauxcelles had
invited a number of painters and sculptors, including many famous
names. Introductions were made and for me it was an occasion to stand
back and observe. I remember distinctly that the host passed Debussy
a print of which he was very proud, and pointed to the signature
'A.D.' The composer said with deep respect: 'Dürer!', and then moved
off to look at the quantity of modern pictures and sketches hanging
on the walls, among them works by Signac, Seurat, Henri Martin
and Renoir. Vauxcelles was the pace-setter of Impressionism and of

the more avant-garde artists, so that here Debussy found himself in his rightful place.

It was soon after *Le martyre de Saint Sébastien* that I heard Debussy play for the first time. In the salon of a musically inclined countess, he showed at the piano that colour depends on the correct handling of the overtones, which must not be obtrusive. He did not play for long, but there was in his gentle playing a narcotic/erotic note, a sweet dreaminess like that of a woman's hand. D'Annunzio was one of the celebrities present. I noted down on the spot the following words with which he described Debussy: 'He's a painter, the colour of the sky, who uses angels' wings for his brush.'

Debussy had no wish to be didactic, or to found a school. Among my notes of that time, I find these words of his: 'A Master who takes himself for a Master is no Master.' I heard Debussy say these words after a young aristocratic enthusiast had been continually addressing him as 'Cher maître'. When the lady of the house said that her nephew showed talent as a composer, Debussy advised her not to send him to a teacher, 'for the love of God!'

Karl Lahm, 'Erinnerungen an Claude Debussy', *Melos*, 21/11, November 1954, pp. 314–15

HENRY MALHERBE

I was fifteen when I was introduced to Claude Debussy. I saw him later at the Concerts Colonne, before the first performance of the song 'Jet d'eau' which he had just orchestrated. The excellent singer who was to perform it came to see him. He asked her:

'Sing me a little music.'

'Would you like Duparc's *L'invitation au voyage*?'

'You haven't got anything less ordinary?'

'Mozart, then, or Bach?'

'Splendid. They are the gods of music.'

During rehearsals he confided to Edouard Colonne:

'If I had to write *Pelléas et Mélisande* all over again, I'd produce something quite different from what's played now.'

'That,' said Colonne, 'is exactly what Gounod said to me about *Faust*.'

'Well, with *Faust* that's hardly surprising!'

Henry Malherbe, 'Deux maîtres que j'ai connus', *Candide*, 717, 9 December 1937, p. 19

RENE PETER

After a difficult beginning, *Pelléas* turned Debussy into a world-famous composer, and a new perspective on happiness appeared to him in the form of another woman. She was a distinguished singer and she loved him . . . The fact that she was rich attracted unkind comment, but certainly Debussy loved her sincerely. He continued to compose in the new surroundings he had chosen for himself, but works now came more slowly. Here again, there is a striking contrast between his daily life and the works that he wrote. He, an atheist, a pagan even, with a wife who was not a Roman Catholic, proceeded to compose *Le martyre de Saint Sébastien*.

Are we to conclude, after all this, that Debussy lived what is generally called 'a busy emotional life'? Certainly woman as an idea interested him more than individual women. But, given his complex personality, how could his dream ever have been realized? Until his death, in his life as in his work, he had the need for exploration and renewal.

Some may think; 'Poor women!' I am not sure that they should be pitied for the brief time they spent with him. They themselves would be hurt and offended by the idea. When some years ago the monument to the memory of my dear Claude was inaugurated, three of those women who had, for a longer or shorter time, been part of his life were there, listening to the speeches and perhaps even a little proud.

René Peter, 'Debussy et l'amour', *Comoedia*, 4 July 1942

Under the fine lines of his fierce mask, he concealed, almost with shame, a quick and individual sensitivity, divinely manifested in every note of his works. I am proud to say that I knew him better than anyone. He had the heart of a child, prouder of a pretty tie than of a compliment on his genius – not that he doubted it, but it seemed to him something so natural as not to be worth talking about. Or only in a certain rough and ready manner which we who valued him before he was famous came to know well.

'Have you been working? – No. – A little? – Very little. – How's it going? – Not bad, and you? – If yours turns out to be a masterpiece, we shan't be pleased; it's getting too much. – Go on, you idiot!'

I saw him for the first time, when I was eleven or twelve, at dinner with the poet Maurice Vaucaire, where I had been taken by my parents. At that time he was called Achille. His Assyrian countenance, his dark complexion, his clipped way of speaking and his mythological name terrified me. He was on holiday from the Villa Medici, from which he had escaped as though it was a prison, because he could never stand any authority, except Mozart and, for a long time it has to be said, Wagner. After that his views changed, but that evening he played *Tristan* (I can still hear his metallic way of pronouncing the name Brangäne!), the Magic Fire scene and the end of *Die Walküre*, then the Prelude to *Parsifal*.

You can imagine what it must have been like. He himself was moved and remained silent. Then he suddenly turned towards me:

'Do you like that, young man? Good, excellent. It's important to love very beautiful things when you're very young. That way you have more time to get tired of them.'

A simple joke; his Wagneritis then seemed irremediable. Being poor, he talked of making the journey to Bayreuth on foot! He was asked to play some Debussy. 'Another time, if you don't mind,' he replied, 'but we also have some Carolus Gounod to hand!' and at the top of his voice he began to sing:

> *Faites-lui mes ave-û . . .*
> *Portez mes voeû . . .* *

Ideas came to him freely, but he was fastidious about writing them down. A detail would hold him up. And he would spend nights lying in wait for a nuance, like a wild beast in its lair. Five acts planned out did not for him, at least in the short term, come up to a chord of the ninth placed in the right spot.

---

*Siebel's aria at the beginning of Act III of Gounod's *Faust*.

'Yes, that's it . . .' And he would smile behind his curly beard.

This care for minutiae showed itself not only in his music, but in his letters, and in his way of dressing and expressing himself. Such was my admiration for him that I thought he was incomparable in whatever he might choose to undertake, and I had the curious idea of asking him to be my first teacher . . . of playwriting! He was happy to accept and, for about eighteen months, he gave me two lessons a week. However, he was quite the opposite of a craftsman and his method of prolonging a scene, preparing an entry or managing an effect had little to do with the rigorous technique of a Scribe or a Sardou. My first efforts painfully reflected this fact. I remember Antoine's* bewilderment on hearing three acts worked out in this fashion which had everything in them except what makes 'a piece'; which, for us, was exactly what was to be despised. Antoine suggested some improvements, fundamental ones, it's true. But Debussy had never taken more than a passing interest in the rise of the Théâtre Libre, and would have nothing to do with these improvements when I mentioned them.

It was in this state of mind that we began a collaboration on a fairy tale with fourteen scenes, which never got any further than the title: *Les mille et une nuits de n'importe où et d'ailleurs* [The Thousand and One Nights of Anywhere and Other Places], and a dramatic satire, of which we wrote two scenes. It was called *Les F. E. A.* (*Les Frères en Art*). It was the story of a nasty painter, highly respected, who had founded a league (F.E.A.) over which he exerted absolute control, and by means of which he could snuff out budding talent and seduce the wife of his favourite pupil. This plan was conceived with enthusiasm . . . and without a disagreement, because at the finest moment of Scene 3, looks were exchanged, then a silence, then simultaneous smiles, and the manuscript more or less closed itself and the ten pages of writing slipped into a drawer and dusty oblivion.

I always remained for him the lad he had once known, which explained the special affection with which he treated me to the end of his life. I had a clown's licence. One evening I said to him:

'For all your boasting, one day you'll be decorated . . . Yes, my

*André Antoine was the director of the Théâtre Libre.

fine friend . . . And you'll enjoy it . . . and you'll be a member of the Ins-ti-tut!'

He began to laugh so heartily that I was stung and promptly offered to make him a bet. Then and there he signed for me three lines, more or less as follows: 'I promise never to accept a decoration and under no circumstances to become a member of any academy.' Six months later he had the red ribbon of the Légion d'honneur, and he wore it. And he was right, since the ribbon was for *Pelléas!*

Pelléas brought with it both pleasure and pain. In making judgments on others Debussy sometimes gave rein to the same severity he showed towards himself, and as he knew nothing of hypocrisy he was not without experience of enmities. His masterpiece was listened to without indulgence, the fifth scene without patience. This put Debussy into rather a bad mood and he barricaded himself in Albert Carré's office. I found him there and we went outside for a short walk in the street, and to talk about something else. The next day the notices were dull and, worst of all, polite! I can still see, at the third performance, the popular singer Paulus leaving the theatre in fits of laughter! This was the first sure sign of victory. A week later the composer, who until then had hardly been known except to a small, select band, was famous. *Pelléas* had 'arrived'.

Only those who did not love Debussy as I did could have missed the unmistakable signs that, from that moment on, he began to leave us. Not that he changed; but despite him, despite all of us, he moved into a different category of being.

People came to the fore called 'Debussystes'; and we, the real Debussystes of yore, we now belonged only to a vague past era which had lost its raison d'être. It was curious, but our Claude, still young and enthusiastic, began to take on a sort of patina and ceased to look like himself. Our conversations were no longer the same; he was no longer a god, but a *maître*. Genius was blurred by fame. And this fame did not give us all that we had once hoped for, when it was still a distant dream. A score of concert societies fought to put on his works, his name leapt out from a hundred posters and from double spreads in the newspapers. The Institut was open to him, if he had wanted; and many a time, on this point, I thought of the second part of our wager.

Where had he gone, the Debussy I had known throughout my

youth, the Debussy who played a bad game of backgammon, at which the reprehensible side of his character became so delightfully visible? And an appalling game of tennis, which he played with a pianist's hand and heavy feet? He no longer had the time, now that he was harassed by reporters, greedy editors and loathsome worshippers – even if he did send them packing – to play badly at anything. The 'enfant terrible' henceforth owed it to himself, whatever he did, to do it well. Supported by a wife he loved, he took the brave decision to exile himself and, as he could no longer belong to his friends, to belong from now on only to his work. But, without meaning to, he had created a formula, and this formula surrounded him! He began to write more slowly . . .

Months passed. He wrote once, in 1914 when my first play, *Chiffon*, was put on; I had sent him the initial idea for it, which he liked. Then came the war. I was to see him only one more time.

It was 12 May 1915, the day of the general meeting of the Société des Auteurs et Compositeurs Dramatiques, and I was amazed to meet him there. It was election day. I shall never forget his beautiful smile as he greeted me. He had on a black bowler hat, something he had never worn until then.

'What are you doing here?' I asked him.

'I've come to vote for my friend Messager.' (He was always very fond of Messager and was happy to express his gratitude for all Messager had done over the production of *Pelléas*.) 'But now that's done, we can go and have a chat.'

He was a magician. From the first moment I was with him, I no longer breathed the same air, I no longer heard or saw the same things. But it was clear already that he was very ill. The conversation turned to his devotees. Or perhaps I should say 'turned against' them. As we parted, I risked saying:

'You know, Claude, the Debussystes irritate me.'

'They're killing me,' he replied.

We went our separate ways, promising to write and arrange a meeting or to telephone. But neither of us kept our promise.

René Peter, 'Du temps d'Achille', *ReM*, 2, 1 December 1920, pp. 159–64

'The great secret,' he said, 'is to tell women that your love for them is on a vast scale, but let them realize intuitively that you feel it only in a pocket format. Like us, women are quite happy to be entertained, as long as one doesn't become bothersome or complicate their life. Using the method I have just described, one could satisfy their amour-propre and true love could operate freely with the maximum of embellishments and arabesques, like a melodic work evolving from the sonata to the symphony according to the mood or the whim or the virtuosity of the players, unfettered by any constraints. So there you are, dear boy; repeat that three times a night before you go to sleep and pass me one of your ghastly cigarettes.'

'But suppose what you feel is really the de luxe article?' I ventured to ask.

Debussy seemed to consider this for a long moment, and 'retire into his study' as he used to put it; then he blew out a large cloud of grey smoke:

'That, my dear fellow, is a point on which so far I have had neither the time nor the opportunity to reflect. Try me again in a year or two. Perhaps then I'll be able to give you a reply from the vantage point of greater experience. Anyway, it's not important.'

*

At the time we first became friends one of the facets of his personality, which I still find the most striking, was the astonishing maturity of his mind, that rather rough-hewn culture he had made his own, simply by the exercise of his imagination, and that decisiveness in his tastes and ideas which meant that he was never at a loss. One evening, an uncle of mine asked him, in the free and easy manner one uses with artists: 'What are your musical likes?' Debussy replied with almost mechanical conviction: 'The whole of Wagner and Schumann, and certain pieces by Bach and Offenbach.' My uncle didn't know whether to treat it as a joke or to take offence, but for the record I hasten to say that Debussy's answer was an entirely serious one. It was he who, together with Etienne Dupin, guided me in my early reading: Verlaine, Laforgue, Rimbaud, Poe, and Mallarmé, whose work he knew and really understood; he had already written his songs on 'five poems by Baudelaire', was unusually familiar with Shakespeare (which he read in the translation by Montégut, not the one by François-Victor

Hugo which he found too 'romantic') and preferred *Ruy Blas* to *Hernani*.

*

His playfulness was a deeply ingrained habit and invaded everything he did. He was playing a game when he used to roll the tobacco of his cigarettes in a sheet of ungummed paper and then flatten it all the way along, without moistening it or ever spilling more than the tiniest speck of the contents. He was playing a game when he won the Prix de Rome by applying a set of old-fashioned tricks, because having the Prix de Rome was rather fun! His whole style is playful; he juggles with grammar, paradoxes and unexpected expressions which suddenly and for no good reason disrupt the train of thought . . . 'You weren't expecting me, but here I am!' The arabesques of his handwriting make up a game, like pass the parcel, where the words are shot through with magic threads, and in the 'y' of his signature you can see the grace of a mischievous iris with its long stem, losing itself in the watery depths. He loved the circus and clowns and playing with hoops, and would spend hours watching his cats at play – always grey semi-angoras, whom he adored. Each was regularly replaced by another because they had a habit of falling out of the window (I saw three of them killed like this), but they were all called Line. Even the piano sometimes became, beneath his spatulate fingers, an arena for his crazy jokes: Chopin's 'Funeral March' was turned into something wild and uproarious, or else *En revenant de la revue* was transformed into a funeral march.

'If that isn't enough for you, here's another one: the march of the *Butchers' Boys!*'

That was his name for Ganne's *Marche lorraine*, and he would yell at the top of his voice:

> '*Nous sommes les garçons bouchers,*
> *çons bouchers,*
> *çons bouchers . . .*'

and then burst into mad fits of laughter.

One of his favourite occupations was to sing and play Chabrier's operetta *L'étoile*, sometimes from one end of the score to the other; his enthusiasm for its imaginative discoveries and its truculent zest was unbounded. Another item was 'Les lauriers sont coupés', a lovely old popular refrain which, under his fingers, was filled with meanings, tender beauties and hidden symbols.

Playful though he was, he did not enjoy card games; except bezique – the Chinese version, of course – which amused him by its irrational ordering of the card values. He would put his pipe down beside him, like a cowboy with his revolver, ready to take aim at anyone who dared to dispute a victory which might depend on the combination of Queens with Jacks of the opposite colour. Then he would cheat, quite openly, turning up the corner of the top card of the stock and, if it was a card he wanted, pretending that it was his turn to play. But if it was in fact my turn, I would deliberately play my highest card, even if it meant losing the game, just so as to parry his coup. 'As for you, my young lad,' he would say, when he realized his ploy had been spotted, 'if you do that again I shall bury you in the coal bucket!'

*

I was the first to hear two of his *Chansons de Bilitis:* 'La chevelure' and 'La flûte de Pan', sung in Debussy's house by one of his favourite singers. After the second song, I allowed my feelings to be tempered by this simple remark:

'You're a bit naughty towards the end there. I imagine it's intentional.'

'Towards the end? What do you mean?'

'The chord under the last word: "*Ma mère ne croira jamais que je suis restée si longtemps à chercher ma ceinture perdue . . .*" '

'It's the thing I like best in the whole song,' he retorted instantly.

'I'm not surprised, it's wonderful. But I still find it a bit disconcerting. Play it again and let me see.'

Sung by him, the effect I referred to was accentuated even more, not so much its mischievousness, which I had exaggerated to make my point, as its feeling of anxiety . . . '*Perdue!* . . .'

'You're right,' he declared, after repeating the exquisite dissonance two or three times. 'And so much the better! That'll teach the young reprobate to let her lover kiss her while he's teaching her the flute, and then tell stories to her mother! Anyway, I owed her that for all the trouble she gave me. The little minx.'

*

One day, shortly after he had moved to the rue Cardinet, I sat talking with him in the chair he normally used for working in. He was looking at me in a restless manner; then, suddenly, he let out a roar. I gave a start.

'What? What's the matter?'

'What's the matter? Are you mad? Look!'

He pointed to the carpet where, in the thick pile, a few millimetres away from the four feet of the said chair, were four distinctive marks.

'Can't you see, there?'

'Yes!'

'Those holes aren't very pretty, but they're inevitable. Are you trying to turn my carpet into a sieve?'

I got up and Claude carefully swung the chair round until its feet finally found their rightful position. He breathed out.

'But when you're working at fever pitch,' I asked boldly, 'don't you ever get up and sit down again without noticing . . .'

'I always seat myself like this,' he replied. 'Now watch, it's worth seeing.'

It was a simple piece of acrobatics. It consisted of carefully tipping up the back so that the back legs were clear of the floor, thereby creating a little space between it and the desk; into this space Claude gradually inserted himself, facing the desk, until he judged that he had moved far enough to be able to sit in the middle of the chair. At that point he lowered 1) the chair, 2) himself into it. After which:

'Well then, what do you think?'

'Magnificent,' I replied admiringly. 'You're the composer of *Pelléas*, all right!'

These little ways of his were a clear indication of his Baudelairean conception of beauty. Many a time he has brought to my mind the sentence: '*Je hais le mouvement qui déplace les lignes!*' [I hate the movement which disrupts the lines!] A picture hung crooked on a wall sent him wild. Anything could have been happening, the worst sort of domestic disaster, but he would still go and restore to the wall an equilibrium essential to his thoughts. He would often look at himself in mirrors, at an angle, or face on if he came upon them unwittingly; he was very proud of his 'small nose', slim and regular in shape, and

I don't ever remember a single hair disturbing the harmony of the lock which hung over the right-hand side of his forehead, nor an unintentional crease interrupting the scientific disorder of his butterfly bow – generally dark green.

Debussy adored green, of every shade and for every purpose. The carpet in his study was pale green, the wallpaper bottle green and the furniture vegetable green, the whole making a delightful cameo, and he carried a green stick hooked over his arm. One day I too was wearing an emerald green tie and he said:

'That's a pretty tie. Where did you find that? Give it to me!'

'But . . .'

'Give it to me!'

'We can talk about it . . . a little later . . .'

'No, immediately. Not that it'll make any difference. When I want something, I have it.'

We left the matter there. A couple of days later, Debussy, Lily and I were sitting in the Pavillon Chinois drinking cocktails, when I noticed on her hat a sort of circular ribbon which seemed vaguely familiar. I said to her:

'That's a pretty hat.'

'You think so?'

'I like the decoration. Where did you find it?'

Claude began to laugh in diabolical triumph.

'I told you I'd have your tie! If you insist, it can go back in your drawer; but you needed a lesson in how to live. Garçon, three more cocktails; it's my turn.'

*

Edmond Bailly, the owner of the Librairie de l'Art Indépendant said to me:

'Yes, young man, this marvellous artist is kind enough to honour me with his friendship; he is one of the greatest and noblest, and he will be the most famous of them all. With your life still before you, you will see it come about! Just as they were talking a hundred years ago about Piccinnistes and Gluckistes, one day they will talk about d'Indystes and Debussystes!' As d'Indy was then at the height of his fame, this prophecy seemed to me such a splendid compliment that I went round to the rue Gustave-Doré to tell Debussy. Without a moment's hesitation, but with slightly over-deliberate conviction, he replied: 'I hope no one will ever talk about d'Indystes!'

*

He had read with passionate amusement Nietzsche's *Der Fall Wagner* in which the author claims that in all Wagner's work it is impossible to find a passage in which the human heart beats so intensely as in the final phrase of *Carmen*, in the sobbing cry of Don José, driven insane by love, the dagger still in his hand, facing her whom he has just stabbed: '*Vous pouvez m'arrêter, c'est moi qui l'ai tuée./O Carmen, ma Carmen adorée!*' ['You can arrest me, it was I who killed her. / O Carmen, my adored Carmen!']

'Show me on the piano how that goes,' I asked, suddenly curious.

Claude was there before me. In a voice made more beautiful and more bitterly sad by emotion, he sang Don José's heartbroken lament. I was shaken from head to foot. He was weeping, really weeping, with his voice as well as his eyes.

'You see . . . I sometimes feel there is a little of that emotion, of that colour, in my music. Just between us, that may only be French music, but your little Bayreuth friend has got some way to go before he can twist our hearts like that!'

But it was now two o'clock in the morning, too late to start a discussion. I left.

'Goodnight, my respects to your lady friends! My neighbours will sing me an aubade tomorrow for making so much noise in the night!'

As I groped my way down the dark staircase, an echo followed me, step by step. The voice of poor Don José, far above me, was once more secretly lamenting the faithlessness of his mistress, before Debussy went to sleep.

*

Twice a week, Debussy was visited by Satie, who came to pass the time drinking coffee, smoking, talking about music and being enormously happy; then he would return home – if it was the middle of winter to 'warm himself by his cold-side', as he put it. This was an expression he had taken from Claude, the only thing Satie was known to have borrowed in his life. In short, he was a model of simple, serene philosophy. I could see that from this point of view Claude admired

Top Debussy at the Conservatoire, *c.* 1874

Gabriel Pierné, who was a fellow-student of Debussy's at the Villa Medici

Top The Prix de Rome prizewinners on the steps of the Villa Medici. Paul Vidal is second from the left; Debussy is sitting above the others, wearing a white coat

Above left Nadezhda von Meck, in whose household Debussy stayed during the summers of 1880, 1881 and 1882

Above right René Peter, a friend from 1890 to 1904

Top Paul Dukas, Lily and Claude Debussy

Above left Robert Godet, a lifelong friend from 1888

Above right Debussy, sitting, with Mme Chausson, Ernest Chausson and
Raymond Bonheur

Top Debussy playing the piano, surrounded by Chausson and his family circle

Pierre Louÿs

Top Debussy with Zohra, Pierre Louÿs's Algerian mistress
Gustave Doret

Top Colette
Debussy on the bank of the Marne

Top left Georgette Leblanc
Top right Blanche Marot
André Messager

Above Mary Garden as Mélisande
Above right Maggie Teyte
Right Henri Busser

Left Erik Satie around the time he and Debussy became friends
Right Debussy and Stravinsky

Top Jacques Durand, Debussy's publisher
Debussy and Lily

Top Marguerite Long

Victor Segalen and Gilbert de Voisins, excavating in China in 1910

Top left Jane Bathori

Top right Ninon Vallin with D. E. Inghelbrecht

Debussy and Emma

Top left Ricardo Viñes

Top right Debussy with Dolly Bardac at Pourville in 1904

Louis Laloy and Debussy, preparing to fly a kite

Top Debussy with Chouchou at Houlgate in 1911

Left Debussy and dogs

Right Henry Wood

Left '. . . that dark, bearded Frenchman; his deep, soulful eyes . . . most of all, his enormous head . . .'
Right Arnold Bax

Left Darius Milhaud
Right 'We saw his face become hollow, his gaze become dull'

him; and there was also the fact that Satie, if not exactly Claude's parasite, was at least under an obligation to him, and it seems that Claude's feeling of being a benefactor took his mind to some extent off his own troubles. In this way Claude unwittingly manifested one of the most unjustly ignored facets of his character: that sort of proud goodwill which he hid even from himself under a rough, despotic exterior, better suited, in his view, to the real person he was.

*

He wrote to me, speaking about Siegmund and Sieglinde: 'They love each other . . . very *wälse!*' (Wälse being, as you know, the name of their father) 'and he issues her with an invitation to the *wälse* . . . upon which she invites him to lunch; pale ale and *wälse* rarebit!'

*

Debussy and Reynaldo Hahn were two very different composers and their antagonism sprang from their nature. More than that, there was distrust founded, not on their own feelings, but on what they thought the other felt: each of them used to say that the other didn't like him, that they were on opposite sides by definition, and as a result hostile and determined to pull the other down. This purely personal vendetta deepened, despite all efforts from outside, to the point that these two, who loved music but each in his own way, became convinced that they despised and detested each other. Their greetings became more formal, then more desultory, then ceased altogether.

Marcel Proust, however, maintained a relationship with Debussy that was largely courteous, if never deep. We know how sociable Proust was. One evening he even took Debussy home in the four-wheeler cab which was always waiting outside his door. Both of them remembered the occasion with pleasure, but with reservations. Proust felt he had not really been listened to, that Debussy had not followed the intricate subtleties and profundities of his thought; Debussy found Proust long-winded, gossipy, hairsplitting and slightly vulgar. It should be said that at that time Proust had published only a volume of imaginative pieces and that, apart from the charm of his conversation, nothing about him foreshadowed the astonishing figure he was one day to become. He even invited Claude to a reception which he arranged at his house for the composer including several interesting friends, either artists or good conversationalists; but Claude refused very simply. 'I'm a boor, you know. I'd prefer to meet in the café. Don't hold it against me, I was born like that!'

*

It was an occasion to be proud of if he asked you to his apartment to share some sausages and scrambled egg – which he cooked to perfection, juicy and golden – or to go and watch a horse race. You felt that in his eyes you were someone; and if he said: 'Did you see that girl's frightful ankles?' you almost felt like thanking him, such was his aura of power and authority. That was why he didn't believe in God – except as a great blind force unaware of the role it had been allotted – because a will superior to his own diminished and offended him. He preferred death and annihilation to the idea of a future life in which he would be simply one of the many. It was enough to have been through that already on earth! And then, who was one going to meet up there? Friends limp with perfection, numb with beatitude, women refusing to flirt . . .

'And then,' he said, 'suppose God didn't like music?'

'Oh, as to that,' I replied, 'I'm not worried, because I imagine that, like real and false virtues, real and false talents will be put in their true place.'

'In that case there are going to be some changes in staff and some fairly curious revisions in the hierarchy . . .'

*

The morning after Debussy had been made a member of the Légion d'honneur, he put a light overcoat on top of the ribbon and hailed a cab to go to the corner of the suburbs where his father lived. Debussy *père* was standing out on the lawn of his tiny garden in his shirtsleeves, a waxing brush in his right hand, his left inside a large shoe which he was polishing. As he didn't see his son at first, Debussy gave a loud cough.

'Ah, my dear boy, what a nice surprise!'

That was not the end of the surprises, for Claude came towards his father and, without saying anything, briskly opened his overcoat. His father too was speechless; he stood stock still, looking dazed and pale; two large tears, nourished by twenty years of disappointment, rolled down his cheeks and into his moustache before he could recover himself. Then suddenly he embraced Claude in a frenzy of love.

'Ah, my boy! My boy!'

. . . while the back of the new *chevalier* was subjected to furious, repeated blows from the ecstatic brush and the grateful shoe. Claude loved telling this story.

'You see,' he said to me in the course of a simple, excellent dinner, 'in that brief moment I could feel pride at having been good for something.'

*

He held more or less categorical opinions about everything in life, principles from which he would not depart lightly: for instance, that superficial kindness is often no more than laziness; that obliging a borrower in whom you have no personal interest is in most cases the result either of the embarrassment you feel about getting rid of him, or else of your fear of appearing attached to money (he was, in fact, very generous with his, when he had any); that if a man holds to one idea in the face of everyone, he is necessarily in the right, given the fallibility which is the defining element of the human spirit – from which it follows that the more people agree about something, the more chance it has of being wrong (did he foresee the battles he would have to fight and the triumph that would finally crown his efforts?); that it was a good idea, before going to bed, to blow your nose thoroughly (which he did noisily and repeatedly until his nasal passages were completely clear), so as not to snore, which, in the case of those who did not sleep alone, he felt to be the height of impoliteness – he himself, apparently, slept like a child; that smoking through a cigarette-holder is a nonsense as ridiculous as kissing a woman on the mouth by telephone (his exact words); that being able to roll your own cigarettes is one of the most elementary duties of any citizen worthy of the name; that not being adroit with your hands is an indication of a careless, inferior character; likewise, wearing ready-made ties; likewise, using safety razors (it was all very well for him to say this, having a beard); and likewise he thought that anyone who could boast, like a well-known composer of the time, that he didn't touch alcohol or tobacco, must lack the instinct of curiosity that is essential to the artist who, wishing to express everything, must have experienced everything –

and even if he had a great deal of talent, as was the case with this man, he must be considered a '*marheureux*', as he liked to say, or else simply a liar, which he thought far more praiseworthy.

However serious matters were, whatever emotions he was labouring under, no one ever saw him open a letter or a packet without arming himself, in the case of the first, with a long dagger with a jade handle. He kept it for a long time, although it was broken. He would insert this into the tiny opening at the top of the envelope – not at the bottom, under any circumstances – with the care of a burglar trying to spring a lock. As for the parcel, if it was covered on all sides with a mass of tight knots, Claude, the scrupulous artist, would introduce into the knots a small knife which he turned and twisted and lifted and turned again, until there were only the wrappings to work through. These he would detach one by one, then lay them out flat on the table. After that the mystery packet was ready to reveal its secrets. If I happened to be present during all this, I'd be dying of impatience. I'd say to him;

'But why on earth don't you just break into it?'

He replied: 'Because it's bad luck.'

I don't know whether he ever changed the habit, but when I knew him he would never go to bed, first without the noseblowing, and second without arranging his slippers so that the toes pointed away from him. It's well known that to have them pointing the other way tempts God. Whenever he saw a magpie, which allows you to make a wish providing it ends in 'ie', he used to follow, the rule, shouting out: '*Cheval pie, donne-moi des louis!*' which then led to: '*Cheval pie, donne-moi Pierre Louÿs!*' and similar jokes. But he never failed to make his wish.

*

Why did he pronounce the word '*malheureux*' as '*marheureux*'? Probably for the same reason that he sometimes said '*bolhomme*' instead of '*bonhomme*' or, when he'd finished a successful piece of work: '*Je crois que c'est assez soi-soi*' (a childish version of '*soigné*'), or: '*C'est chic anglais*' – or, criticizing someone: '*mâs il est fou*' instead of '*mais il est fou*', the contraction of 'ai' into 'â' appearing in his eyes to give the word more energy. But this was the only expression where he used it. '*Mâs il est fou*' meant, 'he's really crazy, not half-crazy, but cr-r-razy.'

And it was always couched in the third person, even if the addressee was present. He seemed to ignore his interlocutor and call Heaven to witness this madness which had been revealed to him through a word he didn't like or a quip he judged to be out of place. His constant childishness was one of his dominant traits. There was nothing so droll as seeing this careful, profound artist uttering such juvenile phrases which seemed to spring out of his beard and, for that reason, to sound strange and diabolical!

He loved children's books, and the pictures in them. He used to insist that nothing is so restful as being stupid; not that he ever was for a moment, but I know what he meant! Innocent games allow the brain to escape from itself, and that is why Claude was so fond of patience; he used to say, when he got a game out: 'After that, my brain is like a tidy room.' Artless books, too, act on our tired brains like Swedish gymnastics on tense muscles, and that's why Claude had a passion for Hans Andersen's fairy tales, which set him up for further assaults on Tolstoy or Schopenhauer. In the same way, he would sometimes abandon Mussorgsky for light music; though taking with him a return ticket, needless to say.

But he did not like Dumas *père* and for a long time this surprised me. It was that Debussy was not a romantic, not interested in the exterior of things, not struck by fine words. Even Victor Hugo, whose beautiful prose he respected – to the point of being alien to it – seemed to him slightly brazen. I doubt very much whether, even at the time, he would have been one of the young Turks at the first night of *Hernani*. As for Gautier, the less said the better . . . He was amazed that Baudelaire, with his taste, should have dedicated *Les fleurs du mal* to him; he supposed it must have been out of simple politeness for the helping hand that Gautier, with the power of his reputation as a journalist, gave the obscure genius, anxious, like all poor poets, to be read. He held *Mademoiselle de Maupin* to be an irritating example of suppressed vice, vice for consumption by young girls; he only just brought himself, on this front, to excuse the *Chansons de Bilitis*, for their grace and the frankness of their language . . . and even then, not all of them! He detested *Les liaisons dangereuses*. What arguments we had on the subject of this work, the only ones maybe where I never gave way! For him, it was merely tales of seduction, complicated by skin-deep relationships in which true psychology played no part. 'Why should I care whether Valmont gets his Présidente? To get a woman by those means, those strategies, these devious devices . . . when it came to the day, I'd find it wasn't worth it. Give me Eugénie Grandet instead, or impure, uncomplicated Coralie . . .'

Balzac? I think he had read practically all of him, which, given the care with which he sifted and weighed and went back over the tiniest details, was an astonishing performance. He particularly liked *Le lys dans la vallée*, *La recherche de l'absolu* and *Les secrets de la princesse de Cadignan*; also *La fille aux yeux d'or* and, of course, *Le père Goriot*. He was less attached to *Splendeur et misère des courtisanes* which, in his view, was rather in the nature of a newspaper serial. But his best and oldest companion was Dickens. He fitted every mood, an infallible antidote and indefatigable healer for all ills. Spleen could be cured by a swift dose of Pickwick, Sam Weller and his father the coachman, Micawber, the old sea wolf in *Dombey and Son* and many others; a poor opinion of women and love by Bella, Dora and even the safe and sound Agnes in *David Copperfield*; misanthropy by the family of Boffin with the heart of gold, Jarndyce, the theories of the astonishing Mr Skimpole . . . and so on. Debussy was irritated at the disdain shown by some of the English, among the upper crust at least, for their great national writer. Unlike Proust, he thought Dickens was superior to Thackeray, who in England was far more highly regarded by the *cognoscenti*. Certainly Dickens is not without his faults; such as his attraction towards low life and the loose, disconnected nature of his plots. In this respect Claude placed *Bleak House* far above Dickens's other works, and the 'risqué' character of the noble lady on her return seemed to him to express itself in terms that were unexpectedly violent and disturbing, coming from an author who, in his other works, seems to be unaware that there is any other kind of love apart from marshmallow idylls and matrimonial exchanges. But what beauty, what spirit!

Claude maintained that *The Old Curiosity Shop* seems to soar on a wave of antique, Sophoclean inspiration, notably when the old dealer, ruined by gambling, and his granddaughter Nelly decide to abandon the unproductive shop and its difficult customers to go and beg on the highway, free at last and drunk with the pure air; also the passage where they both come to the village where Nelly feels she is going to die and is happy. He used to say that this marvellous dénouement

reminded him of the one in *Oedipus at Colonos*; only here the roles
are reversed; it is no longer the old wanderer, but Antigone who is
to know the deliverance and serenity of death. Then there was the
passage in *Dombey and Son* where the moneychanger gives a cold,
utterly cruel reception to his gentle, loving daughter who has come
looking for some small show of affection and to beg his forgiveness
for not being the son he would have liked; he dismisses her as though
she were a stranger, an intruder, so that she puts her head between
her hands and gives a long, despairing cry. There the writer too, out
of control, gives a long cry, of indignation and disgust. He has, at a
stroke, destroyed the end of his book by revealing what is to come;
but no matter. We have to be told that this wicked hardness of heart
will be punished. *Let him remember it in that room, years to come. It
has faded from the air, before he breaks the silence. It may pass as quickly
from his brain, as he believes, but it is there. Let him remember it in that
room, years to come!* Claude's voice used to fail him when he read that
out loud.

Pain inflicted on a child seemed to hurt him personally, making
him angry and almost physically ill – the strong oppressing the weak
used to cause him the very deepest distress. Children aside, he extended
his compassion to any being that suffered unjustly and without means
of defence. It goes without saying that he was a great lover of animals.

He was working one morning when his cat began to circle round
his legs. At first he paid no attention. The cat miaowed.

'Yes, yes, you're a lovely cat!' said Claude, stroking her but keeping
on with his work.

More miaows.

'Yes, you are!'

'Miaow!'

'Line, you're being a bore!'

Silence. The cat goes back to her cushion and goes to sleep. Claude
concentrates on his music. There's a knock.

'Come in!'

The maid appears to announce lunch; but instead of that she gives
a scream.

'Oh, the dirty animal!'

'What?' says Claude. 'What's the matter?'

'There, monsieur.'

'Oh!' says Claude as well. 'My carpet!'

The indignant maid makes as if to strike the cat.

'And if you beat her,' says Claude, suddenly calm, 'will that solve anything? Or do anything for my carpet? The poor animal, she did her best to warn me, and I was the one who didn't respond. She didn't have her little tray, it's not her fault. What would you do, I wonder, if you'd been shut in without your little tray?'

René Peter, *Claude Debussy* (Paris, 1931), pp. 11–12, 30, 39–43, 47–8, 52–5, 56–9, 69, 72, 98–9, 102–3, 109–10, 141–4, 155–62

MADAME DE SAINT-MARCEAUX
(1850–1930)

> Madame de Saint-Marceaux was one of the leading salon
> hostesses of the turn of the century. Ravel and Fauré were
> also among her regular guests.

The young Englishman Cyril Scott has formidable aplomb. He has some musical feeling but the disorder of his music makes it painful to listen to. Debussy, after hearing one of his pieces, said: 'I don't like these five-storey houses.'

Madame de Saint-Marceaux, diary entry for 22 January 1904, in: *Cahiers Debussy*, a.s. 3, 1976, p. 9.

VICTOR SEGALEN
(1878–1919)

> Victor Segalen was a diplomat and writer with a strong
> interest in exotic civilizations. At Debussy's suggestion,
> his study of Maori music, 'Voix mortes: musiques maori',
> was published in the *Mercure Musical* in 1907. Segalen
> sent both the transcripts of conversations and the letters
> that follow to his wife. Sadly, his *Orphée* did not in the
> end prompt Debussy to write any music for it.

Conversation: 8 October 1907

DEBUSSY: How are you?

SEGALEN: Hullo. I'm well. And you?

DEBUSSY: Not bad.

SEGALEN: So you've come from Dieppe!

DEBUSSY: Don't talk about it . . . An absurd visit . . . Can you work by the sea?

SEGALEN: I work more or less anywhere.

DEBUSSY: You're lucky!

SEGALEN: It's probably because I'm not in control of the life I lead, so unconsciously I conform to it . . .

DEBUSSY: I regret not having a career that's quite different from my leisure activities, as you do.

SEGALEN: Oh! 'Regret' is rather strong . . .

DEBUSSY: I mean it. Because that would have prevented me from living all the time with myself. It nearly happened. My father intended me for the sea. Then he met somebody . . . I don't know how it happened. 'Ah! He can play that? Very good. But he must be taught music . . .' etc . . . So my father then got the idea that I should study just music, he being someone who knew nothing about it.

SEGALEN: I don't see there's room for regrets. That would be to deny the whole of your past, which has been a success in that it has made of you what you are . . .

DEBUSSY: You say that because you don't know me.

SEGALEN: I know some very definite things about you.

DEBUSSY: Yes. But not my faults. Everything with me is instinctive, unreasoned. I'm not the master of myself at all. And then there are times when I can't do anything, when I come up against a wall, and wonder whether I'll get over it or not.

SEGALEN: Those times must have been painful in the past, when you were going through that inevitable period when one wonders whether one will ever create anything, and what it will be. But now that doubt has been removed.

DEBUSSY: Absolutely! I've written *Pelléas*. So what? Pelléas! That gentleman's a bore! I wonder now if I'm not going to repeat him indefinitely. I certainly don't want to. It would be a dreadful grind going over that again, or producing some equivalent in sound. I must go further. In any case, I'd rather practise . . . agriculture.

SEGALEN: Doubt is already some sort of reply – ambiguous, but quite promising. And then, every creative, instinctive person has gone through times like that. How is *Tristan* coming on?

DEBUSSY: Mourey has read me the first act; which hangs together. And he's going to read me the rest tomorrow. This is the plan of the first act, in three scenes:

1) The King's bedchamber: the dwarf Froncin reveals that Tristan is the Queen's lover. Mark doesn't believe it. The proof. They are taken prisoner.
2) The lepers. Yseut abandoned among the lepers.
3) The hollow path. Tristan, unarmed, rescues Yseut. They escape.

Second Act

The forest. The runaway couple are sad and tired of living in poverty.

Third Act

The white moor . . .

Fourth Act

1) Yseut of the White Hands.
2) Tristan's madness.
3 or 4) The treachery of Yseut of the White Hands – The death of Tristan – And, which is excellent, 'My life is now too much to bear'–

Gabriel Mourey's prose is not very singable, and there are many passages which don't exactly 'demand' to be set to music.

SEGALEN: Have you started on it?

DEBUSSY: No. I've still got to finish some things which don't want to be finished. Orchestral pieces which I can't bring myself to botch. I've never left anything unfinished so far. It's not something I want to do.

You are one of the few people to whom I talk 'music', or even to whom I talk about myself. That's not flattery. But I don't talk music even to my wife – or only musical chitchat.

10 October 1907

DEBUSSY: You asked me for a line of music. (He meticulously copies a line from *Pelléas*.) There it is. I don't often give them out. I get so many requests! I rather fancy writing out false ones and distributing them. I've had postcards from Buenos Aires and an American lady put five hundred francs in her letter for my reply. I kept the five hundred francs and the reply – But with you it's completely different.

If there's anything I have to say to you about the words of *Orphée*, it is the obscure suggestion: 'Pay attention to what the characters say.'

SEGALEN: ???

DEBUSSY: By which I mean that what the characters, Orphée and Eurydice, say must be very closely adapted to what they would say, to the décor, to the situation. Without that, we realize at once that we're in an opera house.

SEGALEN: But what about the characters who don't understand, the priests, the warriors who don't hear what Orphée hears?

DEBUSSY: Oh, as for them, make them talk like concierges. And I promise not to talk about this project to anyone.

SEGALEN: I do too.

DEBUSSY: As much as anything so I'm not besieged by a host of people saying: 'You've written the role of Orphée? But that suits my physique perfectly! You must reserve it for me.'

12 November 1907

DEBUSSY: Obviously, at the beginning Orphée won't speak his words, he'll sing them. *He might even sing wordlessly through the whole piece.* But that's an unrealizable utopia.

14 November 1907

DEBUSSY: I've wasted the whole morning with young people coming
and playing my pieces to me. 'La soirée dans Grenade', for
example. A Spaniard among them. Do you know how he plays
it? Like Hungarian music! He's amazed when I ask him to play
it in the Spanish style. I told him: 'You can't be *listening*.' (I
break in with a request for a performance of *L'isle joyeuse*; and
wonder where the inspiration for this joyful piece came
from . . .)
DEBUSSY: Purely imaginary. But I have to admit my technique isn't
up to playing it.

Conversation: 6 May 1908

Debussy takes *Orphée* out of a red cardboard file and, for a good ten
minutes, flips through it without saying anything. Then:

DEBUSSY: In the fourth act here, too much . . . too much . . . (He
expresses himself with a gesture)
SEGALEN: Too much material?
DEBUSSY: Yes . . . No, altogether too much lyricism. There's a lot of
it and it's good. But I don't see what ear could ever take it all
in. First of all I read it straight through, saying to myself: 'It's
very beautiful.' And it was through reading it all at once, and
imagining the music for it, that I realized there was too much.
SEGALEN: Well, you yourself can help me with cutting it, because
Pelléas has given you great experience with lyrical prose.
DEBUSSY: Not experience, not at all. Instinct, that's all.
SEGALEN: You must be assailed with librettos?
DEBUSSY: Yes. It's a long business. It wastes time. You can't show
people the door. I've just seen a gentleman from Brittany who
was intending to make a libretto out of his family papers and
entrust them to the 'po-et' Jean Aicard – and then to me after
that. Now I tell everyone that I have work on the stocks for
twenty years at least. I also had another meeting with a professional librettist, Georges Cain, whom I'd seen some time ago.
He said to me: 'You've done *Pelléas*, that's good. But now this
is exactly what we need . . .' I didn't want to know about it . . .

On the education of girls in general and of Chouchou in particular

DEBUSSY: Girls are being turned into equivocal beings, who play at being half angel, half little beast. It's disturbing. I shall try and inculcate into my daughter a little loyalty and also a little goodness. But to do that, I shall even have to fight against her mother.

Paris, 8 May 1908

Segalen to his wife

Debussy, first of all, was utterly absorbing, keeping me from 11 o'clock until 2.30. We looked at the third act and it'll be easy to arrange it as he wants it. He likes Eurydice's ecstatic death. He congratulates you on 'He does not know that everything within me can change – *if he so wishes*', which he knows you were responsible for. The fourth act now seems to him to hold together better.

As for the lunch, nothing new. Madame Debussy and Miss Chouchou both friendly. Afterwards, I obtained a showing of the three *Images*, which did not convince me they are a necessary part of his output. But 'La lune descend . . .' gains a lot from his playing.

He's on bad terms with Messager 'who took upon him my own task of organizing my life', and spoke to the composer on the subject. But Debussy is still very fond of him.

Conversation: 12 May 1908

On Rameau and Hippolyte et Aricie

DEBUSSY: Not a good production at the Opéra. Not in the rhythm of the work. You only have to look at a portrait of Rameau to see that everything needs to be controlled and clean – And they don't play it in period style, with that element of fantasy and convention, but like a modern piece – A good tenor, with a free-sounding voice, who doesn't impose a tragic character on the music when it's not needed, and even when he is being tragic preserves a sense of taste – But the rest of them play it like Gluck.

It's an absolutely French work, in its exact character and in its perfect equilibrium. The libretto is idiotic, of course. But we have to accept it, since Rameau chose it – After him, all the French quality was lost: that wonderfully balanced expression, so clear, so proper, with such simple means – Especially in the extremely moving fourth act, at the death of Hippolytus. Those simple words *'Hippolyte n'est plus'* are underlined by one admirable bar, and not by thirty-six themes one on top of the other! Not that I don't admire beautiful things which are foreign, from Germany or elsewhere, but I consider them as foreign. Let us preserve our own beautiful things.

Conversation: 17 December 1908

On orchestration

DEBUSSY: Composers no longer know how to separate out the sound, to produce it pure – In *Pelléas*, the sixth violin line is as necessary as the first. I try and use each timbre in its pure state; as Mozart does, for example. And that's why no one can any longer play Mozart. Everybody has got so used to mixing timbres, making them stand out by shading or mass, and not letting them sound with their own identities – Wagner went a long way along that road. He combines most of his instruments in pairs or threes. The ultimate is Strauss, who made a complete mess of everything. He combines the trombone and the flute. The flute's inaudible and the trombone sounds peculiar. I on the contrary try to keep each timbre pure and in its right place. Strauss's orchestra is nothing but a compound like an American drink, which mixes eighteen ingredients; all the individual tastes disappear. It's a cocktail orchestra.

SEGALEN: (One of Debussy's preoccupations is with the inadequacy of the percussion section. – Note: bring back from my Far Eastern trip a set of gongs and cymbals. – Another is with the use of the chorus. They're ridiculous. But it's impossible to ask people to play and sing in eight or ten parts which only work on paper. He wants to find a manner of choral writing that's 'stylized' and very simple.)

DEBUSSY: Ricardo Viñes – too dry. I've only heard two fine pianists: my old piano teacher, a small, fat lady who threw me into Bach and who played him as no one does nowadays, making him live (just because Bach wore a wig, is that a reason to bewig his music as well?) The second pianist was Liszt, whom I heard in Rome. As for the disposition of the orchestra, the strings should make, not a barrier, but a circle around the others. Split up the wood-wind. Mix the bassoons up with the cellos, the clarinets and oboes with the violins; so that their entries don't sound like somebody dropping a parcel.

Paris, 5 September 1913

Segalen to his wife

Lunch today with Debussy, more confident and expansive than ever; a shade sad, too: he's writing, more or less on commission, some small works that are annoying him: *Khamma*, an Egyptian ballet for Maud Allan, a nude dancer; and *Crimen amoris*, on pieces by Verlaine stitched together by Charles Morice. He can't even please himself by finishing his two little Poe operas. He's thinking of moving out to the suburbs for more peace and quiet, and for a house that's not so ridiculously expensive to run . . . He's giving me a completely free hand to publish *Orphée* and it may be it will be produced by Crès with a preface of my own devising.

Victor Segalen, Annie Joly-Segalen and André Schaeffner (eds): *Segalen et Debussy* (Monaco, 1962), pp. 70–71, 74–5, 77–8, 80–81, 83–5, 96–100, 107–8, 134–5.

MAGGIE TEYTE

'To describe one's impressions of Debussy is a difficult matter,' the singer replied thoughtfully, when the question was asked. 'His was such an unusual personality. With most geniuses their work, their dreams, colour the rest of their lives. It was not so with him. It was as if someone had taken a bit of genius, put it in a box and thrown it violently at his head. It stuck, yes, but it was not a part of him, of his everyday life, his modes of thought. You see what I mean?

'In his personal life, his methods of dealing with the problems of life, Debussy was primitive, self-centred and as relentless and pitiless as life itself. His music, on the other hand, is the essence of exotic refinement. He gathers up all the colour of modern life under his hand, as if it were the strings of a piano. Sometimes he thumps and sometimes he lays delicate arpeggios, but always it is the discord on the subtle harmonies of modernity – never that of the primitive, the barbaric.

'He had a most noticeable way of breathing, a sort of whistling,' she says. 'I do not know if it was caused by heart trouble or simply nerves, but the effect was to key one up; one was always conscious of that powerful, nervous force at work, directing and controlling. With all his nervousness and irritability he was most fair-minded and open to conviction. Once, I recall, I sang a passage slightly different from the way in which it was indicated. He looked up quickly, thought a moment, and then said, "You are right, quite right; that is the way you should sing it," and passed on without further comment.

'If you look at Debussy's portrait you will see at once what I mean when I say that his genius did not permeate his personality, that it was a thing quite distinct and apart. His head had bumps, great knobs almost, on it here and there and his eyes were dark, brown I think, and very small and piercing. Altogether, he gave one the impression of immense physical power and primitive vitality. His singleness of mind was evident in the love he had for his little daughter; she was the centre around which his affections revolved and everything else in his life was subordinated to this dominating emotion.

'I think if Debussy had been a wealthy man the world would never have heard of him, as he had an inordinate distaste for appearances in public. We always had a saying that we knew when Debussy needed money, for he never made any appearances except when he wished to add to his finances. I do not mean to imply that he was poor; he had a charming home in Paris, but he was not a man of means in the usual sense of having plenty of money to do with as he would.

'One of his idiosyncrasies was his great dislike for having his picture taken; he could not endure the thought and I was very proud indeed when he posed once for a picture for me at my earnest request.

'Did you know that Debussy hated Wagner vehemently? To me that was another of his contradictions – that he should so hate Wagner and so admire Mozart. He had a theory that just when Wagner got a lot of lovely jewels of thought together and was about to transmute them into music, something came along and joggled his elbow – and Debussy didn't care for people who allowed their elbows to be joggled.'

Maggie Teyte, 'Debussy, the man, as Maggie Teyte knew him', *Musical America*, 13 April 1918 (in interview with May Stanley)

PASTEUR VALLERY-RADOT

> Pasteur Valléry-Radot was a doctor who attended both Debussy and Ravel during their final illnesses.

Another man's soul is a thick forest in which one must walk with circumspection.

Debussy quoted in: Pasteur Valléry-Radot, 'Claude Debussy et le culte de l'amitié', *ReM*, 258, 1964, p. 107.

V

Pianist and coach

After *Pelléas*, Debussy soon gave up regular piano teaching, but he was always willing to offer advice to performers whom he found talented and sympathetic. From time to time he would also appear on the concert platform to play his own music, though it seems that his playing was undoubtedly heard to best effect in private.

EMILE VUILLERMOZ

All those who have had the privilege of seeing one of Debussy's works well up from under his fingers know what a miraculously gifted pianist he was. Personally, I have never heard more supple, elegant or velvety playing. He obtained sonorities from the piano which softened the angles and asperities generated by his forward-looking inspiration. He had discovered the exact finger technique to suit his harmonic system. Anyone who never heard him, in playing a chord, delicately mould the outline of an unresolved appoggiatura so as to emphasize its 'suspended' character as well as its allusive function, can have no idea of the charm attached to that way of suggesting a note, by a discreet approach which brushes it without sounding it fully. Debussy's playing was one long harmony lesson.

I shall never forget the cunning balance he was able to give to the beautiful, rich chords in the 'Sarabande' from *Pour le piano*, with its unexpected sonorities and progressions, and at the same time the way he maintained the framework of a courtly dance. He played it with the 'grave, slow elegance' which he asks for at the head of the score and, without forcing nuances or accents, but with the easy simplicity of a good dancer from the sixteenth century, recaptured, bar by bar, the feel of a vanished civilization. And no one else had his gift of transforming a dissonant chord into a little bell made of bronze or silver, scattering its harmonics to the four winds.

Emile Vuillermoz, *Claude Debussy* (Paris, 1962), pp. 54–7, 80–81.

HAROLD BAUER

(1873–1951)

Harold Bauer was an American pianist who lived in France for a number of years. Ravel dedicated 'Ondine' to him in 1908.

Debussy was the most violent of all the critics I ever met, in spite of his enthusiasms and the delicacy of feeling he seemed able to express, in words as in music. He satirized Wagner, he despised and detested Brahms, and he attacked Beethoven with such bitterness and sarcasm that it made one's blood boil. Once, in my hearing, he mentioned that he had 'escaped' the previous evening from a concert where a Beethoven quartet was being played, just at the moment when 'the old deaf one' (*'le vieux sourd'*) started to 'develop a theme'. There was something so hateful in the tone of his voice as he said this that I rose up indignantly and denounced him for his disrespect to the name of a great genius; and the result was, I regret to say, that our relations were broken on the spot and not renewed for a number of years.

A mutual friend, who was responsible for an annual series of concerts, each devoted to the work of one composer, came to see me one day in 1908 with a request, purporting to come from Claude Debussy, that I should introduce at one of these concerts a little suite he had just written entitled *Children's Corner*. I was touched and pleased, and of course I consented. When I had learned the pieces, I wrote to ask him to hear me play them. He gave me an appointment and I went to his house.

Contrary to my hope and expectation, our meeting was quite formal. I played the pieces, and he expressed himself satisfied. One little thing alone broke the stiffness of the occasion. After I played the last piece, 'Golliwog's Cakewalk', he remarked:

'You don't seem to object today to the manner in which I treat Wagner.'

I had not the slightest idea what he meant and asked him to explain. He then pointed out the pitiless caricature of the first bars of *Tristan and Isolde* that he had introduced in the middle of the 'Cakewalk'. It had completely escaped me. I laughed heartily and congratulated him on his wit.

The concert came off. The hall was full. To my chagrin, Debussy was not there. I played the suite and went out into the courtyard of the old house whose ballroom had been converted into an auditorium. I found the composer walking up and down with a very sour face. He came up to me and said, 'Eh bien! How did they take it?'

I was immediately filled with an immense pity for him. I realized that this great man, who had struggled so long to obtain recognition of the new idiom he was bringing to our art, was *nervous*, scared to death at the thought that his reputation might be compromised because he had written something humorous.

I looked him straight in the eye.

'They laughed,' I said briefly.

I saw relief pour through him. He burst into a stentorian roar of glee and shook me warmly by the hand.

'*Vous savez? Je vous remercie bien!*' he said.

It was enough. We were friends.

Harold Bauer, *Harold Bauer, His Book* (New York, 1948), pp. 82, 141–2

MAURICE DUMESNIL
(1886–?)

Maurice Dumesnil studied the piano with Isidor Philipp at the Conservatoire. He later toured widely in Europe and the USA.

The scene: a large parlour, discreetly lighted through lovely curtains with long blue-gray draperies matching the colour of the heavy wall-to-wall carpeting. Louis XV furniture; a bookcase containing volumes bound in rare leather or fabric; on a low table with a marble top, a collection of precious little objects made of crystal, jade, or gold delicately chiselled. Almost in the middle of the room, the black Blüthner grand stood, free of music, book or photographs. The general atmosphere was in keeping with the aristocratic neighbourhood of the Bois de Boulogne, where gracious living prevailed.

Debussy greeted me with placid courtesy. He talked little, but the words he said were significant. Somehow he gave the impression of being distant from the world, his dark eyes fixed on unearthly horizons. He held a cigarette between his fingers, depositing the ash carefully in a small china tray. He was proud of his grand piano, and before I played he showed me a new device invented by Blüthner: an extra string set on top of the others. Although not touched by the hammers, it caught the overtones, thus increasing the vibrations and enriching the sonority. This was a piano he had rented during a stay in Bournemouth, and liked so well that he had bought it and had it shipped to Paris.

I started playing the 'Hommage à Rameau' on this lovely instrument. But I didn't get very far. After the first two lines, Debussy stopped me: 'I do not hear the triplets in time,' he said. I tried again, inwardly counting so as to be sure of the values. But he was not satisfied. He put his hand on my shoulder and gently pushed me away. Then he sat down and played. Frankly, as intently as I listened, I couldn't see any difference between his way with those triplets and mine. But it dawned upon me that his powers of perception were extraordinary and could not be duplicated by anyone.

Probably he became satisfied after all, for we continued. Soon, however, I was interrupted: 'Start again; in those first bars I would like the right hand slightly more prominent than the left hand. Octaves sound flat when played with the same tone volume in both hands.' For a while I continued without being stopped. I felt his presence behind me, however, as he paced the gorgeous Oriental rugs, smoking his eternal cigarette. At the crescendo leading to the climax, marked *ff*, he stopped at my side: 'Please do not overdo this crescendo. It sounds too dramatic; start more softly and you will reach the same effect without impairing the quality of your tone.' Finally Debussy sat down again at the keyboard for a sort of recapitulation of the entire piece. He played a number of passages and the tone he extracted from the Blüthner was the loveliest, the most elusive and ethereal I have ever heard. How did he do it? I noticed that at times the position of his fingers, particularly in soft chordal passages, was almost flat. He seemed to caress the keys by rubbing them gently downward in an oblique motion, instead of pushing them down in a straight line. I tried to imitate him and apparently he was pleased, for he said, 'Bien.'

Now that 'Clair de lune' has become so tremendously popular, it is possible that if Debussy were still alive, he, like Rakhmaninov with his C sharp minor Prelude, would hardly want to play it or hear it any more. But at that time it was still unknown, and I played it for him only because it happened to be no. 3 of the exquisite *Suite bergamasque*. Again the matter of triplet values came up. Now he found them too strictly in time. It was all right in a way, he said, but they ought to be included 'within a general flexibility'. He advised me to depress the two pedals before starting, so that the overtones would vibrate immediately upon contact. Remembering his previous remarks about dramatizing, I tried to keep the middle part moderate. But I guess I still overdid it: 'No,' he said, 'you exaggerate both the crescendo and the rubato. The latter must be done within the entire phrase, never on a single beat.' And the expression had to remain dignified.

Anything suggesting a climax *à la* Mascagni or Leoncavallo must be avoided. Debussy often thought in terms of orchestration. Concerning the second section of 'Clair de lune', he said, 'The left-hand arpeggios should be fluid, mellow, drowned in pedal, as if played by a harp on a background of strings.' But he did not tolerate any confusion and insisted on the purity of each harmonic pattern. In the recapitulation the C flat in the left hand was to be brought out, thus emphasizing the change of colour. As to 'Clair de lune' as a composition in itself, Debussy didn't seem to give it any special importance, at least not as much as he gave to *Estampes* or *Images*. Among the latter I felt those he preferred were 'Reflets dans l'eau' and 'Poissons d'or'.

The remarks dealing with 'Reflets dans l'eau' were illuminating. From the first, the chord background ought to be subdued; played with laterally moving fingers, drowned in pedal, once more. 'I do not hear the bells,' Debussy commented. I gave more tone, but it was not of the proper quality. 'Keep your left hand hanging loosely from your wrist. Then let it drop, and let the tip of your third finger play those notes,' he said. He also gave me a wonderful object lesson in pedalling fast passages. I realize how many interpreters are misled by the famous blur so often associated with Debussy's piano music. He wanted the pedal used in long harmonic strokes, without breaks or confusion. Occasionally he allowed the pedal to encroach a tiny fraction from one harmony into the next, similarly to what one does when practising the five-finger exercise C,D,E,F,G legato by lifting one finger just an instant after one plays the next. In any case, the blur should be used only for special effects, and with utmost discretion.

It was the blur, of course, that caused Debussy to be called an Impressionist. Whenever the term was mentioned in his presence, however, he became irritated and would have nothing of it, claiming that, on the contrary, he descended from the French eighteenth-century harpsichordists.

With 'Poissons d'or' it was indeed difficult to satisfy Debussy. *'Jouez plus librement,'* he would repeat. I thought I did play with great freedom, but it was not enough. Then those initial accompaniment figures – they had to be lighter, almost immaterial, so one could hear 'two clarinets' up above. Toward the middle he spoke again: *'Plus gracieux, plus élégant.'* But when I complied, he said: *'Jouez plus simplement.'* I came to the conclusion that the interpretation of Ricardo

Viñes, to whom 'Poissons d'or' is dedicated, had become inseparable from his own conception; so I took it as a model and subsequently won approval.

It would be a mistake to believe that Debussy always spoke in terms of softness, elusive approach, two-pedal effects, etc. In the suite *Pour le piano*, for instance, it was another story. Here he demanded a totally different conception, one of robust precision. The same holds true for *L'isle joyeuse*, *Masques* and the study 'Pour les octaves,' to mention only a few. Some of his remarks regarding the 'Prélude' from the suite are in order here, because one often hears it played with disregard for its style. Debussy wanted the opening theme and its restatement later on in big chords played in time, with no rubato of any kind. He required that the glissando scales be brushed off in virtuoso manner and straight up to the final C, with a follow-through comparable to the gesture of a tennis player after a strong drive. 'D'Artagnan drawing his sword,' he commented with a smile, on one occasion. Further advice on those glissando scales: never play them to the B, then strike the C with another finger. It simply ruins the effect. The 'Sarabande' had to be played in the same style as the 'Hommage à Rameau', and the 'Toccata', fast, but not too fast. '*Il faut que cela reste clair*,' he said. Clarity was certainly one of his major preoccupations. Another was simplicity in expression. '*Pas d'affectation, surtout!*' No affectation, no mannerisms. Here once more one finds an echo from the great harpsichordists' creed, from the supreme good taste of Rameau, Couperin, Lully, Dandrieu, Chambonnières, Daquin and others.

At one time Debussy interested himself in pedagogy so much that he thought of writing a piano method of his own, because he considered those in existence unsatisfactory, uninspiring, tedious and mechanical. What a pity it was that the project did not materialize, and how much one could have learned from a practical exposition of his theories.

An amusing story comes to mind concerning Paderewski. The illustrious Pole once featured 'Reflets dans l'eau' on one of his programmes. Moved by curiosity, Debussy went to the recital. He was surprised when Paderewski played this piece daintily, with charm, with refinement, and with a pearly technique that would have better befitted a set of variations by Haydn or Mozart. 'It was delightful,' he said to Paderewski. 'Not at all what I had in mind. But please do not change an iota in your interpretation!'

Debussy seldom played in public. But when he did so, at the Société Nationale or the Concerts Durand, it was an excellent demonstration of his principles. Once at the Salle Erard he played several of his *Préludes*. As usual, an attendant raised the lid of the concert grand. But when Debussy came on, the first thing he did was to lower the lid. '*C'était pour mieux noyer le son*,' he said. Drown the tone . . . how wonderfully he did just that in 'La cathédrale engloutie'. It was truly unforgettable.

Although Debussy once played the entire *Children's Corner* at a festival of his works in Budapest, he never did so in Paris. Here are a few recollections of Debussy's comments on interpreting the *Children's Corner*:

'Doctor Gradus ad Parnassum'

'*Pas trop vite*' (not too fast), with a little humour aimed at good old Clementi. Faster and brilliant toward the end.

'Jimbo's Lullaby'

'*Jouez plus gauchement*' (more clumsily), for the first page. Emphasize the 'wrong' accents.

'Serenade for the Doll'

'*Délicat et gracieux*', with nothing of the passion of a Spanish serenader.

'The Snow is Dancing'

This is a mood picture as well as a tone picture. It must be '*brumeux, triste, monotone*' (misty, dreary, monotonous), and not too fast – not fast at all.

'The Little Shepherd'

Differentiate clearly between the improvisation of the shepherd on his flute and the dance motive.

'Golliwogg's Cakewalk'

The first and third sections '*très rythmé*', with a strong, sharp, rhythm. As a contrast, the middle part must be very free. There is a suggestion of the trombone in the part marked '*avec une grande émotion*'. Don't be afraid to overdo it here.

From time to time he spoke on relaxation; it was becoming a fad among pianists, and they carried it to the extreme. 'It is not advisable to use relaxation constantly,' he said. 'In pianissimo chords, for instance, the fingers must have a certain firmness, so the notes will sound together. But it must be the firmness of rubber, without any stiffness whatsoever.'

It has been noted that Debussy's pedal indications are extremely scarce. In fact, their presence in his list of compositions for the piano can be counted on the fingers of both hands. 'Pedalling cannot be written down,' he explained. 'It varies from one instrument to another, from one room, or one hall, to another.' So he left it to his interpreters: *'Faites confidence à votre oreille'* (entrust it to your ear), a remark that is not surprising from a musician whose aim had always been the pleasure of the ear as against rigid rules and pedagogic pedantry.

Maurice Dumesnil, 'Coaching with Debussy', *The Piano Teacher* (Evanston, USA), 5, September/October 1962, part 1, pp. 10–13.

GEORGE COPELAND

Punctually at eleven, we were shown into M. Debussy's salon. The room itself constituted my first surprise. It was very long, very formal, and very well kept, whereas I had expected to find myself in an entirely bohemian ménage. A moment later the door opened and I received a second shock.

As I have said before, I had entertained a preconceived notion of my host as being thin, nervous, effete, with the unhealthy look of the habitué of Paris night spots – and, most certainly, untidy and careless in matters of dress; in short, a typical denizen of Montmartre. To my amazement, I found myself rising to face a tall, dark, heavily built man, impeccably dressed, who gave the impression of relaxed, almost feline strength, and who had the most penetrating black eyes I have ever encountered – like two pieces of shiny black jet.

Señora d'Alvarez made the introductions: 'This, M. Debussy, is M. George Copeland, the pianist, who has introduced your beautiful music to America.'

'Vraiment!' was the laconic reply, and with a brief glance in my direction M. Debussy crossed the long length of the room and seated himself on a stiff green sofa at the far end. Apparently he was as undesirous of meeting me as I had been of meeting him; and although

he must have been aware of the fact through J. Durand, his publisher, he appeared completely indifferent as to whether his music was played in America or not.

As conversation at that distance was impossible, I suggested to Señora d'Alvarez that perhaps we should leave.

'Nonsense!' she retorted. 'You must play for him.'

'But he hasn't asked me to play,' I replied angrily. 'Perhaps he doesn't even wish to hear me.'

'Of course he does! Go and ask him,' Nina replied in an impatient whisper.

So I rose and, feeling as awkward as any schoolboy, crossed to where he was sitting bolt upright on the sofa. 'Would you like me to play for you, M. Debussy?' I asked cautiously.

The composer eyed me calmly. '*Mais oui*,' he replied. I waited, but there was no further comment.

'Shall I play you some Spanish music?' I asked, as this was one of the things I specialized in.

'Spanish music!' he exclaimed in surprise. '*Mais non!* Why should you play me Spanish music? It does not interest me at all.' Then, lowering his voice, as if thinking aloud, he continued: 'No, the only music that interests me is Bach's and my own. *Après tout*, Bach has said all that there is to say in music – the rest of us only say it in different forms!'

The piano, at the far end of the room, was draped with a silk scarf held in place by a heavy cloisonné vase. I asked permission to move the vase, so that I might open the piano cover.

'*Absolument non!*' he replied with obvious annoyance. 'Do not touch it! I never permit that anyone should open my piano. As it is, everyone plays my music too loud.'

Sensing the futility of argument, I seated myself and played through the shorter piano music – 'Reflets dans l'eau', 'La cathédrale engloutie', *Suite bergamasque*, *L'isle joyeuse*, 'Pagodes', 'Hommage à Rameau', 'Poissons d'or', 'Voiles', the 'Danse de Puck'.

M. Debussy had risen shortly after I began playing, and had seated himself close to the piano. When I came to the closing bars of 'Reflets dans l'eau', he got up from his chair in apparent excitement and, pointing a long finger, exclaimed: 'Why did you play the last two bars as you did?'

'I don't know – ' I was puzzled. 'Perhaps because that is the way I feel them.'

'It's funny,' he said reflectively, 'that's not the way I feel them.' But when I said, 'Then I will interpret them as you intended,' his reply was a definite 'No, no! Go on playing them just as you do.' He made no further comment until I had finished and had risen from the piano. Then, with an audible sigh, he said simply, 'I never pay compliments. I can only say that I have never dreamed that I would hear my music played like that in my lifetime.' In that brief moment, our relationship had undergone a sharp metamorphosis.

Señora d'Alvarez and I left almost immediately, but as I took my leave M. Debussy asked me to come again at eleven the following morning. In a daze I consented, and on reaching my hotel I immediately called the steamship line and cancelled my passage.

I remained in Paris, in close daily association with Claude Debussy, for the next four months.

Every morning I would arrive at the same hour, and we would spend the day together in almost elemental companionship, reading, or playing music – sometimes not exchanging a single word throughout an entire morning. If, in his reading, Debussy happened upon something provocative, or something which he thought would interest me, he would rise from his chair and point to it in silence. It was his belief that conversation was unnecessary unless there was something essential that one wanted to say. I did not miss the conventional chatter.

One of the basic factors in Claude Debussy's genius was, I think, his ability to eliminate the obvious, the unnecessary, and the trivial, and in this way to conserve much vitality. He was in no wise a misanthrope, for he was deeply attached to his friends, but he was not at all interested in the nature of man. He believed that only a few arrive at any sort of maturity, and he avoided the fool and the commonplace. He achieved in his music (with only a few exceptions) an almost complete elimination of personal equations, regarding himself (the musician) as a species of sounding board held up to nature. To this end, he had to keep himself free from interference; and he indubitably heard sounds that other people have never heard.

Debussy's study was an extremely simple room, containing one or two good pictures and those jade animals and pieces of Chinese pottery that were, apparently, his one personal extravagance, and about the acquisition of which his biographers have told many tales, real or invented. The room had a Pleyel upright piano, at which he worked on manuscripts which he was composing, as well as on those which required further polishing.

I spoke to him of my desire to transcribe some of his orchestral things for the piano – music which I felt to be essentially pianistic. He was at first sceptical, but finally he agreed, and was in complete accord with the result. He was particularly delighted with my piano version of *L'après-midi d'un faune*, agreeing with me that in the orchestral rendering, which called for different instruments, the continuity of the procession of episodes was disturbed. This has always seemed to me the loveliest, the most remote and essentially Debussyan, of all his music, possessing, as it does, a terrible antiquity, translating into sound a voluptuous sense that is in no wise physical.

Claude Debussy would, not infrequently, inject into some current discussion his reaction to, or estimation of, other composers. Among his contemporaries, he was most fond of d'Indy, Chausson and Ravel, although he thought the last of these too lush in his orchestrations. He admired César Franck greatly, describing him affectionately as 'a man without guile, and full of trustful candour'. Whatever Franck 'borrowed from Life', said Debussy, 'he restored to Art with modesty verging on self-effacement.'

Debussy spoke of Scarlatti as 'an inexcusably forgotten composer', whose *Passion of St John* he described as 'a little chef-d'œuvre of primitive refinement and beauty, in which the style of the choral music is seemingly of pale gold, like those lovely backgrounds to the profiles of the Virgins in the frescoes of his period'.

On the other hand, he ridiculed Grieg, whose music he described as 'a pink bon-bon stuffed with snow'; and of Saint-Saëns he exclaimed: 'I have a horror of sentimentality, and I cannot forget that its name is Saint-Saëns!'

Debussy liked Mozart, and he believed that Beethoven had terrifically profound things to say, but that he did not know how to say them, because he was imprisoned in a web of incessant restatement and of German aggressiveness.

He came to hate Wagner as much as he had first admired him, describing his music as 'strange, beautiful, seductive, and impure' – remarking of a performance of *Das Rheingold*, 'It took two hours, and

one hesitated between a desire to go away and the desire to go to sleep!'
Debussy himself wished to write an opera on the theme of Tristan and
Isolde, which would be in exact style variance with the Wagnerian
version. How much of this he completed, we do not as yet know.

Perhaps the composer whom he most admired, and upon whom, if
at all, he most consciously patterned his music, was Rameau, whose
genius, compounded of delicacy, charm, and restraint, he regarded as
being in the true French tradition. It is probable that Rameau opened
for him, if only a crack, the door which led to that other-dimensional
music of which Claude Debussy became the high priest, and which
he discovered and explored so extensively.

Musically, Debussy felt himself to be a kind of auditory 'sensitive'.
He not only heard sounds that no other ear was able to register, but
he found a way of expressing things that are not customarily said. He
had an almost fanatical conviction that a musical score does not begin
with the composer, but that it emerges out of space, through centuries
of time, passes before him, and goes on, fading into the distance (as
it came) with no sense of finality.

When I asked him why so few people were able to play his music,
Debussy replied, after some reflection: 'I think it is because they try
to impose themselves upon the music. It is necessary to abandon
yourself completely, and let the music do as it will with you – to be
a vessel through which it passes.'

George Copeland, 'Debussy, the man I knew', *The Atlantic Monthly*, January
1955, pp. 35–8.

E. ROBERT SCHMITZ

(1889–1949)

> Robert Schmitz was a French pianist whose later career
> was in the USA. As founder of the society Pro Musica,
> he was responsible for inviting to North America a number
> of important French musicians, including Ravel.

Debussy was not a careless, sensual pagan, drifting wherever the wind
of inspiration might blow him. He did not 'toss off' his pieces as a
diamond cutter might chip off a fleck of diamond dust. He did not

sit down at the piano, close his eyes, and compose a confused jumble
of notes. Rather, he was a typical Frenchman of the bourgeois class –
neat, precise, with a beautifully ordered mind and a habit of thinking
clearly about everything he did.

Even in his personal appearance, Debussy was methodically neat.
Fairly tall, he wore black suits which were always beautifully pressed.
His beard was well clipped, his hair combed. His necktie was always
kept correctly knotted. Without being dapper or elegant, he gave the
impression of being a well dressed, scrupulously clean person. Had
it not been for that strangely jutting forehead, which thrust itself
forward as though bulging with intellect and ideas, he resembled in
every sense a typical French merchant or professional man. He said
little, but what he said was well thought out and pertinent. His voice
was deep and quiet. He was polite, with the exquisite natural manners
of a Frenchman of good family. He was not a man to rant on a subject
or to mouth wild statements.

Everything about him had to be well ordered and perfect. His
house, surrounded by a garden, off the beaten path of the square du
Bois du Boulogne, was always quiet and smooth running. He seldom
entertained. It seemed almost as though he felt that a great many
visitors would have disturbed the ordered serenity of his home, so
necessary to his creative life.

His study, the 'sacred room of the house', was typical of its master.
It was not a large or a cluttered room, such as one is accustomed to
associate with a busy composer. Everything in it was carefully selected
and refined. In spite of the fact that he was a man of wide reading,
the books in his study did not number more than a hundred or so,
and these were only authors that Debussy had chosen as his particular
favourites – Rossetti, Maeterlinck, François Villon in an old edition,
Mallarmé. There was a small upright piano, in one corner between
the light high windows, a desk on which there were several small
carved wooden animals, a bowl of beautiful goldfish. The colours of
the room were subdued, the furnishings practical. Only a few precious
prints and watercolours adorned the walls.

Debussy was very particular about everything in this room. He
could not work properly if a picture hung crooked or one of the small
wooden animals on the desk were turned the wrong way. Perhaps best
illustrative of this trait is an incident now recalled. I was one day

accompanying Miss Maggie Teyte, the soprano, at the piano for a rehearsal. Debussy was standing near the instrument. Again and again he stopped us, saying, 'No, no, it is not right.' Although we were used to endless interruptions and corrections whenever Debussy rehearsed a piece, it seemed that he was exceptionally restless that morning. At last he stopped us for a long time and stood there in silence. We waited for him to give us the signal to start again; but instead, he stooped down and picked up a pin – a single straight pin – which was lying on the carpet, put it into a little box and stuck the box into his pocket. Then, with a relieved expression on his face, he motioned to us to go on. All was right again.

Debussy was as particular in his habits of work as he was in these peculiarities of his personal life. He wrote very slowly, and he never released anything to the publisher until he was sure of every note. The 'Passepied' to the *Suite bergamasque* he refused to release for months, just because the last four measures were not exactly right. This in spite of the fact that he had promised it to his publisher long before.

Time and again I have seen him look at a page of music, his head a little to one side, knowing something was wrong. He would not know just what. Then suddenly the idea, the remedy, would come to him. He would lean forward, his face lit up, and change – a single note. In my possession there are original editions of his *Préludes*, which, even though they were published, he still insisted upon correcting. In tiny handwriting, meticulous, in lavender ink, the corrections run all over those pages – illustrative of Debussy's restless desire for perfection.

The nuance, to Debussy, was everything. He loved miniatures for that reason. For over the miniature, small in its framework, he could expend infinite time and patience. He knew that great art takes time, and that the great artist must be patient. He never wrote a note of music until he had the entire conception in his mind.

Debussy had an ear that was ultrasensitive when someone else was interpreting his music. Once he came to one of the concerts I gave in Paris, when I was conducting the orchestra there. We played his *La damoiselle élue*. During the rehearsal an oboe played a wrong note. Debussy said nothing about it; but as soon as the rehearsal was over he came up on the stage and, picking up the score, felt through the pages, not looking at them. Then he put his finger down at random and, with the other hand, pointed to the oboe player.

'You played *that* wrong,' he said.

When I looked over his shoulder at the place on which his finger was resting, I found that it was on the very spot where the oboe player had made the mistake. Debussy knew even the feel of the pages of his score.

The only time I ever saw Debussy lose his temper completely was at another rehearsal – a rehearsal at the Théâtre des Champs-Elysées, where Nijinsky was preparing Debussy's new ballet, *Jeux*. Nijinsky had worked out the choreography for this ballet and had built it entirely around the idea of a tennis game. But Debussy had conceived the ballet as including all kinds of games. He had worked out different rhythms to represent these various games.

When he saw Nijinsky's proposed choreography for the first time, he was horrified. He wanted the choreography changed at once. But Nijinsky said it could not be done. So Debussy, furious over the misinterpretation of his music, demanded the score back. Nijinsky referred him to the conductor. Out to the orchestral pit went Debussy, almost raving over the way his idea had been spoiled, and demanding of the conductor that he be given back the score. He made so much interference, and Nijinsky was so annoyed by the interruption of his dance rehearsal, that he ordered down the iron curtain so that the stage would be separated from him and Debussy. Finally Debussy gave in. But he would not attend the performance of the ballet.

When I think of these things, I cannot help but feel annoyed at the careless, slipshod playing of Debussy that I hear around me. But these things are not all. I remember also the standard of piano playing which Debussy himself had, and which he taught me through years of training.

I met Debussy because I was accustomed to accompany the singers he used in *Pelléas et Mélisande*. From accompanying these singers I went on to performing many of his regular piano pieces. Not one of those pieces or accompaniments, however, did I ever play, without hours, even weeks, of labour, a ceaseless struggle on his part to make the thing perfect. I have worked under him for a week on a particular passage – perhaps only a measure or two. I have heard his annoyance over the slightest deviation from his ideas. I have seen him lean forward and correct, and correct, the music, define the phrasing of almost every note, so that it might be imprinted in my understanding.

Crescendos in those days were one of Debussy's obsessions in piano playing. He liked slight crescendos, a *ppp* increasing into a mere *pp*. Such tiny changes were meaningful and important to his art. So many pianists, who play Debussy today, overlook his crescendo markings. Seeing the sign, *ppp* then a crescendo, they seldom bother to look for the volume mark at the other end of that crescendo. Immediately they spurt out into an *fff*. It is such carelessness which makes so much of Debussy's music for piano sound jerky, heaving, rather than delicately flowing and wistful, sustained, the way it was originally intended by him to be.

Another thing Debussy insisted upon was the proper way to strike a note on the piano. 'It must be struck in a peculiar way,' he would say, 'otherwise the sympathetic vibrations of the other notes will not be heard quivering distantly in the air.'

Debussy regarded the piano as the Balinese musicians regard their gamelan orchestras. He was interested not so much in the single tone that was obviously heard when a note was struck, as in the patterns of resonance which that tone set up around itself. Many of his pieces are built entirely on this acoustical sense of the piano. Played badly, without a consciousness of the fine, almost inaudible, background of overtones, they are mere skeletons. The warm, indefinable, sensitive, inner beauty – the real quality of Debussy – is totally lacking.

One cannot make up for this bareness by thick, gushy pedalling. One cannot substitute for this exquisite and evocative charm, double tempos, hasty phrases, or erratic interpretations. *One must learn to play Debussy's music as he played it himself*, striking each note as though it were a bell, listening always for the hovering clusters of vibrating overtones above and below it.

E. Robert Schmitz, 'A Plea for the Real Debussy', *The Etude*, December 1937, pp. 781–2

ALFREDO CASELLA

While I was still in Paris, I thought of giving a concert for the benefit of the Italian Red Cross. I asked Debussy to take part. He had been in Rome a few months earlier and had brought back a particularly grateful memory of the Augusteo and the unusually great orchestral preparation Molinari had given to his concert. He was enthusiastic about the action of Italy and agreed at once to my suggestion. We decided to play *Ibéria* on two pianos. He said that this transcription, well performed, gave him as much satisfaction as the orchestral original. For our rehearsals, he had the Bechstein upright moved from his studio into the living room, beside the grand piano. We spent a whole week not only rehearsing *Ibéria* but also amusing ourselves by reading much two piano music – Bach, Mozart, Chabrier, and several symphonic poems of Liszt. Debussy enjoyed these sessions a great deal, and they left with me one of the deepest and most ineradicable impressions of my life.

Alfredo Casella, *Music in My Time: The Memoirs of Alfredo Casella*, tr. and ed. Spencer Norton (Oklahoma, 1955), p. 126 [*I segreti della giara* (Florence, 1941)]

MARGUERITE LONG
(1878–1966)

Marguerite Long was born in Nîmes and studied the piano with the younger Marmontel at the Conservatoire. She herself was appointed Professor of Piano there in 1920.

One often finds in Debussy's music simple landscapes, descriptive poetry in which tenderness, humour and gravity are disconcertingly intermingled. How can such original and refined ideas be translated? The virtuoso pianists did not comprehend, and nothing that I heard satisfied me. Their various interpretations simply emphasized the gulf that separated them from the composer; when Debussy played his music it was marvellous, incomparable. I just did not understand.

I myself had played nearly all the great French piano works, some for the first time. That his were always absent from my programmes annoyed Debussy, and I knew it. Now and then, as if by chance, he would let escape, 'You don't like what I do?', or something like that. Then one day he suddenly asked, 'You don't want to play my music?'

'You are mistaken. On the contrary, I admire it too much. But it is too difficult.'

'Difficult? But it is child's play for you!'

'Oh, the notes, yes.' I went on, 'I feel the same perturbation as when I heard *Pelléas*, but now before a new art of the pianoforte – and as an interpreter I feel it impossible to approach your thought, even from afar. I am, as it were, up against a wall.'

'Suppose I made you work at it – really work?'

'Oh, then!'

In order to encourage this enthusiasm Debussy promised me his collaboration for a charity concert which I was to give in May 1914, in the hall of the Conservatoire. Rose Féart was to perform one of his *Chansons* and I was to play three concertos with orchestra. I had faced this kind of concert before. Such a programme was rare at that time, but was to become the touchstone of a career.

That evening Camille Chevillard conducted Fauré's *Ballade*, Saint-Saëns's Third Concerto and Vincent d'Indy's *Symphonie sur un chant montagnard français*, in all of which I was the soloist. Debussy came as he had promised and accompanied the *Chansons* on the piano. His personal magnetism shed a halo on those marvellous songs, which included 'Le promenoir des deux amants' and, in particular 'Crois mon conseil, chère Climène'; perhaps the inclusion of the latter was meant as a hint that my initiation was about to begin! Without delay, extremely flattered that he had chosen me from so many others, I set to work on the programme he had designed for me.

At the end of June 1914, as with everything, music felt the international political tension. On 28 June the disastrous assassination of the Archduke Ferdinand occurred at Sarajevo. War immediately threatened Europe and perhaps the whole world. In the midst of this tragedy I was seized with anxiety for my husband, who was a captain in the infantry. For the enlisted, for the civilians, for all the youth of France, what reprieve could there be?

For a month Paris lived more intensely than ever before. The day after the Serbian outrage the last pre-summer season performance of *Pelléas* was given at the Opéra-Comique. We decided to go. Pelléas sang,

> Do you hear the wild sea?
> It is the wind rising.

> Let us find our way down.
> Will you place your hand here in mine?
> One would embark without knowing and one would
> return no more.

The music revived unforgettable days, yet exuded mystery and anguish. Did *Pelléas*, which had meant for us freedom and an escape from the Wagnerian fire, now foreshadow real drama? Would art survive the destruction to come?

In the interval my husband left our box. 'I met Debussy in the corridor,' he said on his return. And in answer to my mute interrogation he replied simply, 'What could I say to him?'

Beauty and emotion are at times inexpressible. My husband's silence that night later helped me to convince Debussy of our admiration. Strange as it may seem, the composer of *Le martyre de Saint Sébastien*, hearing me once describe the work of another composer as 'beautiful', thought aloud bitterly: 'No one has ever said that to me – it is beautiful.'

At first I was dumbfounded, then realized that, despite his fame, Debussy's sensitivity was vulnerable. I was able to explain to him that sometimes the emotion caused by response to beauty can only remain silent.

In his music Debussy had often evoked Sundays, ever days of poignant memories: *Dimanche sur les villes, Dimanche dans les cœurs, Je suis née un dimanche, un dimanche à midi*. On two sultry Sundays in July 1914 I went to his house with the programme that we had settled on together. He was happy, but I was trembling.

'Play me first *L'isle joyeuse*,' he said. 'I am curious to know what an artist like you will do with it.'

For a moment I looked at the quiet keyboard and at his hands – hands which could do all he wished, the hands of a magician. I would have given ten years of my life for him to have taught me his secret and the interpretation of such a work.

'Oh, I am not going to play it. Don't expect a performance. You will sit next to me – and after the second bar you will stop me.'

He burst out laughing, and we went on working all day.

Those summer months of 1917 could be regarded as the gift of Providence in permitting so great a love of life to a man as ill as was

Debussy. 'Do you hear the sea?' he said to me. 'To be face to face with the splendour of the ocean, that is music itself.' His courage in suffering was a continuing, purposeful example. There was alleviation in music for both of us, and little by little this was to become my sole reason for living.

If Debussy did not go into all his works, he certainly initiated me into their style. The time I spent was unforgettable, as much on the purely pianistic plane as for the affection of himself and of his family, which was a great comfort to me in my loss. We talked, and I played both his music and that of other composers in which he had a special interest. Of the great masters those he admired most were Bach, Liszt and Chopin – especially Chopin, of whose music he never tired. He was, as it were, impregnated by that composer's work, and through his own appreciation tried to convey all that he thought proceeded from the great Polish master.

For three months that summer I did not leave the piano, but the experience and the benefits of daily contact were immensely enriching.

In his journal Eugène Delacroix writes: 'There are no details in Chopin's playing that are negligible.' Debussy underlined his great musical ideas with unbelievably minute precision. Thus he would say, 'Four semiquavers mean 4 ♩. The hands are not meant to hover in the air over the piano, but to enter into it.'

One day Debussy stared at me, his eyes clear and shining. 'The fifth finger of virtuosi, what a pest it is!' What he meant by that is that too often one hammers the melody without attaching sufficient importance to the whole harmony; harmony that, according to him, should never be sacrificed to the melodic idea. Harmony is intimately allied with melody, which in general is a kind of shaded relief. 'One must forget that the piano has hammers,' was one of his most frequent sayings.

Chopin used to speak in this way to his pupils, one of whom, Mme Mauté de Fleurville, became the first of Debussy's teachers. It was she who taught him the attack and the mellowness which he in turn demanded of his interpreters.

Debussy has left us all the indications possible for the execution of his work. He regarded this with the utmost care, and at times was almost fierce about it. I often heard him tell – somewhat angrily –

this story. A pianist once came to play to him some of his pieces. He stopped at a certain passage and said: 'Master, according to me this should be "free".' Recalling this, Debussy would say: 'There are some who write music, some who edit it, and there is that gentleman who does what he pleases.' I asked him what he had said at the time. Scornfully he remarked: 'Oh, nothing. I looked at the carpet, but he will never tread on it again.'

Ravel, who was also always so concerned about his own intentions, often made me recount this tale. It illustrates the same intransigent attitude that, when Debussy was offered an artist of genius to sing the part of Mélisande, made him reply: 'A faithful interpreter is sufficient.'

The following scene proves the degree to which he insisted that the integrity of his thought be respected. One hot morning I arrived as usual at the chalet for breakfast and to pass the day working there; Debussy stood before me in full glare of the sun.

'You realize?'

I gave a start, not knowing what he meant.

'You know that G sharp must be played *piano*. I have been thinking about it all night long.'

I did not understand, and he was bewildered at my lack of comprehension.

Then I said timidly: 'But, my dear master, I am confused. Excuse me, but I don't know which G sharp is in question. Where? What?'

It was a G sharp in 'Mouvement', the third of the first series of *Images*. Debussy had merely changed the shading of a chord.

I have already said how, one day during the last summer of Saint-Jean-de-Luz, I accompanied him on one of his walks. When we reached the cliff he pressed my arm. 'The sea, do you hear it? The sea – there is nothing so musical. All that one could wish for in the way of music.'

Then, suddenly changing the subject: 'Tomorrow we must work at 'Général Lavine'. That "wooden man" was a genius. He was musical.'

Debussy was not talking nonsense. 'Général Lavine, eccentric', was inspired by a clown, a sort of beginning-of-the-century Grock, in the Médrano Circus. This equilibrist, this 'wooden man' masked an over-sensitive heart with drolleries and pirouettes. Debussy's evocation of the clown portrays unconsciously the varied moods of the composer himself.

Now that I was seeing nearer to Debussy, tenderness and irony appeared as distinctive traits. There was also a sharp streak of cynicism. This was reduced by close friendship, age and illness, but in his youth he must have used it as a defence against life, as Général Lavine did his clowning.

Debussy was an incomparable pianist. How could one forget his suppleness, the caress of his touch? While floating over the keys with a curiously penetrating gentleness, he could achieve an extraordinary power of expression. There lay his secret, the pianistic enigma of his music. There lay Debussy's individual technique; gentleness in a continuous pressure gave the colour that only he could get from his piano. He played mostly in half-tint but, like Chopin, without any hardness of attack. Fully preoccupied with Chopin's method, particularly Chopin's phrasing, he liked to say he wore out his fingers on the posthumous *Etude* in A flat of the Polish master, whom he ranked with Bach and Liszt. His nuances ranged from a triple *pianissimo* to *forte* without ever becoming disordered in sonorities in which harmonic subtleties might be lost. Like Chopin he considered the art of the pedal as a 'sort of breathing'. He had noted the details of this technique in Liszt's playing when he heard him in Rome.

Some time in 1917 Debussy went to hear the suite *Pour le piano* played by a famous pianist.

'How was it?' I asked him on his return.

'Dreadful. He didn't miss a note.'

'But you ought to be satisfied. You who insist on the infallible precision of every note.'

'Oh, not like that.' Then emphatically, '*Not* like that.'

How paradoxical! How difficult to please! At times I recall some of his blistering comments on even the best known of virtuosi, such as: 'He grated like a rope in a well!' or 'He plays like a water-carrier!'

And yet, how gentle he was during all our work together: work which initiated me into the secret of so many masterpieces.

At Saint-Jean-de-Luz Debussy was continually harassed by fatigue and illness, but he displayed infinite courage. 'There are', he said, 'mornings when simply getting dressed seems like one of the twelve labours of Hercules; and I await something – I know not what, a revolution, an earthquake – which will prevent my having to make the effort of doing it.'

Yet Debussy always dressed himself and went down to breakfast with his family. Almost every day I joined them before our work session at the Chalet Habas. That house, at least, cheered him up: 'It is Basque and has a pergola and a view of modest mountains.' The comfort of the place had an English character because of the nationality of the proprietor, Colonel Nicoll. 'I expect to see S. Pickwick Esq. coming down the stairs,' Debussy joked.

Sometimes, when relaxing and chatting with me, he let fly his irony on people he could well have spared. For instance, he murmured one day: 'I detest the concertos of Mozart,' adding, 'but less than those of Beethoven.'

I felt the importance that Debussy assigned to the two books of *Études* as much as he did. They are not well enough recognized by people in the pianoforte world but they ought to take their place alongside Chopin's immortal *Etudes*. Debussy once thought of dedicating this work to the memory of Couperin, but he changed his mind, choosing instead Chopin, whom he revered so highly.

It is for this reason that at the last Marguerite Long–Jacques Thibaud Concours Internationale the *Etudes* of Debussy figured on the programme in addition to those of Liszt and Chopin. 'Chopin is the greatest of all,' he used to repeat. 'For with the piano alone he discovered everything.'

Thus the illustrious musician delved into the past in the same way as he did into the future. He passed even the negative aspects of a performance through his mental sieve. 'You know my opinion on the metronome marks,' he wrote. 'They are as proper in a bar as are the roses in the space of a morning.' What caused me much amusement was to see how often the composer contradicted himself. How often he said, 'To the metronome: to the metronome!' Yet 'only imbeciles never change their mind', said M. de Talleyrand. The following anecdote bears witness.

In the *Etudes* the omission of fingering, in which Debussy usually believed, is remarked on in the Preface. The player may make his own decisions. 'One is never so well served as by oneself.' Yet in 'Pour les huit doigts', the last study in Book I, Debussy stated that 'the changing position of the hand makes the use of the thumbs

awkward. Its execution would become acrobatic.' Temptation, however, became too strong for me and, as I found the effect of using the
thumbs satisfactory, I hastened to disobey. ('Let us find our own
fingering', said the Preface.) Confronted with the success of this *fait
accompli* the composer could only applaud. He thereupon decided to
authorize the use of the thumbs.

Marguerite Long, *At the Piano with Debussy*, tr. Olive Senior-Ellis (London,
1972), pp. 6–9, 12–15, 19, 24, 36, 44–5

JANE BATHORI

(1877–1970)

Jane Bathori, whose real name was Jeanne-Marie Berthier,
was a French soprano who specialized in contemporary
music. She gave the first performance of Debussy's three
songs entitled *Le promenoir des deux amants* on 14 January
1911, accompanied by Ricardo Viñes. Four years earlier
Ravel had accompanied her in the first performance of his
Histoires naturelles.

I had the great good fortune to get to know Debussy in 1904. He
lived then at 58 rue Cardinet, and I went to ask him to listen to me.
I played him a few piano solos and sang his *Mandoline* to my own
accompaniment. He stopped me after the very first few bars and said
'It should go twice as fast.' Then I sang to him the *Chansons de Bilitis*.
It was a joy to work with him. His sharpened sense of the French
language and the most subtle accents, to give the most accurate
expression, helped one to achieve this oneself. When I had got to the
end of 'La chevelure' he said to me, 'Above all, no romantic shudder.'

He united in himself the qualities which I value most in music –
elegance, refinement, wit and variety – and he had a natural good taste
which drew him to beautiful things. Raymond Bonheur, who had
sometimes spent his holidays with Debussy, told me that his choice
always fell on works of value, and this did not come from the culture
with which he had been inculcated – it was within himself. He loved
to surround himself with beautiful things and this corresponded to the
very essence of his music. The little Copenhagen cat which I saw on

his piano in 1904 gave place later to the enormous turquoise toad which he used to call Arkel. Anything refined, delicate, complex or strange attracted him. It was for this reason that he was enthusiastic about the new style pre-Raphaelites, and the Nocturnes of Whistler enchanted him.

Debussy did not like accompanying in public. He gave nervousness as a pretext, which he said made his legs tremble so that he was deprived of all his wits. I think this excuse was mostly to avoid the too numerous importunates, and to keep his time free. Nevertheless, I met him one afternoon in the beautiful property in Boulogne, on the banks of the Seine, which belonged to Otto Kahn and which was called the 'Maison du tour du monde'. It sheltered students who had completed their studies. Debussy had gone there to visit the Japanese garden which interested him enormously. That day the company was brilliant; I was asked to sing extempore, Debussy sat at the piano and accompanied me in the *Chansons de Bilitis* with natural and charming simplicity.

Jane Bathori, 'Les musiciens que j'ai connus: II, Debussy', *Recorded Sound*, I, no. 6, Spring 1962, pp. 176, 178, 179; lecture given at the National Sound Archive (then the British Institute of Recorded Sound) on 25 October 1961, tr. Felix Aprahamian.

MAGGIE TEYTE

Did he frighten you with his bad temper?
Oh no. You see, I was too English – I was always quite cold and took no notice! And I also knew my work. I was always on my toes, ready for anything, and he had no real cause to find fault with *me*. But he behaved dreadfully towards other people. I remember one day that a very well-known accompanist came to his home to rehearse some of his songs with me. This poor man had only played one bar when Debussy rounded on him and almost knocked him off the piano stool. He was white with inward rage, and only after he had explained how he wanted this opening bar played did his anger evaporate.

Another occasion I recall is a concert at which Debussy was to accompany me in some of his songs after a performance of his Quartet. While we were waiting in the artists' room, listening to the playing of the distinguished quartet, I noticed Debussy beginning to work

himself up into one of his rages. Eventually the music came to its
end, and the leader of the quartet came into the room. 'How did you
like it, Maître?' he asked – only to be told by the furious composer:
'You played like a pig!'

Now the French, who want us all to believe that Debussy was the
most perfect gentleman of the age, won't accept this impression of
their national genius. But it is true. His bad temper doesn't make
Debussy any less of a genius, but he *did* have these flashes of tremen-
dous rage, and he *was* a quiet, brooding man.

Had he any other particular mannerisms that you recall?
He was fanatically tidy and precise in everything he did. His love of
precision, of course, is reflected in his music – in every note of it.
He was precise and pedantic to the *n*th degree. I remember one day
when he sat at the piano preparing to rehearse me in one of his songs.
He was just about to place his hands on the keys when he happened
to spot a piece of cotton thread on the carpet. Very slowly he took his
hands from the keyboard, very slowly he bent down to pick up the
offending piece of thread. Then, with great deliberation, he twisted
it up into a tiny little ball and began looking all round for somewhere
to put it out of the way. At last, after several minutes that seemed like
hours to me as I stood waiting to sing, he realized there was nowhere
but on the piano to put it. Gently he placed it on the piano – and
began the song.

Was he a good accompanist?
Oh yes, he was splendid – perfect. My test of a good accompanist is
that you aren't aware of him. When you can hear the accompanist
something is wrong. With Debussy, as I found again with Cortot in
later years, there was such perfect rapport between us that I never
gave a thought to his playing.

Was he a good teacher?
I can only speak of him as a teacher of his own music, of course, but in
that he was magnificent. He taught me how to sing Mélisande 'as he
wanted her', and fortunately we had the same conception. He rarely found
fault with my interpretation or musical handling of the part, but
would ask me to sing a passage more softly perhaps, or more quickly.

Maggie Teyte, 'Memories of Debussy' (in interview with Frank Granville
Barker), *Music and Musicians*, August 1962, p. 16

NINON VALLIN

(1886–1961)

Ninon Vallin was one of the most famous, and best, French sopranos of the first half of this century. After studying at the Lyons Conservatoire, she sang the part of the virgin Erigone at the première of *Le martyre de Saint Sébastien* in 1911. Two years later Debussy wrote of her voice that it 'understands the curves that the music describes through the words . . . it's utterly beautiful and very simple'. On 21 March 1914, he accompanied her in the first performance of his *Trois poèmes de Stéphane Mallarmé*.

In meetings with him, his habit of holding himself fenced off, his tense, abrupt gestures and the very tone of his voice used to frighten me – at the time, I was a little provincial girl and he was at the height of his fame. It was difficult to satisfy him, he was very demanding. 'Slowly' had to be executed slowly; he didn't want 'with life' and 'cheerfully' turned into 'quickly'. The numerous expression marks which he introduced into his text had to be observed with complete punctiliousness. Nuances, accents, pauses, changes of tempo, sudden 'pianos', all the things which are so characteristic of Debussy's writing, none of them could be glossed over. His keen, sensitive ear suffered, and at the slightest mistake he would jump up from his chair. He used to say to me: 'Before putting in an accent or a nuance, I sometimes brood over it for several days, thinking about the precious words which form the texts of my songs.'

The duplets and triplets which so often feature in the melodic line of Debussy's songs, and which are nearly always opposed to the rhythmical movement of the accompaniment, had to be perfectly balanced. He hardly ever made any remarks, he only insisted that the performer should look closely at what he had written. He liked to have his little daughter present at all the lessons he gave me.

'Listen, Chouchou, listen, that is how your father's songs should be performed.'

Ninon Vallin, 'O Klod Debyussi', *Sovetskaya Muzyka*, January 1936, 4/1, pp. 61–3, tr. Henry Thompson.

FRANÇOIS GILLET

François Gillet was the first oboist of the Lamoureux
Orchestra for the first performance of *La mer* on 15 October 1905, conducted by Camille Chevillard. Gillet
recalled later that during one of the rehearsals Debussy
said to the conductor . . .

. . . '*un peu plus vite ici*' . . . So Chevillard said: *Mon cher ami,*
yesterday you gave me the tempo we have just played.' Debussy looked
at him with intense reflection in his eyes and said: 'But I *don't feel*
music the *same way every day.*'

François Gillet, letter of 17 March 1974 to Marie Rolf (reproduced by kind
permission of Dr Rolf)

DESIRE-EMILE INGHELBRECHT
(1880–1965)

D.-E. Inghelbrecht began his career as a conductor in
Paris in 1908 and was chorus-master at the première of
Le martyre de Saint Sébastien in 1911. He later conducted
the Ballets Suédois and directed both Paris opera houses
in turn. In 1931 he founded the French National Radio
Orchestra.

Orchestral musicians are by turns ashamed and presumptuous about
their job and excessively touchy about how it is described. Debussy
used to tell a story from the time when 'he did not weigh heavily in
the opinion of his interpreters'. One day, at the start of a rehearsal,
he remarked that a musician was missing. Immediately, from the pit,
came the stern reprimand: 'Here, Monsieur, there are no musicians,
only artists!' To which Debussy replied: 'That's strange, I didn't intend
to cause offence. I'm always so flattered when anyone calls me a
musician!'

Désiré-Emile Inghelbrecht, *Diabolus in Musica* (Paris, 1933), p. 156

In ten years my acquaintance with Debussy had amounted to a casual
introduction and one brief meeting, and it was only when we began

to work together on the first performance of *Le martyre de Saint Sébastien* that we got to know each other better.

The following year saw the foundation of the Théâtre des Champs-Elysées. At the inaugural concert, Debussy had conducted *L'après-midi d'un faune* and we were shortly to give the *Nocturnes* with dancing devised by Loïe Fuller.

One evening, the young conductor and the orchestra were at work, when suddenly the door opened and the composer came in.

'Why didn't you call me earlier?'

'I didn't want to disturb you just for a read-through . . .'

'But I've made any number of changes in this score which you must take account of before you go any further.' That was before the final version was published. 'What's more, you've already played another work of mine here without inviting me to come and hear it . . .'

This was the *Marche écossaise*, which had constituted music's revenge in a concert given by a well-known acrobat on the violin. I confessed not having dared to impose the rest of the programme on him, and he added, in somewhat melancholy fashion: 'You see, my dear boy, I've never heard it.' That was in 1913, and the *Marche écossaise* was written in 1891! In those days, great composers learnt how to wait. The rehearsal of the *Nocturnes* was interrupted on the spot, and the unknown work played to its composer, who was deeply touched and said: 'But it's a pretty piece!'

A few weeks later the ice was broken and Debussy felt at home in this house of music where everyone now had the courage to reveal to Debussy their enthusiasm. Loïe Fuller had more courage than anybody. One day she went up to *her* composer and confided in him mysteriously: 'If only you knew, Mister Debioussy! If only you knew how the children love the miousic of the *Noctiurns* . . . Come with me, please . . .' And opening the door of the main dancing area where, in a mêlée of multicoloured taffeta, sirens and clouds were devouring sandwiches and oranges, Loïe cried out imperiously: 'Children! Mister Debioussy!' And the children began to sing in their little piping voices the song of the sirens:

la la — la la la la — la la   la la la la la la la la

We had got into the habit of playing Chabrier's *Ode à la musique* at the start of every season. After the brief holiday following the inauguration of the theatre, the first concert, given over almost entirely to Debussy's music, therefore began with 'the charming chorus of young ladies' voices'. During rehearsals, Debussy listened attentively from the body of the auditorium. Bit by bit we saw him come to life, then he got up and came towards the orchestra, singing as though unconsciously, with that interior voice he had at such moments, and which was so moving. Finally he spoke, the words came thick and fast and his suggestions multiplied to the point that he was lifted on to another plane, and he became the one person whom players and singers were following, by tacit and general agreement . . . A moment later, in the cosy office where he would spend rehearsal breaks, he apologized in confusion 'for his indiscretion'.

At this same concert he was himself to conduct *Ibéria*. The score had benefited from thirty rehearsals, and Debussy was kind enough to say: 'I can assure you that if your players didn't stop of their own accord, I would not be the one to control them!' As the player whose job it was to strike the bells had not done so to the composer's satisfaction at the early rehearsals, I went and stood with him to show him how they should go. Came the day of the concert, I was happy that all was well and looking forward to going at last to hear *Ibéria* from the auditorium, when Debussy stopped me and said in an anguished voice: 'Oh no, don't go . . . I've got used to seeing your little head up there . . .'

Then came the outbreak of war. To begin with, we tried to re-form the orchestra and chorus of the theatre, at least those who had not yet been called up, so as to break the silence into which music had been plunged. Debussy joined us, at the Palais de Glace, to hear once again the *Ode à la musique* signalling a new venture. But this enterprise did not last either, and the few concerts we were allowed to give for the wounded were the last orchestral music Debussy was to enjoy. We built the programmes together, and it is impossible to forget his enthusiasm for Lalo's *Namouna* and the hunting horns, with bells upwards, in the 'Parade de foire'.

Désiré-Emile Inghelbrecht, *Mouvement contraire* (Paris, 1947), p. 185; (with his wife Germaine) *Claude Debussy* (Paris, 1953), pp. 229–31, 233–4

PIERRE MONTEUX
(1875–1964)

Pierre Monteux studied violin and composition at the Paris Conservatoire and played the viola at the première of *Pelléas*. His long career as an international conductor was launched by Diaghilev who asked him to conduct for the Ballets Russes, including the first performance of *Daphnis et Chloé*, *Jeux* and the *Sacre du printemps*.

Debussy was behind me when we played *L'après-midi d'un faune* for the Russian Ballet, because he did not want anything in his score to be changed on account of the dancing. And when we came to a *forte*, he said: 'Monteux, that is a *forte*, play *forte!*' He did not want anything *shimmering*. And he wanted everything exactly in time.

Pierre Monteux, interview with John Amis, BBC, 28 June 1961

VI
At home

Debussy lived with his first wife, Lily Texier, until 1904 when he abandoned her for the amateur singer Emma Bardac. He and Emma moved to 80, avenue du Bois de Boulogne (now avenue Foch) in the autumn of 1904, and she gave birth to Debussy's daughter Claude-Emma (Chouchou) on 30 October 1905. They were married on 20 January 1908.

LOUIS LALOY

(1874–1944)

Critic and musicologist, Louis Laloy was editor of the *Mercure Musical*, and in 1914 he became secretary-general of the Opéra, in which capacity after the war he was the butt of Satie's gibes. He was interested in Far Eastern culture and wrote a book on Chinese music. The meeting described below took place at the end of 1902, shortly after Laloy had published an article on the first four bars of *Pelléas*. Laloy was Debussy's first biographer.

It was not without some apprehension that I first climbed a rather dark staircase at no. 58 rue Cardinet, where he was living at that time in a little apartment on the fifth floor. His study was on the right of the dining-room; the table in front of the window, an upright piano in Brazilian rosewood further away from the door. A little later, the firm of Pleyel, who were always generous towards artists, offered him a fine instrument in mahogany, which he showed me and played to me delightedly. The visitor's armchair was on the left and almost opposite his. It was there that he sat me down and, lowering his head slightly to avoid my protestations, began to congratulate me. I felt immediately at my ease, first of all because of his sinuous face which reminded me of the calm courtesy of the Far East, and especially because I sensed in him a wariness, exactly like mine, about not being too abrupt with a stranger and not offering any opinion unless he was certain it would be understood.

He spoke clearly in a low voice, either in short phrases or in a long burst and, without ever searching for words, would suddenly come up with a marvellous image. His mind was that of a poet. I don't know whether, as some of his old friends have said, during his years at the Conservatoire he was entirely ignorant of literature. But what is certain is that in the interim he had outshone everyone in making up for lost time. It was not just luck which, on his return from Rome, prompted him alone among his friends to search out the élite among the writers – to consult Henri de Régnier, for example, (who told me about it later) on the subject of his own words for *Proses lyriques*, when Catulle Mendès was there, quite ready to give advice. There was no luck either connected with his frequent attendance at Mallarmé's salon, where the vulgar mob were not admitted and where, I believe, no other composer was ever seen.

Soon, at his request, I got into the habit of coming to see him practically every week, on a Saturday afternoon, when we would be alone. But it was not only my taste which allied me with Debussy. Although our two lives were very far apart from each other, both in the events that filled them and in the resultant emotions, we found it easy to communicate not those emotions themselves, but their deeper resonances, which were in harmony. In this way we exchanged not confidences so much as reflections, silently prolonged, while each of us applied them to our own particular case, and from that would spring a remark which united us once more.

We had no compunction either, when in a different mood, about dispelling serious thoughts and pronouncing in unison on the news of the day, the ridiculous behaviour of one of our acquaintances or our favourite tobacco. Sometimes he would leave the house with me to go to a nearby *pâtisserie* and treat himself to a cake for dessert at dinner-time. He was made for an opulent life and all his life he had been struggling in a poverty from which he did not expect to escape. I could see that it made him suffer, but he put a good face on it and there were even times when he professed himself perfectly happy. I was entirely of the same mind and I think he was grateful to me for that.

'I went to Bayreuth like everyone else,' he used to say to me, 'and I wept my fill at *Parsifal*. But when I came back I got to know *Boris Godunov*, which cured me.' Even so, Mussorgsky could not entirely satisfy an artist who set such store by purity of style and balance of proportions. 'It's never properly finished,' he would say, with a touch of chagrin. But he found in *Boris* an example of music which was brimful of feeling, both in the simple, popular airs, and in the recitative which followed the word stresses without ceasing to be sung. He came to hate Wagner for his emphasis and the indiscreetness of his disputatious heroes who, not content with proclaiming their passion, plead its cause and defend it using precedents from legend, moral precepts and cosmogonical arguments. Debussy hated quibbling and this parading of motives seemed to him infamous. 'Just look', he used to say to me, 'at the contemptible, cowardly way in which Wagner's characters suffer.'

The only occasion when I called to find Debussy not at home, the door was opened to me by a slim, pale young woman,* with her hair in *bandeaux*, as the fashion then was. She seemed nervous and anxious for me to leave; which I did, without waiting for Debussy's return, though that was imminent.

Later, he spoke of her to me with affection, only complaining that they had no children. I remember my reply – 'You mustn't give up hope' – which the closeness of our friendship permitted, and which he received with a smile. And, in response maybe to an objection which I did not put into words, he added that he was happy as he was, having a part of the house where he could be free and on his own, while the rest of his life was secure.

I came back and a few days later, as a mark of the further progress of our friendship, he invited me to lunch. I was their only guest, and both of them jokingly made me admire their earthenware plates, which they had deliberately cracked in the stove to make them look artistic.

Louis Laloy, *La musique retrouvée* (Paris, 1928), pp. 119–21, 123–4, 132–3, 139–40)

RICARDO VIÑES

(1875–1943)

Ricardo Viñes studied piano first at the Municipal School of Music in Barcelona and then at the Conservatoire, where he made friends with Ravel. He gave many first performances of works by Debussy, Ravel, Satie, Falla and Albéniz. His diary mentions a number of meetings with Debussy, both musical and social.

Saturday, 4 July 1903

I went to Debussy's and he again played me his latest pieces, *Pour le piano*, which he will send me a copy of at the end of the month. By chance, I said that these pieces made me think of Turner's pictures

*Lily

and he replied that in fact, before writing them, he had spent a long time in the Turner room in London!

Saturday, 3 February 1906

At 3 o'clock in the afternoon I went to Debussy's to let him hear the *Images*, which I played several times, and he also; he must have been pleased because he called his present wife [Mme Bardac]. Then they asked me to introduce them to Ravel's *Miroirs*, which I did.

Tuesday, 26 November 1907

I had dinner with Debussy. I arrived first and had a long talk with him. Then Louis Laloy and his wife arrived and we had dinner. We stayed until 1 o'clock in the morning, talking mostly about the Schola Cantorum and the damage done by the mediocrities who run it.

Tuesday, 23 January 1912

I went to dinner with Debussy, together with the Laloys and Mme Charpentier. Naturally, there was no music-making and we hardly talked about it, as happens among *real* artists (by which I mean that they are the ones who have least to say about their art). Debussy and his wife grumbled that I so rarely go and see them; they're very sympathetic towards me. We talked of the Chinese and their revolution.

Tuesday, 12 March 1912

In the evening, the third Durand concert in the Salle Erard, at which I played the first set of Debussy's *Images*. It was such a success that I had to play an encore; I chose 'La soirée dans Grenade', which I hadn't played since the first Durand concert a fortnight ago. I wasn't very happy about it, especially since I knew Debussy was there in a box and he never finds this piece played as he wants it.

Ricardo Viñes, diary entries, in: *Revue Internationale de Musique Française*, 1/2, June 1980, pp. 226, 229–30, 232–3

Debussy was a little bit frightening, with his magnificently ugly face and his curious, clumsily sculpted overhanging forehead (rather like Verlaine's). From the shadows of this forehead, two immense, catlike eyes kept watch, casting ironic and ambiguous looks. The whole effect suggested the romantic image of a *condottiere* or even, if I may say so, of a proud Calabrian bandit. Debussy himself was neither pompous nor austere. At times he could enjoy himself in quite childish ways. I remember on one occasion, after dinner, we spent the whole evening, with two other guests, drawing pigs with our eyes closed, and being allowed to take the pencil off the paper only once, to make dots for the eyes! I've always regretted not keeping the hilarious drawings Debussy produced that evening. Another time, I was bold enough to ask if I could play him one of his *Préludes*, 'La fille aux cheveux de lin', and said as a joke: 'You are now going to hear "La fille aux cheveux de ripolin"!'* Debussy was fond enough of making fun of others, but this play on words left him most decidedly unamused.

Ricardo Viñes, script of radio talk given in 1938, Bibl. Nat. LA Viñes 17/7

JACQUES DURAND

In my mind's eye, I see Debussy's study and his charming house near the porte Dauphine, on the avenue du Bois de Boulogne. Winter and summer, Debussy used to work surrounded by flowers; his study overflowed with them. It was a symphony of colours which used to produce music, and I'm reminded of the line of Baudelaire:

Les sons et les parfums tournent dans l'air du soir

a line which Debussy used as the title of one of his wonderful piano *Préludes*.

His study was on the ground floor, with spacious bay windows which flooded it with light, and it opened out on to the garden which surrounded the house. The wide table on which he used to work was cluttered with high-class Japanese objects. His favourite was a porcelain toad which he called his fetish and which he took with him when he moved, claiming he could not work unless it was in sight.

---

*'The girl with the enamelled hair'

Many was the time he lamented to the difficulty of taking his work-table with him on holiday. Debussy was a stay-at-home; he hated change. He was very fond of his upright piano, a lovely instrument from which he drew ravishing sounds. I also remember, in this study, a certain coloured engraving by Hokusai, representing the curl of a giant wave. Debussy was particularly enamoured of this wave. It inspired him while he was composing *La mer*, and he asked us to reproduce it on the cover of the printed score.

Jacques Durand, *Quelques souvenirs d'un éditeur de musique*, 2 vols. (Paris, 1924/1925), II, pp. 90–93

RAOUL BARDAC

(1881–1950)

Raoul Bardac was the son of Emma Debussy by her first marriage to the banker Sigismond Bardac. He studied music at the Paris Conservatoire, where he was a fellow student of Ravel, and then privately with Debussy.

Certainly his happiness had sometimes been compromised by problems of a financial nature, which had forced him to modify some details of the interior furnishing and to undertake a number of tours. But these were the only clouds on his horizon. The life he led there was not one of luxury (because his taste was not luxurious nor aimed towards the good things of life), but of comfort and extreme refinement, devoid of showy gestures. His day-to-day happiness depended on the satisfaction of little habits within an atmosphere of love and devotion.

He loved his garden, which had been laid out according to his own design and which contained flowers and shrubs that he had chosen, and which he looked after himself. He would walk round it slowly for a long time, in silence, then, suddenly, he would turn back towards the house where he would ask the upright Bechstein or the Blüthner (which I still possess) to repeat for him the musical idea he had just had. At other times he would rapidly and clearly jot down an idea in a bound notebook, or perhaps he would simply come back to the house to arm himself with garden implements, with which to perform a painstakingly delicate operation on some undesirable growth or some withered twig.

He never went out anywhere if he could possibly avoid it, except to the bookseller's or to shops that sold Chinese *objets d'art* and engravings.

Among his literary purchases there was always a large number of English books and magazines. He was very taken with the way they looked and would get them translated for him either by his wife (my mother) or by my sister, who was then a girl living with her mother and stepfather.

Debussy was devoted to various objects, silent but faithful companions, which decorated his work-table: very simple pens made of reeds and always of the same make, special blotters, a pot for tobacco, a cigarette box, the toad Arkel, a model of a sleeping Chinaman and so on.

People have referred to Debussy as being very much a gourmand. He was in fact more of a gourmet, but infinitely so – with unction, none the less, stopping short of voracity or excess. He loved the things he found good – as he loved the things he found beautiful – but without the slightest trace of vulgar gluttony.

He was fond of his whisky, which he used to drink every evening around ten o'clock, served in *his* special graduated decanter, and of *his* tea, which he drank only out of *his* teacup.

He liked having friends visit him, but there was never any party or gathering of them. There were intimate lunches and dinners, very often on regular, fixed days – but never did he entertain eight people at the same time.

He had a weak spot for trying his hand at bridge, but his absent-mindedness meant that he was never very good, and he used to poke fun at his own hopeless blunders. He was also attracted by chess, but could never keep his mind on the game. On the other hand, he was happy to play shuttlecocks or diabolo with my sisters. Indeed, he did not take a delight in any pastime that was complicated or artificial.

But the great, supreme and constant passion of his life was always music, which he loved for its own sake and which he could not bear to see brutalized or cheapened or made the vehicle of empty pomposity. He had never imagined that it would lead him to fame, and had expected even that he would remain more or less unknown.

He loved music in its entirety, and responded to its most diverse manifestations, as long as it was true music.

His admiration for certain composers both past and present is well known. Less so are other opinions of his, of an eclecticism that may well disconcert those who are unaware of the breadth of his musical sympathies. Verdi, for example, for his determination and success in developing and renewing his style – in particular *Falstaff* (notably 'Quand' ero paggio del Duca di Norfolk'), certain passages by Gounod (for example, 'Broutez le thym, broutez, mes chèvres' from the third act of *Sapho*), some little bits of Puccini's *La bohème* and the start of a waltz called *La Esméralda*, by Mesquita, I think.

I quote these examples at random from my memory, because of their diverse characters. There were many others – not to mention *Tristan* and *Parsifal*, because one must not confuse Wagner's musical genius with the influence of his procedures.

Debussy composed slowly, forcing himself, as he used to say to me, to eradicate all parasitical development and to replace it by a musical line which reflected the nature of his ideas and the path that they took, a line which allowed these ideas air: too often composers smother them by setting them against a background that is overfull – or overbanal.

He recommended gathering one's impressions without being in a hurry to crystallize them in note form, so as to condense inside oneself the variations on a single viewpoint. He was of the opinion that one should create slowly and with minute care the special atmosphere in which a work has to evolve; one should not rush to write things down, so as to allow complete freedom to those mysterious, inner workings of the mind which are too often stifled by impatience. But once the shape of things was clear in his mind, then Debussy used to write quickly and easily: his facility in this respect testifying to his possession of a *métier* that was as amazing as it was unobtrusive.

Raoul Bardac, 'Dans l'intimité de Claude Debussy', *Terres Latines*, 4/3, March 1936, pp. 72–4

DOLLY BARDAC (Mme Gaston de Tinan)

(1892–1985)

Dolly Bardac was the daughter of the banker Sigismond
Bardac and his wife Emma. When her mother set up
house with Debussy in 1904, Dolly went with her and
lived in the household for six years until her marriage.

For those who were not yet acquainted with Debussy, he seemed at
first very intimidating and cold; he even frightened some people, by
a rather 'closed' look which came from his natural timidity, and also
a certain indifference towards those who seemed to have nothing that
could interest him.

All this concealed a painful sensitivity and a disposition which was
on the contrary full of warmth towards those to whom he had given
his friendship – as one can see in his correspondence with Chausson,
Robert Godet, Louis Laloy and Caplet among others – which reveal
his true nature.

He was very young at heart, at times seeming like a child; he had
a great sense of the comical, but sometimes (rarely, I am happy to
say) he could have violent fits of temper when his thundering shouts
terrified me.

He was very slow in his movements, very meticulous in himself
and with everything that surrounded him. The objects of his work-
table were arranged in an order which never changed. He was never
parted from a big wooden toad, a Chinese ornament called Arkel,
which was on his table; he even took it travelling with him. With
regard to this I found a piece of paper on which Debussy had clearly
written at the moment of departure: 'Do not put Arkel in the trunk;
he doesn't like that . . .'

He seldom went out, in spite of a hired car which awaited his
pleasure for hours in front of the garden gate. When he did go out
it was usually to see his publisher and friend Jacques Durand, or his
bookseller, or a shop selling Chinese antiques which he was mad about
and whose proprietor still wore at that time the national costume and
the long pigtail. Among other things Debussy bought the black lacquer
and gold panel which inspired the piano piece called 'Poissons d'or'.

Debussy was very interested by English literature, which he read in translation as he did not speak the language, and he liked my mother or me to translate for him magazine articles which always interested him very much.

He had a partiality for the paintings of Turner and Whistler and the drawings of Arthur Rackham, one of which inspired the *Prélude* 'Les fées sont d'exquises danseuses'. Neither must we forget other titles of British inspiration: *Children's Corner*, 'Homage to Samuel Pickwick, Esq', 'Puck's Dance', and finally *The Blessed Damozel* of the pre-Raphaelite painter and poet, Dante Gabriel Rossetti. He was equally anglophile in his liking for beautiful silver for the table, for whisky and for the very strong tea which he prepared himself for breakfast, with the slowness and care that he devoted to everything. In his study he had installed a large armchair made of wood and leather in Morris style, which was the last word in English comfort. Debussy had occasion to go to Britain several times. He went on holiday to Jersey in 1904, where he bought a Blüthner piano, the tone of which had particularly pleased him, and then he went to Eastbourne in 1905.

Debussy adored our garden on the square du Bois de Boulogne and did a lot of work in it himself. On fine days, he walked along a garden path and noted down his musical ideas in a little red leather notebook which never left his pocket. He did not work out the harmony on the piano when he played a piece; it was already finished. All in all, he was an incomparable pianist, not only in his own works, but in those of all the composers he liked, from Couperin and Rameau to Schumann, Chopin, Chabrier, Albéniz, Falla and many others. Sadly, none of the recordings made by Debussy on piano rolls and transferred to records gives a genuine impression of his interpretations.

The friends who came to the house most frequently were Louis Laloy, of whom Debussy said that he was the most intelligent man he had ever met, Paul-Jean Toulet and André Caplet, with all of whom he liked to play bridge, very badly, I must confess, and with a slowness that was the despair of his partners. Erik Satie came to lunch regularly. I always awaited his coming with impatience, so unexpectedly comical was his way of expressing himself and his repartee in conversation. His attitude towards Debussy was both curiously humble and lacking in spontaneity, in spite of a terribly malicious look from behind his pince-nez!

I knew Debussy's parents and his sister very well; they were regular visitors at the square du Bois. They were naturally very flattered by their son's fame, although they did not realize the unique place he had won in the history of music. Léon Vallas, one of the first biographers of Debussy, formulated some doubts on the origins of the latter, speaking of a so-called 'mystery' about his birth; but his resemblance to his parents, which came from a mixture of physical traits of both of them, left no doubt as to his legitimacy. Debussy had never been to school, having learnt to read and write from his mother; she was very severe with her children, frequently slapping them, an unpleasant memory that her sons recalled laughingly.

I had the good fortune to live from the age of twelve in the atmosphere of *Pelléas et Mélisande*, being present at rehearsals and performances wherever my mother and Debussy took me (London among other places). It is often thought that my mother and Debussy met at the first performance of *Pelléas*. This is a mistake. My brother. who was a young man at the time, while I was only a little girl, was in the composition class of Gabriel Fauré, with Ravel. *Pelléas* was a revelation to him; he was able to become acquainted with Debussy and later – between 1903 and 1904 – he took him to meet my mother.

No biographer has ever paid enough attention to my mother's personality and appearance. She was small and pretty with auburn hair and topaz-coloured eyes. What is more, she had an incomparable charm, to which nobody could remain insensible, even during the last years of her life.

When Debussy felt too lonely, while he was working, he was in the habit of sending to my mother, from one floor to another, wonderful little notes, full of love and tenderness. 'This unique charm of yours' are the words with which he finishes one of them.

Dolly Bardac, 'Memories of Debussy and his circle', *Recorded Sound*, 50/51, April–July 1973, pp. 158–61, 163; lecture given at the National Sound Archive (then the British Insititute of Recorded Sound) on 18 December 1972

HENRI BUSSER

Long visit paid to Debussy in his private house in the avenue du Bois de Boulogne. He seems to be bored there! He must often think of his little apartment in the rue Cardinet where he wrote *Pelléas*.

Henri Busser, diary entry for 5 July 1909, published in Edward Lockspeiser, *Debussy, His Life and Mind* (London 1962/1965), II, p. 7 n1.

LOUISA LIEBICH

> Mrs Liebich was one of Debussy's earliest English admirers and published a book on him in 1908. The meeting described below probably took place early in 1910.

On account of the description we had been given of him as 'farouche' and unsociable, I felt nervous at the thought of seeing the lion, so to speak, in his den. But when there entered into his bright study a charming, genial, smiling man, saying pleasantly as he shook hands, '*J'ai eu beaucoup de remords à cause de vous, Madame*,' I felt perfectly reassured and at my ease. His 'remorse' was occasioned, as he explained, for not having written to acknowledge my book. That year, and other years, we were always welcomed by him and his wife. We heard much interesting talk at their table and in the little study overlooking the railway and the Bois. But that first conversation remains more impressed on my memory than later ones, partly because I took notes of it at the time.

I have a special love for *Tristan and Iseult*, not Wagner's Teutonic version, but Bédier's French *Tristan*, which has been exquisitely translated by Mr H. Belloc, so I was eager to know when Debussy's opera on Bédier's text would be finished. In answer to this question he made a big circle with outstretched arms: 'It will take very long to write; it is an immense task; every year I realize more and more the difficulty of doing exactly what one wants to do.' I said something about genius doing what it must and he corrected me: 'Genius must find its own equilibrium; it must stabilize and fructify; all that takes a great deal of time; it cannot happen all of a moment; if it did, composition would be too easy'; and he repeated several times, 'It needs a great deal of time.' He agreed that a genius is born – not made, but 'the germ must be present,' he said, 'and then there must be years and years during which it establishes itself and develops.' Apropos of certain singers and his songs, he said: 'People imagine they can do anything they like with modern music – old music is a religion to them, a fetish; people respect and revere every bar of it, but with modern music they think they can take any liberties.' We talked of Weber, whom he loved, of Mozart, of *petites chapelles*, of music critics, cultured and uncultured, London, etc. I learnt afterwards how characteristic of him it was to ask my husband, whenever the performance of any artist was mentioned: Is he (or she) *sincere*? I think sincerity was a religion with him.

My husband was anxious to play some of the *Images* and other pianoforte pieces to the composer, so a day and an hour was arranged of what proved to be the first of many delightful hours of converse on the interpretation and idioms of his compositions. On one occasion, after tea, Debussy played his first *Prélude*, 'Les danseuses de Delphes' to us. It was as yet unpublished. I have never heard more beautiful pianoforte playing. I have been told he did not always play to advantage in a concert hall. He said that afternoon that many of the *Préludes*, especially 'Les danseuses' and 'Des pas sur la neige', should only be played *entre quatre-z-yeux*. But in the intimity of his own room it was like hearing a poet reciting some of his own delicate lyrics. He had a soft, deep touch which evoked full, rich, many-shaded sonorities. He told us this *Prélude* embodied his impressions of the big caryatide of 'Les danseuses de Delphes' at the top of the grand staircase of the Louvre to the left of the 'Winged Victory'. He also played some of the *Children's Corner*, and on another evening some pieces of Erik Satie and his own 'Cathédrale engloutie'. We now treasure an advance copy of the first book of *Préludes* which Debussy sent to my husband to interpret in England with the inscription *en toute sympathie*, 23 iv. 10.

I especially recall his excessive neatness. His room, his writing-table, his bookshelves were always in perfect apple-pie order. Neither had he any profusion of books or pictures or objects of vertu. His handwriting is minute, and yet not in the least cramped; the letters are beautifully formed, and it is especially clear; his writing of music has the same exquisite trimness. This orderliness can be traced in his creative work, where every note is in its rightful place, with no superabundance of detail, no unnecessary effect.

Louisa Liebich, 'An Englishwoman's memories of Debussy', *The Musical Times*, 1 June 1918, p. 250

PASTEUR VALLERY-RADOT

He lived off the avenue du Bois de Boulogne, at the end of a long drive lined with villas and enveloped in trees. You came to a gate, then up several steps, and found yourself in a rather dark hallway. Then you went into a room full of light, which seemed to be invaded by trees from a small garden. The atmosphere was peaceful, everything struck a uniformly sober note, even though the furniture was of different styles. At the far end of the room, a large work-table; to the right, a tiny piano in black wood; a Buddha; several Japanese drawings on the walls; roses.

His gestures were all curved. His voice was gentle and unaffected, and he spoke slowly, searching for the right word which would conjure up a picture. Sometimes he would stop in the middle of a phrase, like a horse hesitating before an obstacle: he could not find the word which clothed his thought. He expressed himself in visual terms like a man who knows how to look at things and how to draw out their dominant characteristics. His speech was often imbued with imprecision, in order to get across the uncertainty of an idea or an impression, using a word which suddenly sprang vibrantly to life. You were charmed by his sensibility but at the same time you were wary of it, because he could be irritated by an unexpected noise, too bright a light or an ill-timed word.

His wife surrounded him with love, knowing that he was given to childish caprices and that he must be protected from all the shocks of life. One of his greatest pleasures was to hear his daughter Chouchou speak, sing or play the piano, or to see her dance to one of the rhythms he invented for her.

Many ideas never progressed beyond the project stage because he was never satisfied! Many a time he talked to me about his *Tristan*, which he intended to write on his own adaptation of Bédier's novel:

'Something quite different from *Tristan and Isolde*,' he used to say, 'something with a French feel to it.'

If he had merely given free rein to his musical ideas, he could have composed with extreme facility. Instead, he worked painfully hard to express what he had glimpsed in the obscure recesses of his unconscious. When I went into his study, I often found him sitting anxiously in front of a blank page; I knew that at that moment the slightest thing might irritate him, so I held my peace. A few moments later he would turn round and say to me with a friendly smile: 'I like you, you don't upset the atmosphere.' At other times, when he had found the 'formula' he was looking for, he would welcome me with a cheerful 'This time I think I've got it!' Then he would go to the piano and ask my opinion: 'I like to assess the impression it makes,' he said, 'on a musical ignoramus like you, who "feels" what I'm doing without being able to analyse the technique. That's what counts, after all! Whatever you do, don't learn to read music!'

Debussy had the reputation of being a loner because he was sensitive and touchy, but he had a number of friends to whom he remained faithful, and to them he showed nothing but kindness. Louis Laloy, André Caplet and I were of this number. Nearly every Thursday, Paul-Jean Toulet used to have dinner at Debussy's, and sometimes I would be invited too, with Laloy and the pianist Walter Rummel. After dinner, we would repair to the *maître*'s studio and Rummel would sit down at the piano, while Toulet and Debussy broached a bottle of amazing whisky, which Mme Debussy used to call a 'secret of the house'.

Pasteur Valléry-Radot, 'Mes souvenirs sur Claude Debussy', *Marottes et Violons d'Ingres*, 46, 1953, pp. 47–8, 50

ARTHUR HARTMANN
(1881–1956)

Arthur Hartmann was a Hungarian violinist who spent most of his life in the USA. In February 1914 Debussy accompanied him in a public performance of one of Grieg's violin sonatas and of transcriptions of the song 'Il pleure dans mon cœur' and of two *Préludes*, 'La fille aux cheveux de lin' and 'Minstrels'.

One day I wrote to Debussy's publisher to send me any and everything which Debussy may have written for the violin. Receiving the reply that as yet Debussy had created nothing for the instrument, I wrote to Debussy himself, meekly imploring him to permit me to see some of his violin compositions. To my amazement and delight, I received a reply from him which, alas, confirmed his publisher's report. Thereupon I secured several of his songs and immediately saw the possibilities of transcribing his exquisite 'Il pleure dans mon cœur'. With the coming of the fall, I was due for an American tour, and again took the liberty of writing to Debussy that I would be in Paris at a certain date for one day prior to sailing. To my delight, he immediately answered, saying it would give him pleasure to have me call at 11 in the morning. I was duly shown into a room which was decorated with choice Japanese and Chinese vases, wood carvings, draperies, instruments and so forth, and was allowed many minutes in which to examine my surroundings.

While thus absorbed, I suddenly heard a door opened and, turning, saw Claude Debussy looking at me. His eyes were strange, and more especially the formation of his head. I bowed low, and he in no manner returned my greeting, but quizzically gazed at me. Yet I felt his nervous and sensitive personality to be keenly sympathetic to my nature. The silence seemed to me interminable, and finally the uniqueness of this meeting struck my funny side so that impulsively I blurted in French, 'Well, then, doesn't one say "How do you do?" ' and I laughed. Smilingly he answered, 'Exactly! How do you do!' Amusedly I continued, 'I believe that you are Maître Debussy,' to which he answered rather vehemently, 'That, my dear sir, is indisputable'; and continuing in his rather hesitating, timorous and almost petulant manner, he added, 'And as I know that I am Claude Debussy, so do I know that you are Monsieur Arthur Hartmann.' He had not yet moved, nor did he offer to shake hands, but puffed his cigarette violently, while with half-closed eyes he studied me whimsically.

Highly amused, I said, 'And so you are he who created *Pelléas?*' 'Sir,' he retorted, 'it is so. I did it – and all alone.' 'Bravo!' I ejaculated, 'and I for one thank you, for to me you are the greatest artist since Wagner.'

He silently lit a new cigarette from the stub of his old one, but never thought of offering me one. Yet what did it matter? I was in the room with Debussy, and what is more, I felt that he liked me; and as for myself, I knew that I loved him! So I said quietly, 'I see that you do not object to smoking?' 'Oh, in that,' he replied with characteristic mock precision, 'my dear sir, you are perfectly right. I do not mind it in the least.' Whereupon I lit one of my own cigarettes, and he laughed outright. 'And now,' he said, 'show me your transcription.' Looking into his eyes for a moment before unlocking my violin case, I exclaimed, 'What a pity you're not dead, for then I could publish my transcription just as it is! But now I have to show it you and you'll not like it. Indeed no, for I have changed some of your things. For instance, at one place I introduce a G sharp major chord against your E major, and you doubtless know that these tonalities are not very affectionately related. But really, I could not do otherwise, for the violin is such a confoundedly exacting animal, and as long as I stick to her I want to do the best by her that I can!'

Debussy's answer was illuminating. 'Monsieur,' he said, 'I do not know you and I have never heard you play, but I have a peculiar feeling that your ideas will not displease me. Kindly play it for me.' Timorously I started, while he placed himself at the piano. We played it through without a stop, and when I got to the end his only comment was a short 'Once more.' Thus I continued five times, and then stared at him, my heart in my mouth. Silently he held out his hand. 'My friend, it is excellent. I prefer it now to my song, and I shall see that it is printed. There is only one point, if you will permit me to comment on it. You have here kept my ideas in the piano part and put your own into the violin. Permit me to change this so that you become the piano and I the violin, and we will thus be more – ' and he finished the sentence by intertwining his fingers, meaning to indicate a still greater union.

I was in the twentieth heaven of happiness, and staying for a few more minutes smoked several cigarettes, being particularly careful to put the burnt matches in one kind of Japanese vase while I deposited the cigarette ashes in another – just as he was doing. Our conversation was limited to detached sentences and monosyllabic comments. Rising to go, I suddenly commented on the curious coincidence of two men facing each other, completely attired in blue! The shirts, collars, neckties, the suits and even the hose, and I said, 'Funny that my family should never understand that everything about and around me is blue, even to my stationery,' to which he replied, '*Ah, ça!* Families are prone to be the ones with whom one is the least at home.' Asking which hotel I had stopped at for the day, he bade me farewell cordially and wished me a safe journey. Later in the afternoon I was overjoyed with the surprise of having the bell boy deliver an inscribed photograph of Debussy, a thing I would not have ventured to have requested. When I called on the publisher and, introducing myself, recounted my day's experiences, he was so amazed that, calling his wife, he made me repeat my story, constantly interrupting me with, 'And he was nice to you, and received you like that? Amazing!'

Returning to Paris about eighteen months later, I married and for a time lived in the same 'square' where Debussy had a villa. A few weeks later I left a note for him and said that if he had time, I should like to see him again. The answer was very cordial and said that any time I felt like jumping across, it would give him pleasure to shake my hand. And now that he is gone, perhaps the most beautiful thing that I can say of him is that on the countless visits I made him, whether in the forenoon, lunch hour, afternoon or evening, whether he was working or had visitors, he received me immediately. Many times I came to his room when he was working, and I almost had the feeling as if some spirit were doing it for him, for his desk – a huge, long, flat table – was always in perfect order and I never saw an ink spot on the blotter. There were never any manuscripts around, nor any on the piano.

Knowing that he had spent several years in Rome, I once asked him if he spoke Italian well, to which he replied like a characteristic Parisian, 'My friend, after struggling with books to ascertain how to purchase pens and ink in Italian, I found that the clerk spoke so much better French than I ever could Italian that I never made another effort to learn a single word.'

Wagner he had seen but once, but the impression he gained was a frightful one. 'His eyes', he shrieked, 'were terrible. Ouf! they were frightful! But Liszt, ah, that was different. He was goodness itself.'

One morning I found him in his garden with his little girl, and a trowel in his hands. Suddenly the gate bell rang and ere I was aware of what was happening, he had seized me by the neck and dragged me with himself behind a bush. Peering forth to see who it was, while we heard the servant calmly saying, 'Monsieur is not at home', he winked at me and we emerged. We were speaking of religion and I had said that instead of going to church to hear a man tell me things of which he knew nothing, I preferred a long walk in the woods and then to play Liszt's 'Faust' Symphony. I was rather eager to see how he regarded this work, and to my great joy he answered, 'My friend, if there are certain people who permit themselves to judge and proclaim things of which they know nothing, it is no reason why we should follow the herds. And as for the 'Faust' of Liszt, it is one of the few works which stand removed from any possible criticism.' And digging in the earth, he found a worm and was about to cut it in two when pausing an instant he said, 'Chouchou, ask l'Oncle Arthur if he should let this worm live,' and I murmured indifferently, 'Why not! There are so many more miserables who breathe and crawl! As for me, the contemplation of a single tree is dearer than all of mankind,' to which he silently held out his hand.

Suddenly, one afternoon, his servant brought me a note – 'Dear friend; Will you be "at home" this afternoon? If yes, I would have great pleasure in coming to see you. Affectionately your friend, Claude Debussy.' A few minutes later, he with Madame Debussy and Chouchou called. He came in timidly and glancing around hastily said, 'We are quite alone?' 'Quite,' I said, 'except for my wife.' 'Then we will leave the ladies to get acquainted. Where is your room?' By this time he was half-way in my apartment and preceded me to my room. Ensconcing himself in my chair at the desk, he examined my pens, inkstand and papers; then the pictures on the walls and my books. Presently drawing a sheet of paper from the drawer of my desk and smoking silently, he looked at me and said, *'Bien, oui c'est comm' cela,'* and his eyes winked humorously. To which I retorted, *'Oui, c'est certain que c'est comm' ça,'* and he made a dot on the paper. After a long pause, he repeated *'Oui, c'est certain que c'est comm' ça,'* to which I replied *'Ah, ça, c'est indiscutable! C'est certainement comm' ça,'* and he made another dot. Presently my thoughts turned to a set of six antique silver vest buttons which I had collected with great difficulty on a recent concert tour of Norway. They were extremely old and I had

begged these heirlooms from different individuals in Norway, some
coming from the most obscure coastal towns, some from the far north
– from Tromsoe. I had collected these in hopes of getting a set together
and then presenting them to Debussy. I handed them to him and gave
him the story of their rarity and the difficulties I had had in getting
finally six that would match. Silently he took the set and put it in his
pocket without a word, and rising suddenly, rang for the maid.
On her appearance, he peremptorily stretched forth his hand and
commanded, 'Du thé!'

Returning to the ladies, we all had tea together and presently my
wife, inquiring whether I had given Debussy the buttons, proceeded
to recount to Madame Debussy all the difficulties that had to be
overcome in order to get different individuals to part with them.
Debussy produced the set, without any comment, and his wife immediately rhapsodized over the unusual carving, their oddity, the almost
undetectable evenness in the pattern, and so on. When taking his
departure, Debussy suddenly said to me, 'My dear friend, you have
something in this apartment which I should very much like to have.'
With a mock curtsey, I said, 'Ah, at last – doubtless you wish my
autograph,' to which he whistled and shook his finger at me. 'Or
perhaps my photograph with autograph?' Again the same sort of reply.
'Let me see,' I said reflectively, 'the set of Poe? Or the picture of
Lafcadio Hearn?' Seizing me by my arm and dragging me back into
my room, he advanced his arm rigidly and pointing to a queerly
shaped pebble on my desk, exclaimed 'Ça!' It was a little pebble which
an octogenarian had given me, and which he had picked up on his
bridal tour, a half century ago, on the Mountain of Black Ice in
Norway. Laughingly I told Debussy that he was more than welcome
to it, and his effusions and joy over it were simply incredible, while
I inwardly regretted the unique vest buttons. I may add that, ever
after, the curious pebble kept its place on his writing-table alongside
of almost priceless Chinese and Japanese oddities.

Debussy's sense of humour was as keen as it was delicate. Once,
commenting on different French composers, I had remarked that
Vincent d'Indy's religious fanaticism coupled with mediaeval learning
made of him quite a figure of, let us say, the fourteenth century; to
which his brief comment was 'Oui, en bois!' Again, writing him that
I had just made a transcription of one of his piano Préludes, 'The girl

with the flaxen hair', and should like to show it him, he answered, '*Je demande à entendre "la fille aux cheveux de lin" jouer du violon, car je ne doute pas qu' elle n'ait un considérable talent!*'*

A simple tea at Debussy's was as lavish as most dinners, while a dinner at his house was nothing short of sumptuous. I well recall a bizarre dinner when everything was in red, from the tablecloth and napkins to the champagne. (Mind you, red champagne, if you please, and not sparkling Burgundy!) The last time I saw him was on his birthday, 22 August 1914, when I took him a few blue cornflowers and teasingly asked him how he was relishing his plate of lentils or macaroni at noon . . . Dukas, the composer, was there, and I well recall Debussy's characteristic comments about the Germans and their music. 'Ouf,' he said with disgust, 'those people drink whether they are thirsty or not! Everything with them is "*en gros*". A theme must be long, regardless of its contents or value; the longer the better. Then another interminable episode and then another endless theme. Then, after sixteen quarts of beer, they begin a development so long, so long, that there is scarcely room in this house to hold it. Take, for instance, the symphonies of Mahler (which he, of course, pronounced Mal-air), with its thousand voices and whips, submarines and whatnot . . . Or Monsieur Strauss, who is clever in that he knows how to write nothingness itself . . . Well, my friend, with it all, their noise does not sound any louder than the finale to Beethoven's Fifth, produced by a small orchestra with only the addition of a contra-fagott!'

In answer to my apprehension that the Germans might pass Namur and head for Paris, he whistled and winked several times, and as I insistently reiterated that this might become a possibility, he put his hand over his heart and solemnly said, 'My friend, I assure you on my word of honour that the Germans will never come to Paris. Do you believe it now?' And, offering him my hand, I told him that I believed him fully, to which he blurted in fury, while his eyes bulged almost out of their sockets, 'Besides, let them come and you will see something that you overlooked in your reckoning, for do not forget, dear friend, that every female concierge in Paris would go out and

---

*I would like to hear 'la fille . . .' play the violin, as I am sure she must have considerable talent.

fight them with knives and forks. Do you hear me – with knives and forks, thus, piff, pouff, one in each eye. *Voyons*, you forget what the women of France are, my dear friend.'

Arthur Hartmann, 'Claude Debussy as I knew him', *Musical Courier*, 39, 23 May 1918

VII
On tour

Emma Bardac's uncle, the financier Osiris, died in 1907 and in his will disinherited her. From then on, Debussy reluctantly took on a number of foreign engagements to make money. In addition to the visits to London, Turin and Amsterdam described below, he travelled to Vienna, Budapest, Moscow, St Petersburg, Rome, The Hague and Brussels. His last journey abroad was to London in July 1914.

SIR HENRY WOOD

(1869–1944)

Henry Joseph Wood was born in London and studied at
the Royal Academy of Music. In 1895 he conducted the
first of the Promenade Concerts and was still conducting
them nearly half a century later. He was knighted in
1911. Sir Edgar Speyer was a philanthropist and music
lover who took over the financial management of the
Queen's Hall Orchestra in 1901.

Another characteristic about Speyer that won my gratitude was his
willingness to have any great composer of foreign nationality over here
to conduct his own works. Speyer, it must be remembered, was by
birth a German; but he was more than willing to have Claude Debussy
at Queen's Hall – and Germans did not look so kindly on Frenchmen
in those days.

'You must go to Paris,' said Speyer. Then he wondered whether
Debussy was anything of a conductor but concluded that, whether he
was or not, London wanted him and London must have him.

'You must go to Paris next week,' insisted Speyer, 'and you must
make him promise to come next year. You will be given a cheque for
your expenses. Tell Debussy what you like, *but make him come over.*'

This was a delicate mission. Even though Speyer told me to say
that his house was at Debussy's disposal and that he would be entertained royally, I was none too comfortable about it. I thought of the
lovely Italian garden at 46, Grosvenor Street (knowing that Debussy
would have his own suite of rooms there) and summoned up all my
diplomatic powers to persuade the great French composer to make his
first visit to London.

Speyer and I had a good talk about the fee we were to offer. We
had paid conductor-composers such fees as thirty or forty guineas but
such sums hardly seemed to suit the present situation. At last we
decided on a hundred guineas, and off I went to Paris. How to break
it to him, knowing he was reputed to be of a very retiring disposition
and averse to appearing in public, I really was not quite sure. However, I made up my mind to tackle him through Madame Debussy
who, as it happened, spoke perfect English. With the fee in my mind

I thought of how so many English composers had spoilt things by conducting for next to nothing. Elgar told me he often conducted with hardly so much as his railway fare being paid. I tactfully approached Madame Debussy and revealed my mission. When she told her husband and mentioned the fee he jumped up, furious.

'What? A hundred guineas . . . for *me?* And yet you pay Caruso four hundred guineas?'

I corrected this immediately, 'We never engage Caruso or any other singer at such a fee,' I told him. Debussy calmed down and offered to think it over. I felt things were not too good, all the same; so I went out after lunch and wired to Speyer, suggesting two hundred guineas. Speyer wired back his agreement, repeating his assertion that we must have Debussy whatever the cost.

Fortunately, it did happen: Debussy agreed to come. He seemed quite unable to realize that the London public wanted him at all, even though he was inclined to think his music was more popular with us than in Paris. He certainly never regretted coming, for he loved London and thoroughly enjoyed both his visits.

On 1 February 1908, he came and a crowded audience was present to give him a real English welcome. I recall most vividly my first impressions of that dark, bearded Frenchman: his deep, soulful eyes; his quiet and rather grating voice; most of all, his enormous head. I have never seen such a head on a man of his stature; it reminded me of heads of the early Egyptians.

Debussy seemed delighted – almost like a child – because he thought that we in London appreciated his music more than his own countrymen in his beloved Paris. It may be that the French capital has always been hard on its composers. Berlioz, you remember, suffered agonies of mind because his popularity was greater outside France than in it, and César Franck complained bitterly because recognition was so slow in coming.

Debussy certainly had nothing of which to complain regarding the reception accorded to him in London that afternoon; for not even Strauss had received a warmer welcome. Moreover, I had thoroughly rehearsed *L'après-midi d'un faune* and *La mer* with the orchestra, paying the greatest attention to the fine, gossamer-like effects which pervade both works. At the rehearsal Maurice Sons acted as interpreter, for

Debussy spoke very little English. Sons was useful in that way, being a most accomplished linguist.

In fact, nothing could have been happier for all of us; we liked him and he liked us. So that when Newman, the manager, suggested a return visit to Queen's Hall on 27 February 1909, he was more than willing to come. We repeated *L'après-midi* because of the ovation it had received the previous year, but instead of *La mer* we produced the three *Nocturnes*, Smallwood Metcalfe's Eastbourne choir undertaking the choral parts in 'Sirènes'.

Again, I had rehearsed the orchestra until there was practically nothing left for Debussy to do. The rehearsal went off smoothly enough but at the concert there was a peculiar accident. I do not remember ever witnessing anything quite like it. In the second of the *Nocturnes* (a movement called 'Fêtes') the time changes a good deal. To the surprise of all of us, Debussy (who, quite candidly, was not a good conductor even of his own works) suddenly lost his head, and his beat! Realizing what he had done, he evidently felt the best thing was to stop and begin the movement over again. He tapped the desk, and tapped again.

Then the most extraordinary thing happened. *The orchesra refused to stop*. It really was an amazing situation. Here was a famous composer directing a work of his own and, having got into difficulties, was asking the orchestra to stop and was being met with refusal. They obviously did not intend to stop: they knew that the audience would think the fault was theirs. Moreover, the work (which they liked immensely) was going beautifully and they meant to give a first-rate performance of it; which they proceeded to do and succeeded in doing. I never knew them more unanimous.

The audience by no means missed the fact that something had gone wrong because it was so evident that he had tried to stop the orchestra. At the end, in truly English fashion, they recorded their appreciation to such an extent that he was compelled to repeat the movement. This time nothing went wrong and the ovation was even greater than before. Debussy was nonplussed and certainly did not understand the English mind; but I was proud of my orchestra that afternoon and had the satisfaction of seeing that he had been proud to conduct it.

'They *wouldn't* stop!' he told me in the artist's room afterwards; I fancy he went back to Paris with something to think about.

Sir Henry J. Wood, *My Life of Music* (London, 1938), pp. 157–8, 228–9.

VICTOR SEGALEN

London, 31 January 1908 (*Segalen to his wife*)

So I've been spending nearly all my time with the Debussys – who are both the same as ever. Thanks to the excellent means of transport in London, their hotel is only ten minutes away from where I'm staying. But I found Claude rather annoyed about the small number of possible rehearsals, just one instead of the four he asked for. But everything has been sorted out and this evening he seems much more confident. I didn't have dinner with them yesterday because they were detained elsewhere, nor today, when they were going without fail to be with the conductor. And in any case, after seven hours or so of music one needs to be alone. I went to collect them from their hotel this morning at 9.30; and from there the conductor, Wood, took us to a small hall quite different from the Queen's Hall, where the sectional rehearsals take place. So the brass, woodwind and percussion were working from 10 o'clock until 1. To begin with it was dreadful, even though they were willing enough. I was with Mme Debussy who called it 'the sea in lumps'. One had the unpleasant impression of laboriously chewing all the composer's essays in musical construction. Then, little by little, it began to take shape. Debussy on the rostrum didn't change, very much the *maître*, very cool, not extrovert. But the impression of the whole morning was of tantalizing incompleteness, as though one had been shown fragments of a rich mosaic bit by bit. From there we were firmly taken off to lunch by the obliging Wood, who was very solicitous of Debussy's well-being. Back to work around 2 o'clock, with the strings this time; much more in the way of polish and nuances; not far from being a satisfactory ensemble. Debussy cheered up. He told me that these English, 'as soon as they had to play under a Japanese

or Negro conductor, made enormous efforts to satisfy him, and
would rather die on the spot – yes, on the spot – than not get things
right.'

Victor Segalen, Anni Joly-Segalen and André Schaeffner (eds.): *Segalen et
Debussy* (Monaco, 1962), pp. 90–91.

GEORGES JEAN-AUBRY

It was, in fact, at that moment that Debussy was invited to appear at
one of the Queen's Hall Symphony Concerts, on Saturday 1 February
1908. The works to be conducted by him were the *Prélude à l'après-
midi d'un faune* and *La mer* (first performance in England).

I was most anxious to see Debussy conduct, and particularly before
an English audience. His cordial wish that I should accompany him
to London, or that we should at least find each other there, would
have conquered any possible resistance. However, I feared for a
moment that the state of my health might not permit the journey which
I desired with all my heart to make. He wrote to me on 22 January
1908:

*My dear friend, – I assure you that I heard with the greatest regret that
you have been ill. I thought of you on Sunday, and hoped that I might see
you. The London concert is fixed for 1 February, and I shall stay at the
Grosvenor Hotel (Victoria Station).*

*I trust that you have had time to recover sufficiently to embark on a
journey which I fear will be strenuous, considering you will have to cross
the sea to hear 'The Sea' and then to return by the sea.*

> Believe me, My dear friend,
> Yours affectionately
> Claude Debussy

I was present at that concert. We lunched together – the composer,
Madame Debussy, T. J. Guéritte, and myself – and I must say that
in spite of the fact that he was greatly pleased with the orchestra
after that morning's rehearsal, yet he was extremely nervous and
uncomfortable. We did our best to reassure him, and told him that
he was no stranger to the London public, that he would be sure of
the warmest reception, and that there was no cause for any apprehen-

sion. But, sensitive and nervous as he was, this first encounter made him restless.

The ovation he received from the English public at that concert was like nothing else I can remember. I can still see him in the lobby of Queen's Hall (where I went to shake hands with him immediately after the performance), trying to hid his emotion, and saying repeatedly, 'How nice they are, how nice they are!'

The London papers – I kept the cuttings, and they lie before me as I write – were unanimous in emphasizing two facts, neither of which displeased Debussy: the enthusiasm of the public and the physical resemblance of the composer to Dante Gabriel Rossetti, which some of the papers went so far as to designate as 'striking'.

At the door of Queen's Hall, and even to the door of his carriage, Debussy, fatigued by all his emotions, was the victim of the avidity of autograph-collectors, who thrust threatening fountain-pens at him from every point of vantage. Shrinking into the corner of the carriage to escape a kind of enthusiasm to which he was anything but partial, he yet repeated again with a tired patience, 'How nice they are!'

George Jean-Aubry, 'Some recollections of Debussy', *The Musical Times*, 1 May 1918, pp. 204–5

PERCY GRAINGER

(1882–1961)

Percy Grainger was born in Australia and, after studying with Busoni in Berlin, embarked on a career as composer and pianist. He was a close friend of Grieg and Delius. The meeting described below probably took place in 1908.

I met Debussy at the Speyers, and he was like a little spitting wild animal. Lady Speyer had invited some friends to tea and he said, 'Tea? I won't be in the same room with anybody. Bring me my tea in here!' . . . where he could drink it alone.

Percy Grainger, in interview with John Amis, BBC, 15 June 1959

ARNOLD BAX

(1883–1953)

Arnold Bax studied at the Royal Academy of Music, where
his piano teacher was Tobias Matthay. He wrote seven
symphonies and a number of symphonic poems, as well
as short stories and poems under the pseudonym Dermot
O'Byrne. In 1942 he became Master of the King's
Musick.

In 1908 or thereabouts was founded the 'Music Club', a dressy concert-
cum-supper affair presided over by Alfred Kalisch, critic of the *Star*,
and a pious thurifer before the altar of Richard Strauss. The Club
members were mostly elderly, and notable for wealth, paunchiness,
and stertorous breathing. Bulging pinkish bosoms straining at expensive décolletages, redundant dewlaps and mountainous backs were
generously displayed by the ladies, whilst among the men ruddy
double-chins, overflowing their collars at the back of the neck, and
boiled eyes were rife. The assemblage indeed was ever inclined to
bring to mind Beardsley's famous drawing – 'The Wagnerites'.

In the year 1909 Kalisch and the Club, seized with overweening
ambition, decided to invite several eminent foreign composers as their
guests, and to glut them with copious food, strong wines, and selections
from their own works. The four musicians earmarked for these
delights were Debussy, Vincent d'Indy, Sibelius and Schoenberg; and
I may tell you at once that their sufferings were prodigious!

Of the four guests Debussy's torments were certainly the most
excruciating.

The majority of the meetings of the Music Club were held in the
Art Galleries in Suffolk Street, where the ordeal by two arts at once
might be undergone by the more resolute British penitent, but for
some reason that I have forgotten Debussy was led to human sacrifice
on the boards of the Aeolian Hall. The proceedings were to be preluded
by an address welcoming the composer, and embodying a short
appreciation of his work. A speaker of French was an essential, for
Debussy could understand scarcely a word of English.

Trouble began at once, for although Frederick Corder, who was a
good French scholar, had been invited and had declared himself willing

to make the address, he at the last moment failed to turn up, excusing himself on the plea of sudden sickness. (The fact was, as we discovered next day, that his artistic conscience had worked mightily within him all the afternoon, and he had decided that he could not bring himself publicly to extol a musical idiom that he was unable to appreciate.)

His place was finally taken by Kalisch himself, whose French was of the school of Stratford-atte-Bow – or possibly at Oxford, – it was difficult to hazard which, as he was largely inaudible.

The great composer, an inordinately shy man, was planted in a chair in the exact centre of the platform facing the audience. He was clearly utterly nonplussed, and could only attempt to solve his problem by rising and making a stiff little bow whenever he recognized his own name amid Kalisch's guttural mumblings.

This part of his ordeal over, he was permitted to shamble dazedly to the rear of the hall, where he confided to Edwin Evans that he would rather write a symphony to order than go through such an experience again.

I believe that a fairly representative programme of the master's songs and instrumental works was performed, and I remember that I played the piano part of *Ariettes oubliées* for some American singer.

After the concert I had word that Debussy would like to meet me and thank me for my share in the evening's music. Never shall I forget the impression made upon me by that thick-set clumsy figure, the huge greenish, almost Moorish face beneath the dense thicket of black hair, and the obscure dreaming eyes that seemed to be peering through me at some object behind my back. As he lumbered vaguely forwards, extending a cushioned hand, he looked like some Triton arisen from 'the glaucous caverns of old Ocean'. 'A mythological survival!' I said to myself.

Recalling that morbidly sallow complexion of his I must conjecture that even so early the malignant foe, destined to be his death in his early fifties, was already prowling within his body.

Evans passed on to me the composer's remark that I had interpreted his songs very sensitively, but in rather too pianistic a fashion. This verdict interested me deeply, for never before had I been arraigned on the count of playing like a pianist.

Arnold Bax, *Farewell, My Youth* (London, 1943), pp. 58–9

VITTORIO GUI

(1885–1975)

Vittorio Gui was brought by Toscanini to conduct at La
Scala in 1923 and in 1928 founded the orchestra in Florence from which the May Festival was to spring. The
following memories relate to Debussy's visit to Turin in
1911.

I confess that when the Paris train came in my heart was hammering
away almost as loudly as the pistons of the locomotive. Not one of us
had met Debussy in person: there was just one photograph of him
(very well known now) going the rounds in Italy, rather an uncompro-
mising one in comparison with those of some of his colleagues in
flamboyant attitudes. So our eight eyes anxiously scrutinized the crowd
which emerged from the wagons-lit. Many faces appeared, but none
resembling the dark bearded one suggested in the famous photograph.
We were already deep in conjecture about lost trains and other imaginary causes of delay when at last a little group descended on us in good
order from the last compartment: a group composed of a little woman
(very chic), a little girl of seven or eight, a nurse, and finally a tall
man with dark eyes and beard, gentle of demeanour and laboured in his
movements, sparing of gesture, with the resigned and good-humoured
expression of the father of a family on holiday. It was he with all his
family. (I remembered all at once what one of his acquaintances,
perhaps Pierné, had said of him, not without a spice of irony: '*Oh,
Debussy aime beaucoup ses aises.*') And so he had come for a week's stay,
bringing with him all his dear ones because he could not bear to be
parted from them even for such a short time.

Rapid conventional introductions, hasty handclasps and an appointment in half an hour at the Hotel d'Europa where he was to stay. We
rejoined him there, and he received us in his room in shirt sleeves,
apologizing, with an adorable *sans-gêne*, with such lovable simplicity,
that when I recall that scene now and then look around and contrast
it with the swollen-headedness displayed by nonentities puffed up with
their own imaginary importance, I am profoundly moved. It seemed,
or at least it seems to me now, that he paid the most cordial attention
to me, who was the youngest there; and I noted to myself, with great

satisfaction, the natural way in which he disassociated himself from the habitual deference that nearly all men ostentatiously display towards those whose position entitles them to be considered 'important' in society. I was certainly the least 'important' person there, and yet it was to me that he chose to display particular affability. I felt born within me, besides the high admiration which I already had for him as an artist, something new that attracted me towards the man and which was shortly to become real affection; and the timorous respect which I showed at first towards him soon developed into open expression of that affection.

When Depanis, after having touched on all the most salient points about the rehearsals, orchestral parts, etc., came to the more delicate point about the help which I was prepared to give him in the preparation of the orchestra, to our great surprise Debussy, in a decided tone which allowed of no discussion for the time being, announced (declining the offer) that conducting was an old unfulfilled passion of his, and that he would be only too pleased to be left to do everything on his own! Hasty retreat of the undersigned, who immediately passed into the happy band of onlookers, from which however, as we shall see, he was soon to have to emerge.

Scene two: start of rehearsals. The rehearsals, for reasons above all of convenience, were to take place on the stage of the Teatro Regio: only at the 'generale' were we to move to the Festival Hall at the Valentino Park. The orchestra, in which were many brilliant youths fresh from their studies, and also composers in embryo (some of them have since passed with honour to the conductor's rostrum), was well conscious of the importance of the musician who had come in person to work with it, and was prepared to treat him with the greatest respect. Had not the music world been discussing him rabidly for nearly ten years, and even the public been stirred from their habitual lethargy? This was the real event of the season of concerts: not the coming and going of a famous conductor, lionized by the 'fans', – that is a more or less commonplace event in the life of an orchestra, but the contact with an authentically great creative artist who, even then, they could sense was destined for immortality. The entrance of this man who seemed so indifferent, a cigarette drooping from his lips to be thrown away only a few minutes after he had actually reached the rostrum – and most unwillingly, it seemed – provoked considerable surprise and, perhaps, disillusionment. It was inevitable; popular collective imagination always clings to its steadfast childish illusions.

His beat was uncertain, his head was always buried in the score (and it was his own music!), he lacked control over others and over himself, and even turned over the pages of the score with the hand that held the baton! He did this more than once, losing a beat to the great confusion of the orchestra. Never as much as then, in the growing painfulness of such a spectacle, have I wished so fervently to see the dream come true before my eyes of an ideal orchestra, composed of superior beings, all capable of putting forth their best intellectual and intuitive forces to help, not the conductor (there wasn't one), but the composer, the creator, who with his superfluous and obstructive physical presence seemed to be there as an argument for the abolition of an intermediary stage between thoughts and the expression of them in sound. Even in this (I thought, carried on by my absurd vision), this revolutionary creator of new and anti-bourgeois music seemed to push audacity beyond all limits. Would the time never come when music could be communicated to men without these material obstacles? (And the human element is often much more hostile and refractory than gut or brass.) Would music *ever* be liberated from the tyranny of the executant? But reality brought me down to earth with a bump, and I had to dash over with the excuse of being his interpreter, and with my authority as permanent conductor quell the confusion and the first ironic reactions which were spreading among the less reverent: to quell in short that flood of natural disorder which is evident in a group of men, especially Latins, when the influence of a leader is not vouchsafed to them. Things became really desperate during the unravelling of the suite *Ibéria*. It was the first time an Italian orchestra had been faced with this difficult score. Even now its delicate blendings of light and shade, its complicated rhythms, are no joke at the first run over. Just think of the confusion produced in the circumstances I have been describing! There was such a mix-up that Debussy himself, feeling that he was not succeeding in making the orchestra understand a note of his score, began to get worried; and, completely engulfed in the intricate chaos of noises, he took the way of least resistance by conceding the customary ten minutes' intermission, and vanished in obvious vexation into the room reserved for the conductor.

Depanis, after a short council of war, took a heroic resolution and marched off to propose to Debussy what was now inevitable, that is that he should leave to me the work of preparation, taking up the baton again on the evening of the concert, when everything would be ready and the orchestra would be able to play like clockwork. Debussy seemed to be expecting the proposal, such was the alacrity with which he agreed to it, not dissembling his satisfaction at getting out of a nasty situation. It must be added that by this time I was on very good terms with him; our meeting had led not only to an intellectual understanding, but to a growing friendship which later was to become a real bond of affection.

The illustrious composer was increasingly affable in his dealings with the insatiably curious youth who besieged him with questions, often importune, on all sorts of subjects, letters as well as music (for he had an exceptional literary and general culture), excited as one is at that age to meet people more important than oneself, – thirsting to drink at the fountainhead and not just animated by vulgar curiosity. He was touched by my youth and sincerity and gave himself up to conversations of all kinds, being a conversationalist full of verve, inimitable in the synthesization of his impressions of people and things, seeing always the amusing side and enjoying himself in the play of his subtle but good-humoured irony, so that one could never tire of listening to him. The one-time frequenter of Mallarmé's salon seemed to have retained some of that master's subtle art of conversation which had been such an integral part of his make-up; as an artist completely modern in his outlook, a son of the new times, Debussy's very highly developed critical faculties, which he was forever focusing on his own work, obliged him to examine penetratingly the more important artistic and aesthetic manifestations of his time, in whatever field of art.

His enthusiasm for Swinburne caused me to realize the real significance of the work of the great English poet, steeped as I was then in an excessive admiration for Tennyson. He did not conceal the derivation of the text of his *Proses lyriques* from the sensibility of Laforgue and others of the Parnassians who were spiritually his predecessors. He used to converse now smiling good-humouredly, now with sudden animation; intolerant only of the vulgarity of little people and, above all, of exploiters of that vulgarity. A sense of real aristocracy was innate in his speech as in his whole conduct, a witness of the natural nobility of this prince of good taste. Above all an immense, indisputable honesty, a perfect conformity between man and artist, between his way of living and his high ideals – these were the things which fired me with admiration in those halcyon days when I was his constant companion.

It was decided, then, that I would make a start the following morning by unravelling the first movement of *Ibéria*. I passed most of the night poring over the tiny miniature score – our eyes in our twenties can support certain abuses cheerfully – a score which is now one of my most precious possessions, on account of the words of gratitude Debussy wrote on it after the first performance. I studied it at length, I slept a little, and eagerly set off to the Regio, where I was received with great satisfaction by the orchestra, mortified by the failure of the previous rehearsal, but at bottom only wishing to be able to demonstrate its real ability to the illustrious composer it so sincerely admired. So the players gave of their best, and soon miracles were being performed; so much so that in less than an hour the first movement of the suite was being played with confidence and no little refinement. All at once, the eternal cigarette in his mouth, Debussy himself came quietly into the theatre, with his good-humoured and vaguely sad smile, – perhaps brought by curiosity. We were all pleased. The orchestra, flushed with triumph and feeling itself this time competently led, conscious of the order which had arisen from the unmitigated chaos of the night before, was by now able to appreciate the beauty of the music, which contains some of the most vivid and enjoyable descriptive pages which Debussy ever wrote: as for me, I was fretting at the bit like a young charger, my pulses racing. Debussy asked to hear the result of our labours: I gave the signal for the attack. Under the impulse of all these emotions the miracle happened: the first movement was played easily, delicately, with the clarity of morning light. In the streets of Spain passed sun-bronzed southern girls with a flower in their mouths, prodigal of their smiles, filling the streets and the hearts of passers-by with a sense of the joy of living; here and there an ear of corn still tangled in their hair (according to the imagery of Verlaine so dear to his heart), they passed by, the embodiment of a dreamed-of youth singing of love to greet the life spring of the returning day . . . The two clarinets had hardly ceased to sigh the evanescent major third with which the picture dissolves in a luminous cloud, when I felt two arms encircling my neck (I feel them still), and the great musician imprinted a kiss on my burning cheek; around us a burst of clapping enveloped his gesture and my natural emotion. After this, it was logical that I should take all the rehearsals up to the eve of the concert. He was always beside me, on the left-hand side of the rostrum, approving, advising, and often showing a profound and intimate satisfaction which could be sensed from the sweetness of his expression. These days of working with one of the noblest spirits I have ever had the fortune to be close to passed in the fervour of an activity worth pursuing, and surrounded by the warmth of his esteem. They remain in the memory like an oasis in the stormy path of life; because he, besides being the incomparable artist revealed to us by his music, was full of a generous and serene humanity, able to understand because he had suffered and known life's injustice in the struggle which he had won, but which had been so bitter. He took his victory without presumptuousness, good natured towards the shortcomings of others and aware of his own, for even the occasional irony of his words had never the flavour of spitefulness that so many of his compatriots, in particular, indulge in. He seemed actually to attune his rather blasé maturity to harmonize with my youthful and exuberant enthusiasm: really to value my unbounded admiration for his exquisite music, perhaps because my sincerity was so patent.

At last the day of the concert came (it was postponed for a couple of days to enable the finishing touches to be put to the work of rehearsal), and I gave back the baton to him, whom the public really wanted to see. He took it reluctantly and exhibited quite childlike trepidation! I began then to feel a new sensation; fear for another, almost as if the situation were reversed by some strange wizardry and the younger were he and not I; I trembled for his predicament with an almost fatherly apprehension! He conducted as best he could, woodenly, mechanically, without fire and without really leading his forces; no calamities, but no poetic feeling. The real significance of that beautiful but elusive music was lost without the poetry which is its real essence. The orchestra tried desperately hard to divine the will of its weak leader; but individual goodwill, without a real co-ordinating force, was unable to fuse into a coherent whole, and there was lacking that *je ne sais quoi* which attracts and dominates the public, rousing them to enthusiasm; it remained cold and impassive. The music was new for most of the audience, and (remember the date) they were ill-prepared for it; moreover, the last straw, the wonderful passage of colouring which unites the 'Parfums de la nuit' to the finale, that tremulous and very subtle flower of inimitable poetry, was ruined by a very violent shower of rain upon the glass roof. Materially damaging the tonal effects, it also distracted the attention of the audience to a gloomy speculation on the prospect of having to get home, – without umbrellas! This was the last piece on the programme: there was no chance of redeeming the lost cause, so wantonly lost, too, by a banal chance.

The only item which was applauded without protests was *L'après-midi d'un faune* which was already known to Italian audiences; the 'usual' *Après-midi* against whose popularity Debussy himself keenly inveighed, when he spoke to us in confidence! Certainly, there was not lacking the sympathy of one or two enthusiastic admirers. (I remember still, to our comfort and his honour, young Piero Coppola who had come from Milan, and who seemed beside himself with enthusiasm on the one hand, and with scorn for the *profanum vulgus* on the other.) Debussy himself was quite calm and smiling, as usual; he was, perhaps, prepared for hostility, and instead he had experienced only a little coolness. There was plenty of time: it was the first hearing in Italy of some of the music, and he had found a few isolated disciples already profoundly believing in him. That was enough for him; the anonymous applause of a heterogeneous audience, that wasn't the real reward for work done on so elevated a plane! He sensed around him the wholehearted devotion of a small but faithful band, and this was a greater reward in his eyes than the noisy and superficial approval of the 'animals with a thousand faces' which betrays and flatters with equal readiness! Besides, his critical detachment had exactly appraised his own position in the world of his contemporaries, the position as of one who has taken a big jump forward, and now calls back and waits to be caught up with; he could not, therefore, reasonably expect to gain the approval of those who mix with the common herd, who express its desires and banal sentiments.

He remained with us a few more days; we spoke together, and lived yet a few more hours of unforgettable intellectual and spiritual comprehension; and then came the moment when we had to say goodbye. In the corner which is on the right as one enters the Hotel d'Europa, there was a modest wicker table; it was there that, without being asked, he took from my hands the score of *Ibéria*, already a symbol of precious memories for me, and wrote on it words of affection and gratitude in that tiny and very precise handwriting of his, like that of a Benedictine monk; words which fill me with pride, but also with confusion when I think of all that he, perhaps unconsciously, had done for me in these days and yet . . . the one who got the thanks was I! Yes, the silent message of those few words, and others he wrote to me from Paris, is worth more to me than the noise of many unknown hands applauding.

Vittorio Gui, 'Debussy in Italy', *Musical Opinion*, January 1939, pp. 305–6; February 1939, pp. 404–5.

DR RICHARD VAN REES

(1853–1939)

Richard van Rees was a lawyer and banker in Amsterdam. He was a member of the board of the Concertgebouw from 1884, and president from 1913 to 1922. Debussy visited Amsterdam in the spring of 1914.

The Committee of the Concertgebouw had already tried several times to persuade Debussy to come to Amsterdam and make him understand how much his music was appreciated in Holland, but always without success. People who knew him assured us that he lived a very reclusive life and that he had an insurmountable objection to undertaking tours and appearing in public, so that only by some lucky accident could we hope to have the privilege of welcoming him.

This lucky accident came about when the Swiss composer and conductor Gustave Doret, who often came to Holland and who had a great admiration for the Concertgebouw, offered to act as an intermediary in getting his friend Debussy to come to Amsterdam. He was so keen on the idea, and on Debussy hearing our orchestra, that he was prepared to accompany Debussy on his journey – in his opinion, the only way to overcome Debussy's hatred of travelling.

In this way we succeeded in getting Debussy to come to Holland, though unfortunately at a time when Mengelberg was away, conducting concerts in Frankfurt. The Debussy concert, partly with him as conductor and partly as pianist, took place on a Sunday afternoon.

When he mounted the rostrum, with Doret leading him by the hand, so to speak – he went with the composer everywhere, acting as his mahout and even sitting by his side when he was conducting or playing – the large audience rose spontaneously to their feet, as did the orchestra, giving him an extraordinary, truly royal welcome. Truth to tell, Debussy on the rostrum appeared clumsy and ill at ease. Not because of his external appearance, because his robust physique made an agreeable impression, together with the delicate, noble lines of his face to which only his colouring lent something southern. But there was over his whole personality a faint cloud of lassitude and boredom, such as you find with people suffering from homesickness – a disease which, according to him, never left him when he was far from Paris.

I think he conducted the short orchestral pieces called 'Nuages' and 'Fêtes', which had been rehearsed as carefully as possible under Doret's guidance. He was a bad conductor but the orchestra were very responsive and followed his instructions intuitively, so that the performance of his works was an enormous success. The same success attended his performances on the piano, even though technically these were far from perfect. The concert ended with noisy ovations, which seemed to exhaust the composer and he left the rostrum quite soon, led off by Doret. When he reached the artists' room he expressed gratitude for his reception and for the excellent performance of his music, but without much enthusiasm. He was obviously glad it was all over.

A few hours later, Debussy and Doret came to dinner with me. Doret had accepted the invitation on behalf of both of them on the express condition that there would be nobody at the dinner whom Debussy did not know. As a result I had invited only the leader and the first cellist and their wives, M. and Mme Zimmerman and M. and Mme Gérard Hekking, and several of the Concertgebouw committee who had been introduced to Debussy in the artists' room. To my great regret, I had to disappoint several of my friends who would have liked to meet this famous guest, procured with such difficulty, and who had intimated their wishes to me with some insistence.

Debussy felt at ease in our beautiful old house with its superb corridor and the tall, imposing rooms built and decorated in pure Louis XVI style. It provided my wife with the opportunity to show him the great influence exercised by French taste and style on our ancestors. At table, Debussy's attention was immediately attracted by a small Empire clock, which he admired very much. 'You'll see me looking at it frequently,' he said to his hostess, 'because every minute that passes brings me closer to Paris.' She had put to sit beside him a charming, vivacious woman, very pretty, some of whose ancestors had fled the Terror and who spoke French perfectly, but she was unable to improve her neighbour's temper.

When I thought the time had come for me to say a few words, Debussy took his plate, fortunately still clean, and held it up in front of his face for a few moments, no doubt to hide the timidity and other feelings to which his expression was bearing witness at that juncture. I refused to be put off by this. After thanking him for coming and for the honour he had done us, and emphasizing the great veneration in which he was held in Holland, I finished by pointing out to him that the artists' reception room at the Concertgebouw contained portraits of the most important European artists who had performed for us, but that there was an empty place among them which we hoped to fill one day with the portrait of the great French master. After his visit to the Concertgebouw we were delighted to be able to satisfy this wish and beneath it we had written the words which the Académie Française had inscribed on the bust of Molière in its reception room: 'his fame lacks nothing, but ours did' (*rien ne manque à sa gloire, il manquait à la nôtre*). This speech obviously made a good impression on our guest. It was amusing to see that Doret, sitting opposite him, was making silent but expressive gestures to indicate that he had to reply to the speech that had been made in his honour. He seemed to ignore Doret's attempts, but after a certain time he thanked us for his welcome and expressed his admiration for our orchestra, simply and easily, in an elegant little speech.

Smoking a cigarette after dinner, he was obviously more at ease. He talked enthusiastically about all sorts of things, except music. When finally I suggested we rejoin the ladies in the drawing-room – it was getting late – he said: 'Why? We're perfectly comfortable here.' I had some difficulty in explaining to him that the time had come to go our separate ways and that, consequently, we had no option.

Shortly after we entered the drawing-room, it was announced that the cars had arrived and Doret made a sign to his friend to take his leave. At this, Debussy said to me: 'It seems these people are going away.' So what happened was that our guests, seeing that Debussy was not yet thinking of leaving, made their farewells. He let them go without demur, sat himself comfortably down next to his hostess and said, feeling obviously more relaxed: 'How nice it is here, Madame, I didn't know one could dine so well outside Paris.' And, realizing that my eldest son had no doubt been in charge of the wine in my absence, he turned to him and said: 'Young man, I congratulate you on the wine list, they were exquisite.' Then he talked very freely and easily about his wife and his daughter; he told us that, because of his very sensitive stomach, he regularly used to go to the market himself to choose the food he liked; in short, he spent an hour talking with us about the most ordinary, everyday things. Doret, who was like a cat on hot bricks because they had to leave the next day and still had their packing to do, and who was trying at intervals to get Debussy to go, made no headway with him: 'Leave me alone, there's a good fellow, I'm happy here, I'll just relax for a little longer, go and do our packing if you want to, I'll follow on after.' It was already past eleven o'clock when the two friends left.

Richard van Rees, unpublished typescript, pp. 36–8

GUSTAVE DORET

I imagine Debussy the orator is not a phenomenon you've experienced. After a concert in Amsterdam, there was a lavish dinner hosted by the President of the Concertgebouw. Speech by the President (with the champagne), speech by the Secretary (with the coffee), and no reply. I was sitting opposite Debussy and mimed meaningfully to him as to his duty, indicating that I could not do it for him. I ended up by giving him a sharp kick under the table. Finally he reacted; and I realized then that his silence was merely the result of timidity. He got up and, with a voice drained by emotion, said three words of thanks and sat down again. Then, as though a great weight had been lifted off his shoulders, he became as chatty as a magpie and was the life and soul of the occasion. We got back to the hotel at three o'clock in the morning, smoking enormous Havana cigars which our host had stuffed into our pockets.

Gustave Doret, unpublished letter of 31 March 1918 to Robert Godet

Then came the moment of our dress rehearsal in Amsterdam. First of all, works by Saint-Saëns. Why is Debussy remaining on the platform and listening to the works of his senior with particular attention? Just as I'm climbing down from the rostrum and making my way through the hall he takes my arm: 'Well, my dear Doret, to say I'm a passionate admirer of Saint-Saëns' music would be going too far. But you have to admit it's damned cleverly put together!' . . .

Gustave Doret, *Temps et contretemps* (Fribourg, 1942), p. 191

VIII
Last years

In 1912 Nijinsky produced a ballet on *Prélude à l'après-midi d'un faune* for Diaghilev's Ballets Russes. Although Debussy was not happy with this production, he agreed, largely for financial reasons, to compose for Diaghilev the ballet *Jeux*. The outbreak of war caused him considerable distress, and in addition his cancer developed to the point where an operation became necessary in 1915. He completed only one more work, the Violin Sonata, before his death on 25 March 1918 at the age of fifty-five.

LOUIS LALOY

On a bright afternoon in the spring of 1913 I was walking round my garden in Bellevue with Debussy. We were waiting for Stravinsky. As soon as he saw us, the Russian composer ran with his arms out to embrace Debussy who, over his friend's shoulder, threw me a look of combined amusement and affection. He had brought the piano duet arrangement of his new work, the *Sacre du printemps*. Debussy agreed to play the lower part on the Pleyel piano which is still in my possession. Stravinsky asked if he could take his collar off. Glaring through his glasses, pointing his nose at the keyboard and sometimes humming a part that had been omitted from the arrangement, he led his friend's supple, agile hands into a maelstrom of sound. Debussy followed without a hitch and seemed to make light of the difficulties. When they had finished, there was no question of embracing, nor even of compliments. We were dumbfounded, overwhelmed by this hurricane which had come from the depths of the ages and taken our life by the roots.

*

Just before the war Debussy had introduced me to Satie, and we sometimes met at his table, where we exchanged ambiguous compliments and oblique looks which, I think, Debussy found amusing. Between Satie and himself there existed a turbulent but indissoluble friendship. Or rather, it was one of those family hatreds which are exacerbated by the repeated shock of incompatible faults, but without destroying the sympathy the two sides feel for each other, which is due to a community of origin. It was like seeing two brothers, placed by the events of their lives in very different conditions, one rich and the other poor; the first welcoming, but proud of his superiority and ready to make it felt, the other unhappy beneath his clown's mask, paying his share by means of jokes to entertain his host, hiding his humiliation; each continually on watch against the other, without being able to stop themselves loving each other dearly.

Debussy was not a Christian, any more than Satie was. The only difference was that he never hid his pride. What is more, during the

war years when Satie saw the first glimmerings of fame, Debussy was
depressed at the state of the world, consumed by a disease that nothing
could arrest, absorbed in bitter thoughts and less capable than he had
ever been of any kindly gesture or word of flattery. When concerts
were organized consisting entirely of works by Satie, Debussy was
unable to go; confined to his room, he found it hard to believe the
news of their success, and thought it must be the work of a cabal, or
perhaps a practical joke. Satie got to know of his opinion and was
infuriated, to the point of writing a letter that was little short of
insulting. Debussy read it lying in bed, where he had been for some
weeks, and where he was shortly to die. His trembling hands crumpled
the letter on the sheet, then tore it up. 'Forgive me!' he murmured,
like a child who's going to be scolded, with tears in his eyes. I was
angry with Satie for behaving so cruelly – more cruelly, no doubt,
than he realized. It was only after his death, seven years later, that I
forgave him, when I learnt from his friends how much he too had
suffered, praised by others but refused the approbation he valued the
most in the whole world. And that, through the fault of both of them,
was the pitiful end of their friendship.

Louis Laloy, *La musique retrouvée* (Paris, 1928), pp. 213, 258–9, 261–2

PASTEUR VALLERY-RADOT

I remember the evenings I spent with Debussy at the early performances by the Ballets Russes at the Châtelet theatre, which enchanted
him by their novelty and their explosively bright colours, in general
excellently matched with the music. But Nijinsky's sometimes angular,
ataxic choreography, 'ugly' and 'Dalcrozian' to use Debussy's own
epithets, had a habit of annoying him, and Nijinsky's contortions in
Prélude à l'après-midi d'un faune were very far from what he had had
in mind.

  At the première of *Jeux*, in the Théâtre des Champs-Elysées on 15
May 1913, I was disagreeably struck by the choreography which
seemed to me juxtaposed rather than blended with the music. I couldn't
help expressing my opinion to the composer. He shrugged his

shoulders, meaning: 'What does it matter if they haven't understood me?'

'I didn't see you,' I said, 'during the performance. Where were you?'

'In the concierge's office, smoking a cigarette.'

Pasteur Valléry-Radot, 'Mes souvenirs sur Claude Debussy', *Marottes et Violons d'Ingres*, 46, 1953, p. 53

JACQUES DURAND

(*c.* 1915) After his famous String Quartet, Debussy had not written any more chamber music. Then, at the Concerts Durand, he heard again the Septet with trumpet by Saint-Saëns and his sympathy for this means of musical expression was reawoken. He admitted the fact to me and I warmly encouraged him to follow his inclinations. And that is how the idea of the six sonatas for various instruments came about.

Jacques Durand, *Quelques souvenirs d'un éditeur de musique*, 2 vols (Paris, 1924/1925) II, p. 77

LOUIS LALOY

When I saw Debussy again at the end of 1915, I was struck by how despondent and gloomy he looked. He had just finished his *Noël des enfants qui n'ont plus de maison*, a heartrending threnody for the innocents killed in the burnings and slaughter with which Belgium was punished for her loyalty. That day we made no allusion to this crime: his music sufficed. We didn't talk about military operations either, but about Reims Cathedral and Joan of Arc. He had had the idea for a cantata which would describe her compassion, her courage, her sadness, and in the flames of the fire her prophetic faith announcing the liberty of her country after further hardships. He asked me to write the text, and from that time on this was the main, though not exclusive, topic of our all too infrequent meetings. He would read in a low voice, reflect, scribble an orchestral or tempo indication in the margin of the manuscript, ask me for another rhythm, a repeat, would

often retract what he had done, changing course after all, turning the
sketch around and examining it from every angle, true to that method
of patient approximation and progressive accommodation which ulti-
mately led to the most exact matching between inspiration and style.
It was during one of these working sessions that he said to me,
talking about a strident trumpet call which he had thought of and then
abandoned: 'I distrust the exceptional.' That was the last piece of advice
he gave me. I should like to leave it to posterity.

Louis Laloy, 'Le monument de Claude Debussy', *Revue des deux mondes*, 102/
14, 15 July 1932, pp. 461–2

DARIUS MILHAUD
(1892–1974)

> Darius Milhaud studied at the Paris Conservatoire with
> André Gedalge and made his name especially with ballets
> such as *L'homme et son désir*, *Le boeuf sur le toit* and *La
> création du monde*. He was a member of the Groupe des
> Six and a close friend of Erik Satie.

I had also the possibility of hearing Debussy in concerts – he played
sometimes when he accompanied certain songs – and I was always
extremely moved by the tenderness with which he touched the notes;
he played magnificently. I saw him also once conducting the first
performance of *Rondes de printemps* in the Salle Gaveau, in, I suppose,
about 1912. He had a great precision and simplicity which I loved,
but I never dreamed that I could once meet him. At this time, when
there was no radio, no television, there was still a sort of mystery
about great men, and nobody of my generation would dare to try to
disturb them; which is not the case when sometimes someone telephones
just to know how I spell my name.

Then, during the war, when Debussy wrote his Sonata for Viola,
Harp and Flute, it happened that I was regularly playing chamber
music at a friend's house and we tried this sonata with harpist and
flautist. Then his publisher, M. Jacques Durand, heard about it and
asked me if I would like to give the first performance as violist in
Debussy's Sonata; it was in 1916, I think, during the war. I was

extremely excited about this project and M. Durand told me: 'I'm going to make an appointment and you'll go to Debussy's house and he will give you all the tempi.' Of course I went there with my heart beating hard and I saw the master whom I admired so much. He was sick of the dreadful illness which two years later brought about his death. He was very pale, with a little shawl on his shoulders, and his hands were trembling on the piano; but with extraordinary serenity he twice played his sonata for me on the piano; but I could not get all the details – the tempi, the rallentando, etc.

Then, of course, I did not tell him I was composing myself because we were more shy than young composers might be now. For Debussy I was a young violist full of deference and respect. After so many years I keep for Debussy the same admiration, the same tenderness, the same love.

Darius Milhaud, 'Reminiscences of Debussy and Ravel', in: *Essays on Music*, an anthology from *The Listener*, ed. Felix Aprahamian (London, 1967), pp. 79–80.

ERNEST ANSERMET

(1883–1969)

Ernest Ansermet was a mathematician by training but also took lessons in music from Ernest Bloch and André Gedalge. He conducted the Ballets Russes from 1915 to 1923, and in 1918 founded the Suisse Romande Orchestra which he conducted until 1966.

In 1917, when I gave the first performance of *Parade* by Erik Satie in Paris with the Russian Ballet, Debussy was there and he invited me to his home for the following afternoon. We discussed many of the tempi of his works and I asked him some questions about the *Nocturnes*. He took down his score of the *Nocturnes* and I saw then that this score was full of corrections, with pencil of all colours: red pencil, blue pencil, green pencil. I asked him, 'What is right?' He said, 'I don't know. Take the score with you and bring it back in a few days and choose what seems to you good.'

He was a man of a very reserved, aristocratic nature. And I had the impression always that he was apart from his surroundings. He had a few friendships, an old one with Godet and later with Lacerda. He was very friendly with Satie (every week Satie had lunch with him). But he had his opinion about Satie, he did not take him for a great musician but for a charming one and an interesting man. I had the impression he was very alone, very solitary.

He was convinced of himself. He had his way of seeing things and he would not be disturbed by the others. He could not be in harmony with people who were all interested in political or economic life. He was just for his music. He was not a man for looking at other people's scores, he used to play his own music. He was very fond of Chopin, of Schumann and of Bach. He had a pianist friend, Walter Rummel, who used to come to him and play the Bach chorales.

Ernest Ansermet, interviewed by Robert Chesterman, BBC, 7 September 1969

ANDRE SUARES

I met him twice, with some twelve or fifteen years between the two occasions. The last time, he was nearing the end of his life. He was appearing in a charity concert where some of his works were being played. I was struck, not so much by his thin and wasted appearance as by his air of absent-mindedness and by his profound lassitude. His complexion was the colour of melted wax and ashes. In his eyes there was no light of fever but the gloomy reflection of dark pools. There was not even any bitterness in his shadowy smile: one saw rather that he was tired of suffering. His round, supple, plump hand, a rather strong, episcopal hand, hung heavy on his arm, his arm on his shoulder, his head on his body and life on his head. In conversation, one or two people pretended to be confident, saying they found him in better health than they expected. But when he had sat down, he gazed slowly at the audience, blinking rapidly, in the manner of those who wish to see without being seen and who look furtively at what they can only half apprehend. He was devoured by *pudeur*, as an artist often is who feels disgust and almost a sense of shame at his suffering.

It was even said that he encouraged the disease by pretending it did not exist.

André Suarès, 'Debussy', *ReM*, 2, 1 December 1920, p. 123

JACQUES DURAND

(1918) Paris was under enemy fire. There were constant air raids and one of them, of exceptional violence, had struck the immediate neighbourhood of Debussy's house.

I went there one evening, hoping to see him one last time. I knew that his days were numbered – the ravages of the disease were plain to see on his highly expressive face. When he saw me, he said how pleased he was and that he wanted to talk with me in private. He described first of all the horror of the preceding night when, seeing the danger from the bombardment, he had not had the strength to get out of bed to go and hide in the cellar with his wife and daughter, who had refused to leave him. This physical incapacity, added to the miseries of the war, tormented him. I tried to reassure him, to persuade him that his health would improve. He thanked me, then, looking steadily at me with eyes which could already see beyond this life, he told me that it was all over, that he knew it, that it was now merely a matter of hours. Alas, it was the truth. When I began to protest, he signalled that he wanted to embrace me, then asked me to pass him a cigarette, his last consolation.

Jacques Durand, *Quelques souvenirs d'un éditeur de musique*, 2 vols (Paris, 1924/1925), II, pp. 77–8

LOUIS LALOY

The illness from which he had been suffering for some years now took a turn for the worse, under the strains of wartime. We saw his face become hollow, his gaze become dull. He had to stay in his room, then in his bed. 'Oh! This bed! This bed!' he used to say in despair. The Opéra was preparing a revival of Rameau's *Castor et Pollux*, and the dress rehearsal took place on Thursday 21 March 1918, in the afternoon, because they were afraid of air-raid warnings in the evenings. It was one of his last regrets not to be able to go to it. Seeing I was leaving, he tried to smile and whispered: 'Say *bonjour* to Monsieur Castor!' Two days later the long-range bombardment of Paris began. During his last days he listened to the dismal sound of explosions, and his suffering ended on Monday 25 March.

Louis Laloy, *La musique retrouvée* (Paris, 1928), p. 228

CLAUDE-EMMA DEBUSSY (CHOUCHOU)
(1905–19)

Claude-Emma Debussy was Debussy's only child. She died after receiving the wrong treatment for diphtheria. Raoul Bardac was the son of Debussy's wife Emma by her first marriage.

Letter to Raoul Bardac

My dear Raoul   8 April 1918

Did you receive the last telegram? You must have done. I was the one who thought to send you the first one. I wrote it and then I realized that being only a little girl I didn't have the necessary documents to show at the post office, so I asked Dolly to send it. She was here because I sent for her when I saw Mama's face so utterly distraught. When she'd gone, Mama was called to Papa's bedside because the nurse thought he was 'very bad'! We sent at once for two doctors and they both said he should have an injection to stop the pain. I understood then – Roger-Ducasse was there and said to me, 'Chouchou, come and kiss your Papa.' At once I thought it was all over. When I went back into the bedroom, Papa was asleep, breathing regularly but very shallowly. He went on sleeping like that until 10 o'clock in the evening and then, gently, like an angel, he went to sleep for ever. I can't describe what happened afterwards. A flood of tears was building up behind my eyes but I forced them back because of Mama. All that night, alone in her great bed, I couldn't sleep for a minute. I had a fever and with dry eyes I gazed at the walls and couldn't bring myself to believe the truth! The next day far too many people came to see Mama and by the end of it she couldn't hold out any longer – it was a release for her and for me. Thursday arrived, the Thursday when he was to be taken from us for ever! I saw him one last time in that horrible box – lying on the ground. He looked happy, so happy and then I couldn't control my tears. I almost collapsed but I couldn't embrace him. At the cemetery Mama, naturally, couldn't have behaved better and as for me, all I could think of was, 'I mustn't cry because of Mama'. I summoned up all my courage. Where did it come from? I don't know. I didn't shed a single tear. Tears restrained are worth as much as tears shed, and now it is night for ever. Papa is dead. Those three words, I don't understand them or rather I understand them too well. And to be the only one here struggling with Mama's indescribable grief is truly terrible – for several days it's made me forget my own, but now I feel it more bitterly than ever. You're so far away, Raoul! Think occasionally of your poor little sister who would like to embrace you so much and tell you she loves you. Can you understand all I feel but can't put into words?

A thousand kisses and all my love
Your little sister
Chouchou

It's unbelievable. I don't know how I stay alive, and I can't believe the awful truth.

Chouchou Debussy, in: *Debussy Letters*, ed. François Lesure and Roger Nichols (London, 1987), pp 335–6

PASTEUR VALLERY-RADOT

Debussy wanted to be buried in the cemetery at Passy, which he thought was less gloomy than the other Parisian cemeteries. He would lie there, he said, among the trees and the birds. But the Debussys did not have a plot there. So the coffin had to be taken in the first instance to Père-Lachaise. A year later Mme Debussy, André Caplet and I took it from Père-Lachaise to the cemetery at Passy, where it now lies.

Pasteur Valléry-Radot, 'Claude Debussy: souvenirs', *Revue des Deux Mondes*, CVIII, 45, 15 May 1938, p. 417n

Index